The Moray Firth Coast Line

"A' Gaun Coast Wye?"

David Fasken

and

Graham Maxtone

Published by

THE GREAT NORTH OF SCOTLAND RAILWAY ASSOCIATION

The 8.58am Elgin to Aberdeen entering Knock hauled by a North British Type 2 on 22nd June 1964. The train consists of two full parcel vans and three coaches, indicating the importance of parcel traffic. This was in the twilight of the Coast Line, although the coaches were the comfortable British Railways Mark 1 design. (Roy Hamilton/Strathspey Railway)

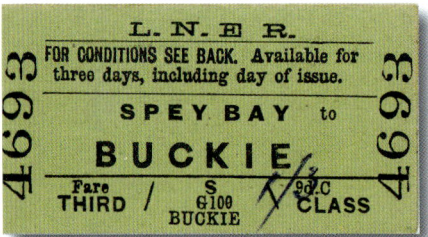
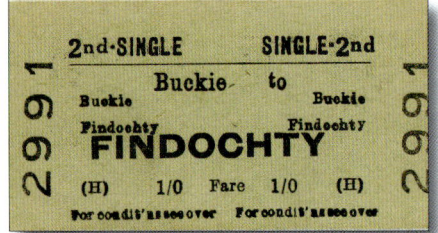

Cover Photographs:

(Upper) Standard Class 4 Tank No. 80028, fitted with tablet catcher, has arrived at Cullen with the three coach coastal portion of an Aberdeen to Elgin service. A small clutch of passengers has disembarked and the porter has unloaded a healthy barrowload of parcels. There is a decent number of vans in the goods yard, although these were possibly being stored. The locomotive and the maroon coaches dates the scene to the period 1956 – 1961. (Graham Maxtone collection)

(Lower) An unidentified North British Type 2 diesel (later Class 21) heads a train for Aberdeen across the viaducts at Cullen. The vans at the head of the train would be for fish traffic. It's late August 1961 and the harvest is in full swing. (Frank Spaven)

Contents

Preface	5
Acknowledgements	6
Introduction	7
Early Plans 1845–1858	9
The Morayshire Railway 1841–1863	11
The Banff, Portsoy & Strathisla Railway 1857–1863	13
The Banffshire Railway and Great North 1863-1883	19
Difficult Years and Fishing Developments 1866-1881	25
The Building of the Coast Line 1881 - 1886	27
The Spey Viaduct	37
Coast Line Stations	43
The Great North Years 1886-1922	55
The LNER Period 1923-1947	69
British Railways: Death by a Thousand Cuts 1948-1968	77
Post Closure 1968	93
The Spycatcher of Portgordon and….	97
….Other Coast Line Anecdotes	99
Accidents and Incidents	107
Appendix 1: Coast Line Stations and Sidings	111
Appendix 2: Coast Line Signalling	113
Appendix 3: Coast Line Operations	119
Appendix 4: Coast Line Excursions	124
Appendix 5: LNER Instructions for the Working of Blairshinnoch Crossing	125
Bibliography	126
Index	127

© David Fasken and the Great North of Scotland Railway Association, 2024
ISBN: 978-0902343-36-8

All rights reserved. No part of this publication may be reproduced, stored in a retrieval system or transmitted, in any form or by any means, electronic, mechanical, photocopying, recording or otherwise, without the prior written permission of the author.

Designed by Keith Fenwick

Published by the Great North of Scotland Railway Association
www.gnsra.org.uk

Printed in the United Kingdom by Henry Ling Limited, at the Dorset Press, Dorchester, DT1 1HD

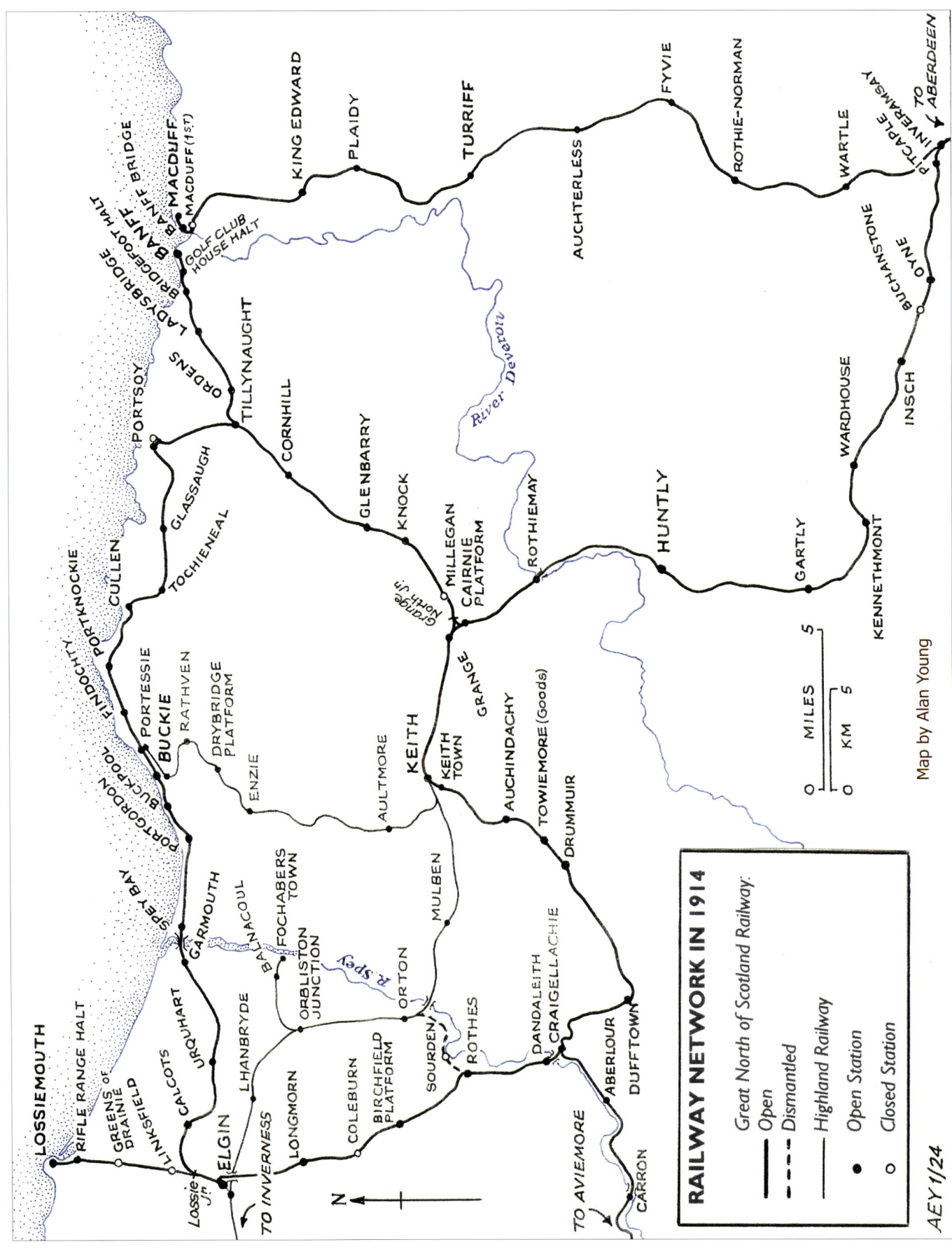

PREFACE

"The Moray Firth Coast"
Waves on the beach, and the wild sea-foam,
With a leap, and a dash, and a sudden cheer,
Where the seaweed makes its bending home,
And the sea-birds swim on the crests so clear,
Wave after wave, they are curling o'er,
While the white sand dazzles along the shore.

Great North of Scotland Railway, Moray Firth Coast - The Scottish Riviera, *railway tourist guide, 1913.*

My father.... had gone East (to Penang) to make a living.... At intervals he could afford to come home for a holiday of half a year and take a furnished house with some shooting and fishing in his own corner of Scotland. First it had been.... near Huntly.... Now, when I was more active (aged 9) and could roam at large, it was at Glassaugh mid-way between the small seaside towns of Portsoy and Cullen. It was and still is a land of little men and little places. Apart from the great Seafield Estate.... it had little farms with bonnet lairds, a little railway with a lot of little stations, little harbours, hummocky hills and tiny burns with tiny trout.... The shire (Banff) lives as much on fish as on farming. Its coast has a string of little harbours stretching west from the county town towards the now comparatively large and important Buckie. I share John Betjeman's love of slow trains and small railways. Our line, as I learned when taken to get my hair cut in Elgin, trickled through a series of tiny stations whose names I have never forgotten. "Almost singing themselves" they ran. After Cullen came Portknockie, Findochty, Portessie, Buckie.... and Portgordon. The old Great North of Scotland Railway had a time-table which made music as it linked Aberdeen with Elgin and Inverness.

Ivor Brown, Scotland's Forgotten Country, *Blackwood's Magazine, June 1972.*

We travelled [in April 1968] by the afternoon train on Saturday [from Aberdeen], which is known as the trawler train because it is normally heavily patronised by fishermen.... About five seconds before the train was due to start a dozen fishermen came pouring down the platform and piled into our carriage. They were in merry mood.... one or two had dined exceptionally well and had to be lifted aboard by their mates.

Distributing themselves in the adjoining seats they dug tins of beer out of their duffle bags and commenced to talk at the tops of their voices about the price of fish, the probable outcome of that afternoon's football matches, the iniquities of the Government and so forth, all but the few who were too much under the weather to talk, but just sat slumped in their places mumbling foolishly or, in one case, crooning a ditty entitled "The tarrin' o' the yole."

.... As we stopped at Huntly the singer suddenly sprang to his feet, exclaimed "Michty me, this is far I git aff", reeled to the door, wrenched it open and fell flat on the platform.

His colleagues, who had for some time been playing an uproarious game of brag, immediately rushed out and dragged him back. "The gype disna ken fit he's deein'", one of them told Enid and me. "He disna git aff or Finnichty." Presently the guard came along the train. "A' gaun Coast wye?" he inquired, and as I told him yes, I nudged Enid. "Take special note of that question. It is one you will never hear again."

One of the fishermen who had been sitting opposite us in a stupor roused himself at Cairnie and lurched over to Enid. "Far ye gaun, quine?" he inquired. "Garmouth" she said. "Ye canna get tae Garmouth," he informed us. "The line's is a' hale't up the tither side o' Buckie.".... This gave rise to a furious argument.... Just as Enid and I were beginning to have an unpleasant picture of ourselves bumping from Buckie to Garmouth over naked sleepers on a railless track, the guard passed by and quashed the argument by stating that Willem was havering.... "he was right"; we made it to Garmouth smoothly.

Donovan Smith, Aberdeen Press & Journal, *January 1971.*

Cullen was one of the many little stations in Scotland. All along the Coast were little railway stations where only about two or three people got on latterly. Of course, hardly anybody could afford to go on a long journey so most people went on at one station and off at another.

The stations were all roughly about the same size. There was a station at every town along the Coast. It would have taken a long time to have gone on a long journey because the train just got going then it had to stop again.

Cullen Primary School, Memories of The Railway in Cullen, *on the centenary of the construction of the Cullen Viaducts, 1986.*

"Farmers up and down the line
check their watches by hell-fires time"

"Hellfire" was Elgin driver James Jack (1886-1961) whose service spanned Great North, LNER and BR days from 1901 to 1951 and who…. had a reputation for prodigious timekeeping particularly when in charge of the 2.15 coastal mail train from Aberdeen to Elgin. The origins of the nickname…. would [be] for the ferocity with which he drove his engine rather than the high speed of this run…. on the Coast line only 40mph was permitted around the Tillynaught area and only 20mph was sanctioned at Portsoy and Cullen. Once past the viaducts the real racing ground unfolded as top speed of 50mph was allowed over most of the section between Portknockie and Spey Bay. The remainder of the run to Elgin saw the return to the leisurely pace of 30mph.

John Ross, Some Gleanings from Elgin Depot, *Great North* Review, *Volume 40 No 159, November 2003.*

Acknowledgements

John Ross

I am indebted to GNSRA member John Ross for allowing me to draw extensively on his excellent booklet *The Spey Viaduct* which was published by the Association in 2006. It largely forms the basis of the eighth chapter and it provides an excellent and detailed account of the construction and life of "Barnett's Monument". John also patiently answered many additional questions, even to the extent of checking out an issue at Elgin station while walking his dog. Sadly John died in June 2024, so it is posthumous thanks that go to him for his invaluable help.

General

A fair degree of the material for this book has been derived from the Association's archives, including back issues of the *Great North Review*. It has not been possible to identify all the members who have (mainly unwittingly) contributed, but some of the regulars are Gordon Casely, Mike Cooper, Bob Drummond, Keith Fenwick, Douglas Flett, Donald Galloway, Keith Jones, Graham Maxtone, Ron Smith and Mike Stephen. Their contributions down the years have provided much invaluable information and indeed some of the anecdotes. For those whom I have missed I offer both my apologies and my thanks.

I would like to thank Peter Donaldson at Grampian Transport Museum for sending me the Donald family information on the Spycatcher of Portgordon; David Ross for allowing me to use statistical information from his 2015 book *The Great North of Scotland Railway: A New History*; the Cullen, Deskford and Portknockie Heritage Group for allowing me to consult their archives in the Heritage Centre in Cullen; and Duncan George of Keith who alerted me to the "story" (and grave) of Karam Dad while we tramped the hills and moors of Aberdeenshire during the winter months.

I record my great appreciation to Keith Jones and David Spaven who both painstakingly proofread my drafts and provided invaluable comments, suggestions and corrections; to Alan Young for his wonderful hand-drawn map of the Coast Line; and to Keith Fenwick for his ongoing advice and support and, not least, for his design, lay-out and publishing skills.

Finally, I thank Graham Maxtone for undertaking the not inconsiderable work of selecting photographs and providing the associated captions. Many of the pictures are hitherto unpublished and Graham's work has complemented the text to bring the Coast Line to life.

David Fasken, Forgue, October 2024.

Introduction

The history of the 39 miles of railway from Cairnie Junction to Elgin via the Coast is not straightforward.

Firstly, there is the definition of the "Coast Line". Strictly speaking it is the section of railway along the Moray Coast between Tillynaught Junction and Lossiemouth Junction; but when this section was fully connected in 1886 the Great North of Scotland Railway Company's services were extended over the whole route from Cairnie Junction and Grange to Elgin. The branch to Banff complemented those services and, of course, the first mile of the Morayshire Railway's line connecting Elgin and Lossiemouth, became an integral part.

Secondly, the history of the route involves a number of different railway companies until all were consolidated in various stages into the Great North of Scotland Railway. Those companies are inextricably linked with each other and the development and operation of the Coast Line.

Thirdly, the Coast Line was the last of three through routes between Aberdeen and Elgin. The first to be completed was via Keith and Mulben (1858), with the section west of Keith to Elgin part of the Inverness & Aberdeen Junction Railway Company (subsequently the Highland Railway Company). Then came the Glen Line (1863), so named because its route passed through the Glen of Rothes and Craigellachie which the Great North of Scotland Railway regarded as its "Main Line" from Aberdeen to Elgin. And, finally, the Coast Line via Buckie (1886) completed the set. In terms of operations these three routes inevitably interacted with each other. The mileage from Aberdeen to Elgin was 71¼ via Mulben, 80¾ via the Glen Line and 87¼ via the Coast Line.

I have endeavoured to concentrate as far as possible on the Coast Line itself. Other lines and companies are covered by a variety of books, some of which have been published by the Great North of Scotland Railway Association.

The Great North of Scotland Railway Company promoted the Moray Firth Coast Line as "The Scottish Riviera". For those living on that coast and who have endured the regular horizontal rain, sleet and snow driven by a Force 10 screaming down from Iceland this may appear a quite fanciful notion. Undoubtedly, however, it is a most beautiful coastline and the scenic sea views from the trains were breathtaking. The towns of Banff, Portsoy, Cullen, Lossiemouth and others with their attractive sandy beaches all became popular holiday destinations; and the remains of old seawater swimming pools are testament to a degree of summer warmth and the hardiness of the folk who patronised them.

This is also a tale of through passenger services between Aberdeen and Inverness, local journeys, fish traffic (people and freight), agricultural produce, whisky, general supplies and wartime effort. Along the way there were adventures, incidents, mishaps and accidents and I have tried to convey a sense of both the history and working life of this rather unique railway line. We shall not see its like again.

Findochty was typical of the smaller fishing villages along the Moray Firth coast with a small harbour and rows of cottages which, even in June 2024, can easily be spotted. The promontory in the distance provides a commanding location for the local church. The railway ran along the coast on the right of the photograph with the station quite a distance up the hill from the village centre. (Keith Fenwick)

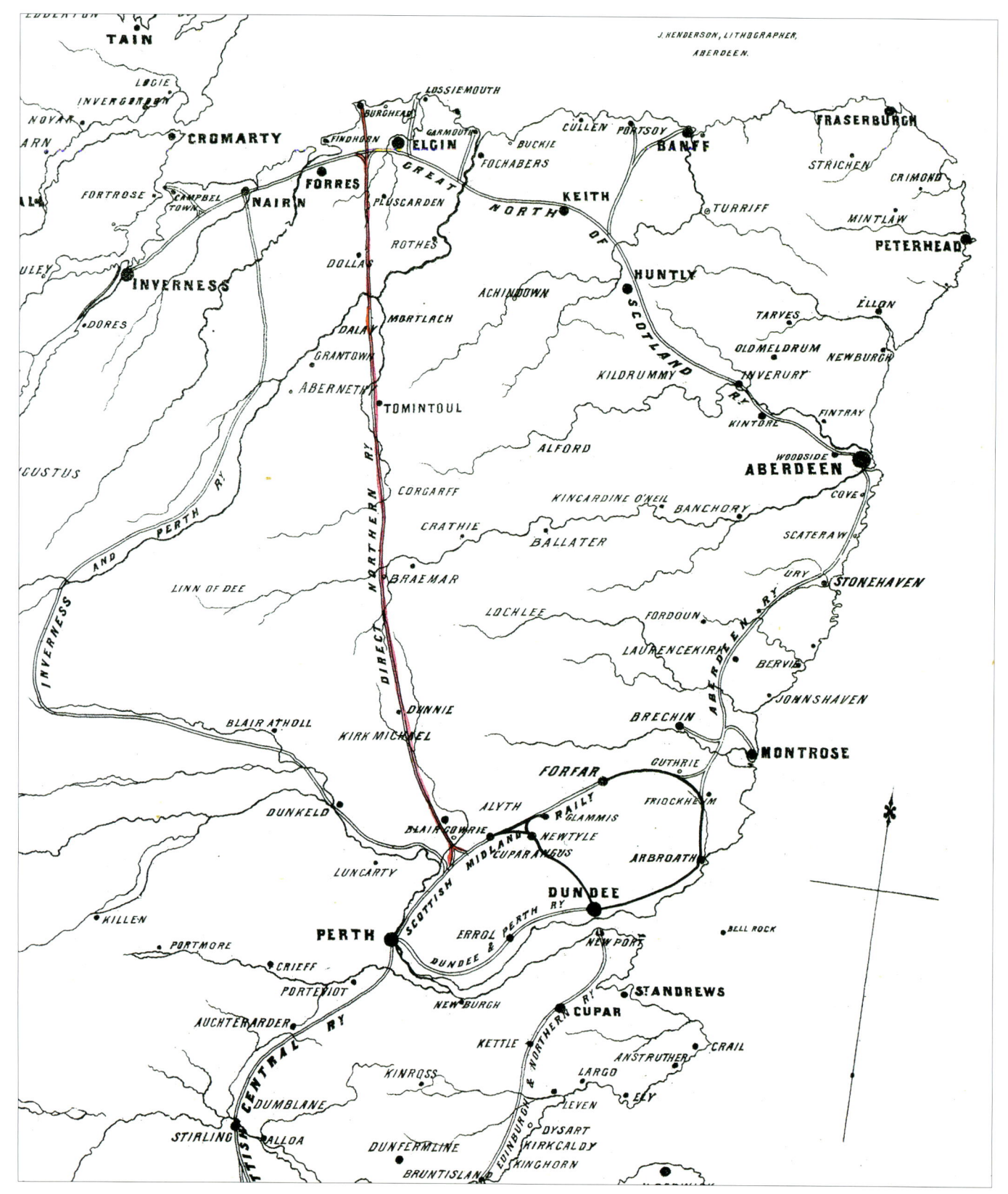

A map prepared in 1845 which shows some of the proposals of that year. As well as the Great North, the Inverness & Perth is shown on the left while running up the centre is an even more speculative scheme for a direct line from Perth to Elgin; it never got beyond the drawing board given that it was to run through Glenshee and Tomintoul.

(GNSRA collection)

Early Plans 1845–1858

The idea of a railway line along the Banffshire coast can be traced to the formation of the Great North of Scotland Railway (Great North) in 1845. Indeed, consideration of routes to the west and north of the Granite City, especially the link between Aberdeen and Inverness, had been prevalent in the preceding years. On 8th March 1845 the new company issued a prospectus for a double-track line from Aberdeen to Inverness and, at 108¼ miles, its proposed route differed little from today's line between the two cities. Banff and Portsoy on the coast were to be linked by a branch from Grange (4½ miles east of Keith) while shorter branches from Orton, Alves and Nairn would serve Garmouth, Lossiemouth or Burghead, and Fort George respectively. An amended prospectus dated 20th March was published and its title "Great North of Scotland Railway from Aberdeen to Inverness in Continuation of the Aberdeen Line from the South" signified the main objective. The proposed branch to Fort George was dropped.

In an era of general proliferation of railway projects throughout the U.K. there also appeared in 1846 the Great North of Scotland (Eastern Extension) serving the north-east corner of Aberdeenshire; and the Great North of Scotland (Western Extension) serving the district between Inverurie and Banff. This latter line would have approached Macduff from the east on a gradient of 1 in 30, passed the town's harbour, and followed the coast over the Deveron to Banff Harbour where it would have met the branch from Grange. These schemes came to nothing.

As the Great North's proposed inland route excluded the fishing ports of Banffshire and Morayshire, this led in April 1845 to the promotion of the somewhat longer Aberdeen, Banff & Elgin Railway which would run north-west from Aberdeen to Banff via Udny, Fyvie and Turriff, before heading west along the coast to Portsoy, Cullen, Buckie and Portgordon, and then inland to Elgin. A separate company called the Inverness & Elgin Junction Railway would connect Elgin with Inverness following the same route via Forres and Nairn as was being proposed by the Great North. Branches to serve Peterhead, Fraserburgh, Newburgh and Macduff were included. However, the Inverness & Elgin Junction soon broke their ties with the Aberdeen, Banff & Elgin and declared its support for the Great North.

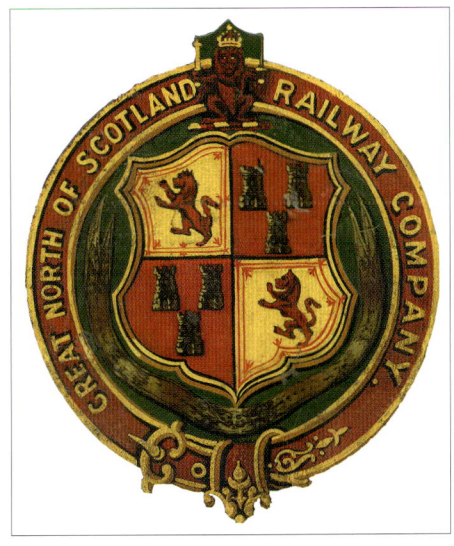

As the three companies prepared their respective Parliamentary bills, the Aberdeen, Banff & Elgin Railway collapsed through lack of funding. That, at least in part, was due to their proposed line along the coast by-passing the important market town of Keith. In any event, the Great North had a new fight on its hands opposing the Perth & Inverness Railway's scheme for a direct link to the south from Inverness to Perth via Nairn, Grantown, the Druimuachdar Pass, Blair Atholl and Dunkeld. That Parliamentary bill was thrown out due to concerns over the gradients required to cross the Grampian mountains and the Great North was able to proceed with little opposition to its Aberdeen to Inverness proposal. It was granted powers through an Act of Parliament on 26th June 1846. However, it was a costly success at £80,000 and further financial impositions were placed on it through stipulations that lodges and gate-keepers had to be provided at numerous level crossings and that financial compensation must be paid to the trustees of the toll bridges carrying the main Aberdeen–Inverness road over the Spey at Orton and the Findhorn at Forres. The total estimated cost of the line was £1.5 million.

The Great North now faced two major problems. It had little money and, completely unconnected to general railway expansion, the UK faced a nationwide financial panic in late 1847. Money could not be raised at any price. The Great North had been making progress in their negotiations with landowners, but the lack of funds and lack of confidence from potential investors led to complete stagnation. Not a sod was turned on the Aberdeen to Inverness line and that early enthusiasm to connect branches to coastal towns had become totally irrelevant. To compound matters the Aberdeen Railway Company (connecting Aberdeen to the south) was reneging on its deal to amalgamate with the Great North due largely to the latter's financial difficulties and the proposed "marriage" was annulled in July 1850. Any prospect of the Great North heading southwards from Aberdeen had gone. The company was at a standstill.

The second problem lay in Inverness. While the prospect of the Great North reaching the Highland capital had diminished for the time being, railway interests there were, nonetheless, keeping a beady eye on developments in Aberdeen. As the financial position eased and the Great North commenced construction towards Huntly in 1852, a new company was floated in Inverness to build a railway to Nairn. The objective was to keep the Great North out of the Highland capital. The Great North reached Huntly in 1854 and the Inverness & Nairn Railway opened in November 1855 and triggered a lengthy period of antagonism between what was to become, in 1865, the Highland Railway Company and the Great North. In 1858 the two companies met head-on at Keith where they enjoyed a most uneasy relationship until the turn of the 20th century. But, at least, the first through link between Aberdeen and Inverness was complete.

Many of the shareholders of the Great North were dismayed at being thwarted from reaching Inverness, although the company had secured representation on the Board of the new Inverness & Aberdeen Junction Railway which had completed the link from Nairn to Keith. The company now turned its attention to pushing westwards to Elgin (and Strathspey) by an alternative route. The Glen Line extended the Great North's railway from Keith to Elgin via Dufftown, Craigellachie, Rothes and Longmorn on completion in July 1863. In due course the Company considered this route as its main line.

A faded photograph of Lossiemouth harbour which nevertheless provides much fascinating detail. The photographer is looking north, with the station behind him. Sidings from the station ran onto both sides of the harbour. On the right, a long line of open wagons ready to carry barrels of fish can be seen. The rails along Pitgaveny Quay on the left are still in situ. (John Ross collection)

The Morayshire Railway 1841–1863

In order to gain a full understanding of the ultimate development of the Moray Firth Coast Line it is necessary to record the establishment of another railway company. The Morayshire Railway's 5½ mile line from Elgin to Lossiemouth pre-dated the opening of the main line from Aberdeen to Huntly and a one-mile section out of Elgin would, in time, become an integral part of the Coast Line.

The prospect of linking the cathedral town of Elgin to the port of Lossiemouth was considered as early as 1841 and a survey of the proposed route confirmed that a line would be straightforward and cheap. Investment, however, stalled and it was another four years before local banker and distiller James Grant, who founded Glen Grant distillery in Rothes and later was appointed Provost of Elgin, resurrected the proposal as the Morayshire Railway. He further proposed to extend his line 16 miles southwards from Elgin to Craigellachie with the possibility of double track and an extension to Aberlour. However, as the Great North was by now in existence, the proposal was amended to build only two sections, from Lossiemouth to Elgin and from Orton to Craigellachie. The two sections would be linked by running over 10 miles of the Great North's proposed main line from Elgin to Orton. This proposed railway was authorised on 16th July 1846, only three weeks after the Great North of Scotland Railway Act received Royal Assent. But the Morayshire Railway was, like others, caught up in the financial crisis of 1847 and the project stalled.

Four years later, in 1851, there was another crisis as the Board of the Morayshire Railway attempted to officially abandon the proposed section from Orton to Craigellachie. Some Edinburgh shareholders disagreed and tried to secure the abandonment of the entire line but were defeated and withdrew their support. That led to another pecuniary crisis and on 10th July the Railway Commissioners formally confirmed abandonment of the Craigellachie section. The company was saved, however, by Elgin Town Council which increased its shareholding by £1,000 and by local landowner Colonel Brander of Pitgaveny, a champion of the railway, who increased his subscription significantly. Consequently, the contract to construct the Elgin to Lossiemouth line was awarded to Hutchings & Company of London. There was an early station north of (what was to become) Lossie Junction at Linksfield Level Crossing from around 1853 to 1859 and a halt at Greens of Drainie over the same period. A third halt called Rifle Range was operated by the LNER in the 1920s on the southern edge of Lossiemouth but it did not appear in any timetables. Lossiemouth station was stone-built on the Down side with curved platform and there was a short extension beyond the station to the harbour. The line opened on 10th August 1852 to the usual fanfare at both ends. Trains ran until midnight and 3,000 passengers were carried on that first day. And so was born a railway line which, initially, was completely isolated.

The Great North's powers to build the line westwards from Huntly lapsed in 1854. The Morayshire Railway at first proposed to complete their line from Lossiemouth to Craigellachie itself, but when the Inverness & Aberdeen Junction Railway constructed the Nairn – Keith line, it reverted to the original 1846 plan to use that new company's section between Elgin and Orton. The Morayshire's rather primitive station at Elgin, built in 1852, was only 300 yards from that of the Inverness & Aberdeen Junction Railway. With much of the material for railway construction

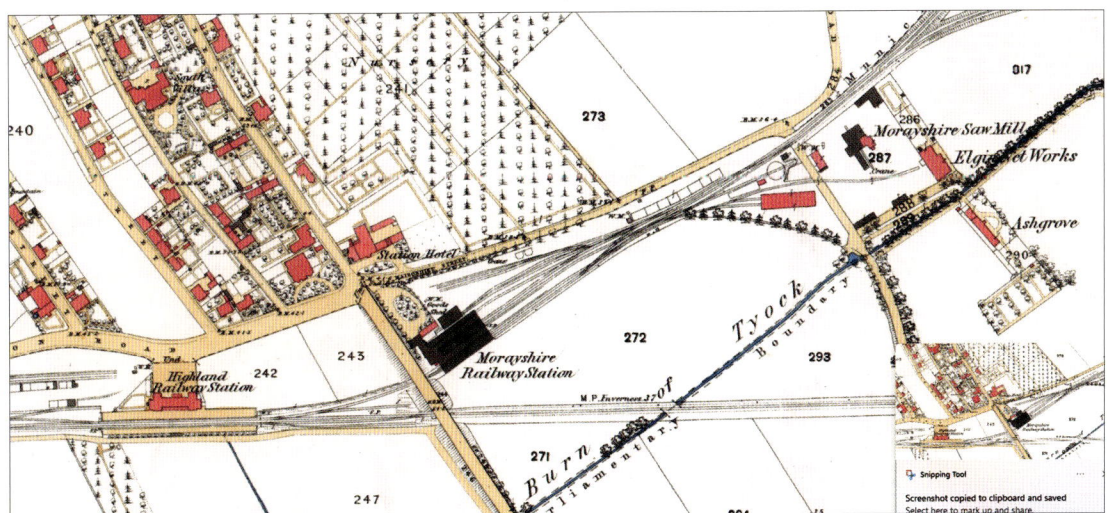

The first OS map of Elgin, published in 1871, shows the distance between the two stations there.
(National Library of Scotland, Creative Commons Licence CC-BY)

arriving by sea at Lossiemouth, a temporary connection between the two stations was made in 1858. When the Board of Trade inspected the railway prior to opening it noted that it had no knowledge of the connection. Both companies' response was that they had not thought of giving formal notification. The "temporary" link remains in place today! A platform on the connecting line was built and additional buildings, made of timber to minimise costs, were later provided to accommodate the Great North. The platforms were unprotected. The spartan facilities were also intended as temporary but they were to serve the public for 40 years. A two-road engine shed was constructed. The 3½ miles from Orton to Rothes opened on 23rd August 1858 and the line opened through to Craigellachie on 23rd December but terminated one mile north-west of the town at Dandaleith to avoid the cost of bridging the Spey.

The arrangement for running over the Elgin – Orton section proved problematic mainly due to the conflicting business interests of the two companies. While the Inverness & Aberdeen Junction concentrated on passenger traffic, the Morayshire Railway's main business was the transport of goods, especially whisky, agricultural produce and timber which had hitherto been floated down the Spey. The quick development of such freight resulted in the Morayshire running more dedicated goods and mixed trains which led to subsequent delays to the extent that some ship departures from Lossiemouth were held up. There were problems with both charges and timetabling leading to constant disputes. This all resulted in the Morayshire Railway promoting and constructing an alternative and shorter (by 3 miles) route of its own between Elgin and Rothes through the Glen of Rothes via Longmorn. It opened on 1st January 1862.

Finally, the one-mile gap between Dandaleith and Craigellachie was bridged and opened on 1st July 1863 from which point the Great North took over the day-to-day operation of the Morayshire Railway. That linked the Great North's new line from Keith and Dufftown to Craigellachie to complete what was to be known at the "Glen Line" and which gave the Great North its first direct link from Aberdeen to Elgin. The Rothes – Orton section struggled on but was by now unprofitable and it closed without notice on 1st August 1866. The junction at Orton was removed, but some intermittent freight services continued from Rothes to Sourden until at least 1880 and possibly on towards the end of the century. The points at the Rothes end were removed in the late 1890s and the line abandoned. The Great North Board *"resolved to remove the rails on the Orton branch which are of old pattern"* on 23rd March 1907, but they were not in fact lifted until the mid-1930s.

When the Great North consolidated a number of the small and notionally independent railway companies in the north-east on 30th July 1866, the Morayshire Railway remained independent despite a willingness in principle by both parties to join together. The main problem was the weak financial position of the Morayshire (partly due to the funding of their new line to Rothes) which did on that same date, however, obtain powers to consolidate with the Great North as and when terms could be agreed. In 1875 the platform at Lossiemouth was extended in order to accommodate longer trains especially during the summer "bathing season". The Morayshire Directors hoped that the Great North would pay for the work although the Great North did not take over the Morayshire Railway until 1st October 1880. The Great North enlarged the goods yard in 1896.

Dandaleith, the original Craigellachie terminus of the Morayshire Railway, was on the north side of the River Spey. The station building, seen in 1936, was unusually long as a large part of it consisted of railway houses. (H R Norman)

The Banff, Portsoy & Strathisla Railway 1857–1863

Meanwhile, with the main line from Aberdeen to Keith completed in 1856 but having been thwarted in its bid to reach Inverness, the Great North pursued a policy of building a network of branch lines, primarily to feed the main line into Aberdeen. The company would, in fact, go on to develop an image of being "all branch". A pattern emerged whereby many of these branch lines were promoted by independent companies reflecting local interests, but with the expectation that the Great North would work them and indeed offer a degree of financial support. All of these companies, except the Morayshire, Banffshire and Deeside Railways, were absorbed by the Great North in the major consolidation of 1866.

Railway interests soon had their eye on the coast again, although the high grounds north of Keith presented an engineering challenge compared to the flat land further to the west. The Inverness & Aberdeen Junction Railway had flirted with the idea of building a line from Elgin to Buckie but it was no more than that. It was a new company, the Banff, Portsoy & Strathisla Railway, based in the county town of Banff, which resurrected the 1845 proposal to build a 16¼ mile line from Grange station (on the main line between Huntly and Keith) to Banff Harbour through the Glenbarry gap with a 2¾ mile branch from Tillynaught to Portsoy. The line was to be built as cheaply as possible with only light earthworks anticipated, although there would be some steep gradients. The Great North greeted a deputation from the new company on 26th October 1856 and declined an invitation to subscribe. It did agree in principle, however, to work the line at prime cost on condition that the rates were the same as the Great North. The Banff, Portsoy & Strathisla Act received its assent on 27th July 1857 with authorised capital of £90,000 and borrowing powers of £30,000. A short branch to Portsoy Harbour was subject to the approval of the Admiralty and the Company was authorised to make an agreement with the Great North for joint use of Grange station. The majority of directors were local landowners and businessmen and, rather ironically, the Chairman was the Hon. Thomas Bruce who was Factor for the Earl of Seafield and also the Deputy Chairman of the Inverness & Aberdeen Junction Railway. Another Director, William Taylor of Glenbarry, also sat on that company's Board. The contractors were B. & E. Blyth of Edinburgh who were paid £49,800 in cash and £12,500 in shares and whose Engineer William Keir managed the construction and then became the Company's engineer.

There were financial problems from the start. Heads of Agreement for working the line were approved by the Great North Board in January 1859 but by the time the line opened

The Banffshire line started in the bay platform at Grange. This is looking towards Keith with the main lines on the left. Once the Coast Line had opened, there was little need for this bay platform but it retained a run-round loop.
(Roy Hamilton/ Strathspey Railway)

on 30th July that year only £46,002 of the Banff, Portsoy & Strathisla Railway's £90,000 share capital had been subscribed while expenditure stood at £63,084. The shareholders in arrears on share calls were threatened with interest being charged on unpaid calls and even prosecution but they, and the wider public, failed to respond to the Directors' pleas for further financial support. The new Company was forced to use its borrowing powers and within six months secured two loans of £15,000 and £13,400 from the North of Scotland Bank and the Royal Bank of Scotland respectively. By line opening the North of Scotland Bank loan was overdrawn by £7,240! Moreover, the new company wanted to borrow wagons from the Great North.

There was another issue. A separate Act of the same date, 27th July 1857, had authorised the extension of the railway from Turriff to Macduff which was only a mile away from Banff over the River Deveron. Both railways expected the Great North to invest and work their lines. The proximity of the two railways opening at the same time (the Banff, Macduff & Turriff Extension Railway reached its first terminus at Gellymill, advertised as "Banff & Macduff," just short of Macduff on 4th June 1860) does not appear to have been taken into account during the parliamentary hearings for the bills. Competition between the two was inevitable. By June 1860 the Banff, Portsoy & Strathisla was complaining about the lower rates to Aberdeen via Macduff and Turriff although the Great North disputed this. Unconsigned traffic was sent by each route in alternate months.

The new line from Grange on the main line, which had opened on 11th October 1856, to Banff and Portsoy was single throughout. At Grange, with the junction to the main line facing Keith, there were no through services and trains departed from and arrived at a bay platform on the outside edge of the main line Up platform. The intermediate stations were at Knock and Cornhill. Problems with a proposed station at Glenbarry due to wet ground resulted in the building of Knock station. That Banff was clearly the main station was reflected in its initial staffing level of Stationmaster, porter, ticket boy, clerk, engine driver, fireman and cleaner. In contrast Portsoy and Knock each had only a Stationmaster and porter while these two roles were combined for one employee at Cornhill. Level crossing keepers were employed at Mill of Boyndie, Ladysbridge and Blairshinnoch. In October the Ladysbridge gatekeeper received a pay rise as he found himself also acting as Stationmaster.

Gradients were capped at 1 in 70 on either side of the summit at Glenbarry and on the Portsoy branch. Drivers departing southwards out of Portsoy faced the daunting prospect of a challenging 1 in 86 start, later exacerbated by the sharp curve of that station after the line was extended along the coast, followed by 1 in 70 for the two miles to Tillynaught. Gradients were easier on the Tillynaught to Banff section despite a couple of stretches at 1 in 80. The passenger station at Portsoy was situated on the south side of the town with single-road engine shed and turntable. Water (for the locomotives) was pumped from the nearby Loch of Soy. A steep 1 in 30 spur was constructed down to the harbour in 1860. There were special safety procedures for working this incline with the maximum load for one locomotive restricted to four wagons and the level crossing gate at the bottom operated by a lever interlinked with the nearby safety points. From May 1862 it was decreed that only tank engines (and not tender engines) could operate the branch. It was an expensive extension through a deep cutting flanked by high retaining walls and crossed by three bridges and it reflected Portsoy's importance as a seaport. Initially, the rails extended onto the quayside but these were later cut back to the foot of the incline. There was a similar, but more straightforward, harbour connection at Banff where the terminus was adjacent to the quay. The very cramped nature of the station only allowed for one line through to the harbour and it operated as a long siding. It opened in late 1859.

The steep harbour branch at Portsoy wound its way between the houses, with high retaining walls on both sides. The trackbed survives as a pleasant walkway and now has a hardcore surface.

(Norris Forrest)

The 1865 25 inch OS map showed the full extent of the harbour branch at Portsoy before it was cut back.
(National Library of Scotland, Creative Commons Licence CC-BY)

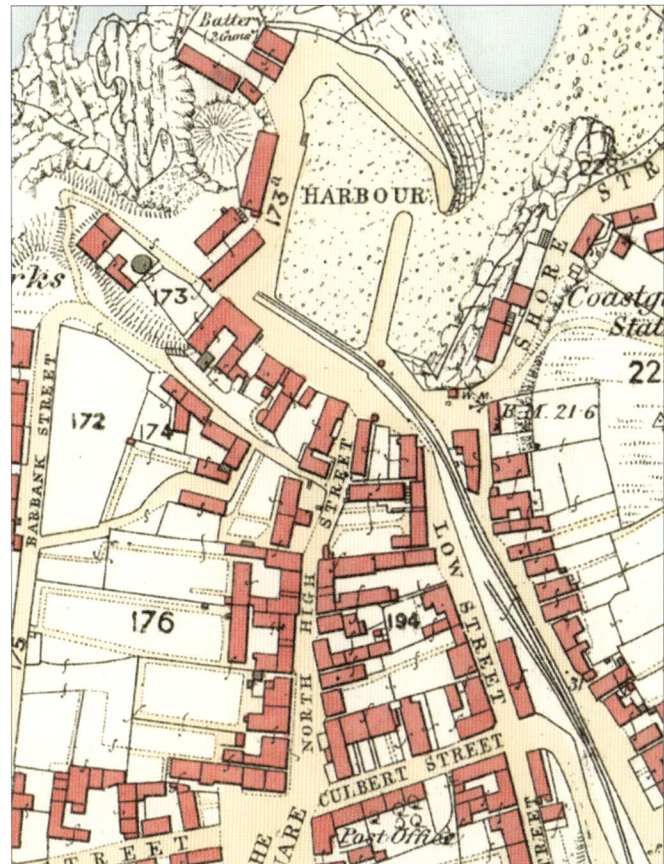

The company failed to reach a working agreement with the Great North and the commenced its own operations. Services began with one 0-4-2 tank engine, No. 1 *Banff*, designed and built by Hawthorns & Co. of Leith. The official opening day, 30th July 1859, was an unmitigated disaster. The celebratory train was derailed four miles north of Grange between Knock and Barry. There were suggestions of excessive speed and defective track and the locomotive ended up on its side, the first carriage across the line and the second coach partly derailed. This resulted in a speed limit of 16mph being imposed. A locomotive was hired from the Inverness & Aberdeen Junction Railway while *Banff* was repaired.

Until the second 0-4-2 tank, No. 2 *Portsoy*, was delivered by Hawthorns, the services from Grange involved running to Portsoy and returning back to Tillynaught before proceeding to Banff. The procedure was reversed in the opposite direction and the trains operated in such fashion from 2nd August until October that year.

From 1st January 1860 there were three trains per day each way between Grange and Banff, increased to four in the summer

The original passenger station at Portsoy which later served as a carriage shed seen in May 1968 from the later passenger station. The harbour branch ran on the far side of the original station. The building is a remarkable survivor and is still in commercial use. The final deliveries of coal had been made to the sidings. Spare ground in the station is being used for vegetable growing, no doubt a perk enjoyed by some railwaymen. A Camping Coach was sited here in the 1950s and early 60s. (Keith Fenwick)

months, with extra shuttles on the Portsoy section to cater for Portsoy to Banff traffic. Journey time from Grange to Banff was just over an hour, although one train was scheduled at 45 minutes. The run between Tillynaught and Portsoy took, on average, 10 minutes, although in 1863 the 5.14pm ex Portsoy took only six minutes while the earlier 2.30pm mixed took 15 minutes. There were no Sunday services.

The private coach service *Earl of Fife* from Fochabers to Banff was cut back to Portsoy by agreement and the mail contract from there to Banff passed to the railway. The coach service was withdrawn shortly afterwards. Almost as an afterthought, and only after the line had been fully inspected, the Board decided to build a siding at Barry for passengers and goods, as well as at Millegan. They opened on 1st October 1859 and became unadvertised conditional stops along with Ordens on the six-mile section from Tillynaught to Banff. "Open sheds" were constructed at Barry and Ordens later in the year to afford protection to waiting passengers. Ordens, along with Portsoy, had portable cattle pens. Tillynaught and Ladysbridge were also afterthoughts as it was not until 24th August 1859 that the Board decided to make the junction a passenger station; and on 22nd October that Ladysbridge was declared a station and to be advertised as such. It had actually opened, along with Ordens, on 1st October. In the following year a siding and signals were installed at Ladysbridge and Knock. Cornhill, Tillynaught and Ladysbridge dragged themselves into the 19th century with the installation of urinals! The embryonic Company's misfortunes were not over. On 1st November 1859 the line was damaged by storms with a bridge washed out near Cornhill which closed the line onwards to Banff until a temporary wooden bridge was in place by 2nd December.

Initially, trains terminated at a temporary station situated on the links five furlongs short of Banff until an agreement was concluded to extend into the town. The first freight train consisting of 11 wagons and a carriage conveying the Company directors was cheered into Banff Harbour by crowds on both sides of the line on 31st March 1860. It was hauled by a decorated locomotive with masonic flag. Passenger services to the new station commenced on 1st May and the temporary terminus closed. The new station had a small single road/platform passenger trainshed (attached to the Stationmaster's house) which was barely fit for purpose. It housed the booking office, waiting rooms, and manager's and auditor's offices. The extremely cramped goods area boasted a main siding, loading bank, shed, water tower and hand-operated crane. Interestingly in 1859, as it was not yet involved with the new line, the Great North introduced two steamer services. One was from Invergordon to Inverness but the other provided a service from the Moray Firth ports to Aberdeen and Granton (Edinburgh). The two services failed due to lack of traffic and were withdrawn after only 10 months. One can only surmise that the objective was to thwart the future Highland Railway before their proposed lines were built.

In November 1860 No. 3 *Keith*, a larger 0-4-2 goods tender engine bought second-hand from the Scottish Central Railway, arrived to be followed in July 1861 by No. 4 *Strathisla*, also purchased from Hawthorns. All four locomotives were painted green, but in a darker shade to the Great North and more akin to the Inverness & Aberdeen Junction engines. The locomotives were stabled in sheds at both Portsoy and Banff where there were turntables and watering facilities. There was also a goods shed at Grange and a turntable which had gone by 1887. Passenger rolling stock consisted of two composite (one First and one Third Class) and two Third Class coaches. Subsequently 30 goods wagons and a brake van were ordered.

Timetable issued on 1st November 1859. Two locomotives were now in use. The Goods train was soon withdrawn but four trains were provided in summer.

From the start the new railway struggled financially with an ongoing deficit on the capital account. There were problems with the locomotives and in August 1860 the company had to hire another from the Great North complete with driver, fireman and cleaner! It requested the Great North's terms for repairing locomotives and it agreed to do so *"to order as at present"*. In October the Company accepted a formal offer from the Great North to undertake this work. By November it was asking if it could employ the locomotive foreman, William Thomson, from Keith.

Freight traffic included fish and agricultural produce, whisky and supplies for the Banff distillery and metalwork goods manufactured by Fraser's Foundry in Banff, but volumes were disappointing. Coal was handled in large quantities both for the local merchants and to supply the nearby Banff gas works which was shoehorned between the goods yard and the sea. However, passenger receipts exceeded expectations and were sufficient to meet working expenses, with a net surplus of £2,200 recorded in the first year. This was swallowed up servicing debts and interest charges. Nevertheless, a dividend of 2% was paid in 1861.

However, the opening of the Great North's line from Turriff to Macduff (Gellymill) in 1860 with its more direct route to Aberdeen did not help. To compound matters the Great North Board proposed in July 1862 to construct a goods tramway from the town of Banff and from Macduff station to and from Macduff. Work started but by the following year a deputation from Macduff was asking for it to be made *"fit for passengers"*. Work was suspended but this issue was to rumble on for a few years until, in 1866, the Great North agreed to abandon the tramway in return for an undertaking to extend the Macduff terminus (at Gellymill) towards the town within five years. The financial problems persisted and, in March 1861, the Company secured a temporary loan of £38,000 from the North of Scotland Bank which was substantial given that gross revenue was only £5,531 that year. The Inverness & Aberdeen Junction Railway, of course, had inside knowledge of the Company's finances and it saw its potential as a defence against the Great North expanding further westwards. In April 1862 Thomas Bruce recommended to his Board that the Inverness & Aberdeen Junction should conclude a working agreement with the Banff, Portsoy & Strathisla. However, the Great North was alert to the danger and in June it reached agreement to work the line in perpetuity from 1st February 1863.

The Great North took over the working of the line in return for 65% of the receipts up to £6 per mile, 60% between £6 and £6 10/- per mile, 55% to £7 per mile and 50% above £7 per mile. It was also attracted by the Banff, Portsoy & Strathisla's plans to expand westwards from Portsoy and the two companies

The interior of the roof of the first station at Portsoy in 2010 with its original beams supporting the large span. (Keith Fenwick)

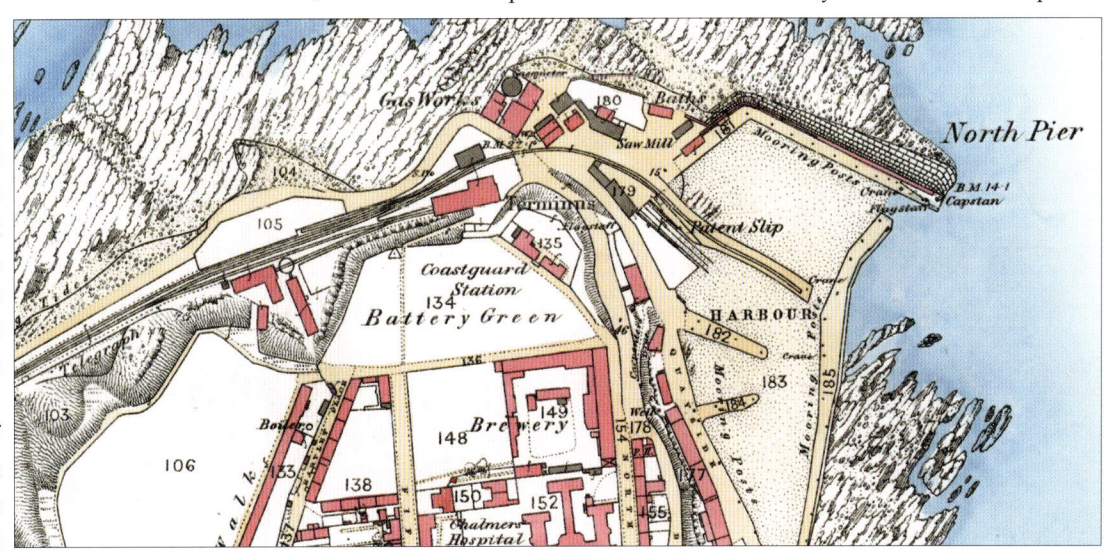

First edition OS map of Banff showing the cramped nature of the station and the extension to the harbour. A cleft in the hillside by the locomotive shed was used for an additional shed accessed via a small turntable.
(National Library of Scotland, Creative Commons Licence CC-BY)

discussed the issue in the summer of 1862. A public meeting in Buckie on 4th June of that year supported such an extension referring to it as the "Banff and Moray Junction Railway". And, simultaneously, the Great North engineer Alexander Gibb was surveying a line from Keith to Fochabers, Portgordon and Buckie for the Company. The Great North agreed to promote a line to Buckie, Portgordon or to "*a point east of the Spey*", to invest £25,000 in the new company and to work the line on completion. However, when the Duke of Rutland objected (as well as Lord Seafield) the Great North decided not to pursue its proposal beyond Portgordon. As well as being a business opportunity, such a line would effectively block the threatening plans of the Inverness & Aberdeen Junction for extending eastwards along the coast from Elgin. On 21st July 1863 the Banffshire Railway Act ratified the agreement and the undertaking was renamed the Banffshire Railway.

As well as guaranteeing the Banffshire's loans, that same Act officially authorised the extension of the line 14¼ miles along the coast from Portsoy to Portgordon with £160,000 of new capital to be raised. The Great North was authorised to contribute £80,000 and there were additional borrowing powers of £33,000.

The proposal was to skirt Cullen at the foot of the cliffs to avoid heavy engineering works (although there were difficulties at the west end of Cullen Bay and a proposed tunnel was a non-starter) before following the coast somewhat inland. However, money problems persisted with 60% of receipts still failing to cover interest charges and, in any event, the Great North had growing financial concerns of its own.

And there was another threat. The Inverness & Aberdeen Junction Railway was now promoting a railway to Garmouth which it planned to build from the original Fochabers Station (later Orbliston Junction) to the town of Fochabers and along the west bank of the Spey to Garmouth. The Fochabers & Garmouth Railway Act of 8th June 1863 incorporated a separate company to which the Inverness & Aberdeen Junction and the Inverness & Perth Junction Railway companies would subscribe £15,000 and £5,000 respectively. This move was seen simply as a move to thwart the Great North's plans to expand westwards. Fortunately for the Great North nothing materialised and the powers were abandoned in 1869. The Inverness & Aberdeen Junction Railway directors later admitted that the line was indeed promoted only to prevent the Great North from expanding along the Moray Coast.

A general view of Banff from above the cottages at Scotstown in the early twentieth century. The station is in the centre distance with the town up the hill to the right. The harbour is hidden behind the station. A mixed train is on its way to Tillynaught on track with very poor ballast. The trackbed is now a footpath.
(GNRSA collection)

The Banffshire Railway and Great North 1863-1883

Although the Great North did not yet own the Banffshire Railway it set out immediately to review its operations. The four locomotives were renumbered 37 – 40 respectively in the Great North stock and the nameplates were removed. Nos. 39 and 40 were transferred to the Deeside Railway, leaving the original two tank engines to work the line from Grange to both Portsoy and Banff, which they did until withdrawn in early 1885. Although official railway documents referred to these locomotives as "Banffshire" engines, local railwaymen called them "Strathisla" engines. The Great North also reviewed some stations. Millegan (variously spelt Millagan and Milligan), which mainly served a local sawmill, was closed to passengers permanently in October 1863, its final appearance in the timetable. It never had a platform but continued to handle goods under the control of the Knock Stationmaster and was referred to as Millegan Siding. Barry and Ordens also disappeared from the timetable, although closing Knock completely and moving the signals to and consolidating local business at Barry was considered. Ordens, between Tillynaught and Ladysbridge, was retained, but only as a conditional and unadvertised request halt under the control of the guard. It was to reappear publicly advertised from the summer of 1915. On operational issues a distant signal was required at Ladysbridge because of the goods siding. Discs were to be erected at Banff, Portsoy and Grange platforms as an additional safety precaution.

In 1864 the parent company was unhappy when it discovered that the Banffshire had advertised for contractors for the Buckie extension, especially in view of the state of the money markets. On 16th September a joint meeting with the Banffshire directors revealed that tender documents had been issued without the Great North Board even seeing them and with only three weeks given for a response. At the Company AGM on 26th April 1865 it was reported that the Buckie extension was to be postponed for one year and this was agreed with the Banffshire directors a month later. However, the Banffshire directors were permitted to continue to secure land before the purchase powers expired, although the Great North took the wise precaution of refusing to take any responsibility for any land agreements. Basically it adopted a *"we'll leave it with you"* stance. The Banffshire's financial position continued to deteriorate to the extent that the terms of the Working Agreement were suspended and the Great North became entitled to 100% of the line's revenue during the period of that suspension.

By 1865 the Great North was in the rather bizarre situation that over 75% of its network comprised subsidiary companies as well as the Morayshire and Banffshire Railways with only the main line from Aberdeen to Keith wholly owned. The Great North of Scotland (Amalgamation) Act of 30th July 1866 brought many of the small nominally independent companies into the fold but the ongoing financial problems of the Banffshire Railway precluded its inclusion. It did also, however, provide three additional years for the completion of the extension to

Ordens seen on 4th May 1968, its final day of service, although there is little sign of use as there were only scattered farms nearby. The station cannot have been very inviting to passengers. Access was by a path behind the small wooden building up to the road. The building itself survived for many years after the line closed.   (Keith Fenwick)

The locomotive shed at Banff was cramped as shown in this view looking west on 7th October 1954. Originally there was another building at right angles to the line in the foreground, accessed via a small turntable. The Banffshire Railway would have carried out all its maintenance here. (J L Stevenson)

Portgordon. Although gross revenue grew modestly it failed to cover working expenses and interest between 1861 and 1867 and the Company was basically insolvent. It took another 12 months of hard negotiation before the Great North of Scotland Railway Act of 12th August 1867 confirmed its amalgamation, with most of the employees of the Banffshire Railway transferring to the Great North and the Great North taking responsibility for the Banffshire Railway's debts of £45,000. The Banffshire Railway secured representation on the Great North Board. At the same time powers were obtained to abandon the extension from Portsoy to Portgordon for which the Great North was committed to expenditure of £78,500. A line along the coast would have to wait and this was a major disappointment to the fishing ports to the west of Portsoy.

With the railway now under its ownership, the Great North continued to review operations. The Board of Trade examined the Portsoy Harbour branch following an accident at the level crossing at the foot of the incline. On 29th August 1867 the Company considered giving up working it by locomotive power and, at the same time, evaluated working both Banff and Portsoy lines as one line with only one engine. By October it was considering three options: close the harbour branch which would allow one engine to be withdrawn; close the harbour branch and continue to work the line with two engines; or continue to work the line as at present but with the provision of a pedestrian footbridge over the harbour branch. The decision was to continue present operations, including the harbour branch, but to investigate if interested parties would finance the cost of a gateman at the level crossing. In May 1868 it was proposed to cut back the harbour branch "*to opposite Mr Young's house*" which would allow the gates to be dispensed with (presumably no one had come forward to pay for a gateman).

The Company was also reviewing Banff and, on 14th May 1868, it served three months' notice to the Banff Harbour Commissioners that it intended to cease working the harbour extension due to poor volumes. The Commissioners requested reconsideration and the Company agreed to keep it open for a further month until 20th September. A deputation from Banff failed to convince the Great North who suggested that the Harbour Trustees continue to operate it by horse on their own responsibility. Agreement was reached and the Great North duly retrenched back to the station.

The issue of amalgamating Knock and Barry was discussed again but a decision was deferred. In August 1869 residents close to Barry were calling for a "*full station*" and additional land was secured in February 1871. In March the Company received a petition against the closure of Knock and for a station at Millegan. It was agreed that Knock should be closed and that there should be a station at Millegan. In June the Company discussed the closure of Knock again. Annual revenue was over

£500 against an annual expense of £50 while the annual revenue of Barry was under £100. Closure of Knock would result in a loss greatly in excess of any saving and therefore it was agreed (only by a majority of six to four) to continue with both stations for a further 12 months. There were objections to the suggestion that Ordens would close and the Company reported that receipts were £2.5.1d in the 12 months to November 1868 for goods and livestock and that 15 trucks of cattle had been forwarded to Aberdeen and Glasgow. The station was still open for passengers (1869) but there was no Stationmaster.

Meanwhile the Great North was still mired in issues regarding the amalgamation of the Banffshire. Some of the Banffshire Guarantors were now in court as the Company attempted to recover the money guaranteed. A compromise proposal was put forward whereby half the guaranteed amount was to be paid but without any arrears of interest. That just brought howls of protest from those who had already paid in full with interest and had received their shares; and from those who had paid in full but without paying the interest and had not received their shares. It was some mess! As the Guarantors continued to resist payment in early 1869 the Company turned to the Sherriff Court to invoke the Debt Recovery Act, although it was also threatening to raise actions in the Court of Session. That did the trick as many Guarantors paid up in the face of this threat.

The issue of Knock versus Barry appeared to have been resolved. Barry, which had still been handling some goods and parcels during its seven closed years, reopened in 1870 on a slightly different site and was renamed Glenbarry on 19th February 1872. Knock was to be retained, and there was no more talk about a station at Millegan. As the Great North prepared to open their extension from Gellymill to Macduff on the Turriff line on 1st July 1872 the town clerk of Banff suggested that the new intermediate station be called Banff South and that Banff Harbour be renamed Banff North. The Company ignored that advice and named the new station Banff Bridge. This resulted in another issue for the Company. Suddenly Banff Bridge became an even shorter, easier and cheaper option for travel from Aberdeen to Banff – and it avoided the need to change trains at Tillynaught.

On 26th February 1874 the timber engine shed at Portsoy blew down and, as additional sidings were necessary there, the Company decided to rebuild on a new site at a cost of £200. A pivot crane was added in September 1876. By 1875 the Great North was wringing its hands yet again over the viability of both Millegan and Knock and was revisiting its option to centralise their business at Glenbarry. This time Knock faced a real threat. It had a single platform of 46 yards in length on an incline of 1 in 72 falling to the south. It had a siding entered by south-facing points outside the station at the southern end and also runaway trap points. Due to widespread opposition in the area, Colonel Yolland of the Board of Trade acted as arbiter between the Great North and local interests and he refused to sanction such a move. This was largely because many local residents claimed they had supported,

Banff looking east on 22nd June 1937. The goods sidings on the left are not very busy. The signal box is still in existence at this time. Gravity shunting was used to allow the engine to change ends for the return trip to Tillynaught, although there had been a short lived crossover in the early days at the station end of the yard to allow normal rounding of trains. (H R Norman)

Ladysbridge looking over the valley to the Banffshire District Lunatic Asylum, one of many established around the country in Victorian Britain. The locomotive is a rebuilt Cowan 2-4-0. The photograph can be dated as between 1880, when the first of that locomotive class was rebuilt, and 1888 when signalling was installed at the station. (R D Drummond/GNSRA)

indeed had invested in, the railway on the understanding that a station would serve Knock; and that, at the amalgamation of the Banffshire into the Great North in 1867, assurances had been given by the Company that the railway and Knock station would be maintained in their current state. There was, unfortunately, nothing in writing to this effect.

Moreover, an analysis of the three stations over the three years 1872 to 1874 showed that, while Glenbarry had receipts of £1,118 against expenditure of £144, Knock was not far behind with receipts of £992 against expenditure of £146. Millegan, on the other hand, had receipts of only £146 against expenditure of £189. The Board of Trade also took account of the additional mileage (2¼ miles on average both ways) which would be incurred by those living to the east and south of Knock to access Glenbarry. And the traders using Portsoy, Banff and Macduff stations contended that they would lose out significantly as residents and businesses to the south of Knock would transfer their traffic to Rothiemay station on the main line which would result in those three towns being in competition with those on the main line to Aberdeen. The outcome, in the Board of Trade report of 28th July 1875, was that it was "*somewhat questionable*" as to whether centralising at Glenbarry would save the rather modest cost of operating Knock. Colonel Yolland recommended that Knock be retained and that Millegan Siding be closed. It had, in fact, already been sacrificed on 1st July that year. Two years later, in December 1877, the Company received a petition requesting the closure of Knock and the substitution of a station at Millegan but the Company declined. Only seven years later, in a commitment to that station's future, the Great North chose Knock as one of the first seven stations on its network to install the new "*telegraph speaking instrument*", a two-position improvement on the conventional electric telegraph. The Great North's long-standing doubts over Knock were erased.

During the Board of Trade assessment of centralising Knock and Millegan traffic at Glenbarry, it came to light that there was some form of written agreement given to a single proprietor by the Directors of the Banff, Portsoy & Strathisla Railway Company, and confirmed by the Great North, to maintain Glenbarry as a passenger station. There was some doubt as to whether this commitment would be upheld in a court of law, but it cannot have done any harm to the station's future prospects.

There was a very interesting barb at the end of Colonel Yolland's 1875 report when he appears to have confused his role as arbiter with his normal role of railway inspector: "*I should mention that neither of these stations* [Glenbarry and Knock] *are fitted with those appliances, which the present requirements of the Board of Trade exact for all new lines of railway*". The original station of Barry/Glenbarry had a platform of about 60 yards for the single line on an incline of 1 in 95 to the south with sidings entered to the north side.

The Great North must at least have been relieved that the operation of Cornhill was relatively straightforward (and continuous) from the start. It was a single platform station on the Down side and a goods yard, mainly for domestic coal which was shovelled by hand into carts for onward distribution, and livestock for the adjacent mart every Thursday. A standard Great North wooden building with parcel store was erected in 1888 to replace an earlier much smaller building. Yard access was by a tablet-operated ground frame (after 1893) and shunting was normally undertaken by the early morning service from Elgin. There were poultry "*plucking sheds*" within the yard from which dressed birds were dispatched by train to Aberdeen shops. Slates were received from Gartly for replacing thatched roofs on local houses. Bulk supplies of oatmeal, flour, sugar and tea arrived and were taken by horse and cart to fill the bins at Chalmers shop in the village. Cornhill shared a summer public holiday with Portsoy and the Great North was not slow to take advantage. On Monday 31st July 1865, for example, a special train departed the coastal town at 5.50am, picked up at Tillynaught (6.00am), Cornhill (6.10am) and Grange (6.35am), and deposited the day trippers at Keith at 6.50am. The train returned at 9.52pm and set down its no doubt weary passengers at Cornhill at 10.32pm and at Portsoy at 11.00pm. It must have been a long day!

The original Tillynaught station was a simple affair with a central platform serving the Banff and Portsoy lines on either side. There was one siding. The main intermediate station was Ladysbridge ("Lady's Bridge" from 1859 to 1886). It had a single platform with wooden station building (which was not constructed until early 1887 along with the lengthening of the platform to 300 feet) and a small goods yard of two sidings and a loading bank on the Up side. Access to the yard was controlled by a two-lever ground frame locked by the section tablet. The station served the nearby fishing port of Whitehills and the small harbour of Blackpots (1½ miles distant) from where fish and crabs were carted to the station for dispatch. The Great North Board had authorised cheap tickets for fisher-women at all relevant stations as early as June 1860 and Ladysbridge was included from November 1864. The local fishwives used the station to travel to and from their regular destinations by special ticket which cost 6d and included one creel (basket) of fish on the train free of charge. There was significant agricultural traffic with livestock, grain and potatoes, including up to 250 tons of seed potatoes annually to England and Wales. Large cans of milk were sent to the creamery in Huntly. Another important function was full examination of all

With only two weeks remaining before the withdrawal of passenger services BR Standard Class 4 No. 76104 sits ready to depart from Banff with a late afternoon service to Tillynaught on 24th June 1964. A youngster appears to be getting possibly his first and last tour of a steam engine footplate.
(Norris Forrest)

tickets and collection of Banff tickets on all Down trains. All Up train tickets were examined at Banff and collected at Ladysbridge from those alighting.

The station also served the adjacent 90-bed Ladysbridge Hospital which opened as Banff District Asylum in May 1865 and the nearby 40-bed Woodpark Succursal Asylum. The two combined in 1889 and became part of the National Health Service in 1948. Excursions from the local station were organised for the residents. For example, in July 1873, 39 men travelled on the 10.20am train to Glassaugh House for a summer picnic. There they joined 40 ladies who had travelled by road and, after an enjoyable day, the men returned to Ladysbridge by regular train. In 1872 and 1878 the summer excursions of the Sabbath Day School of the Established Church in Portsoy saw over 200 adults and children travel to and from Ladysbridge by train for sports, picnic and dancing within the grounds of the hospital. The return to Portsoy in 1878 was by special train. The station was used down the years by both visitors and staff including members of the Mental Welfare Commission in Edinburgh. It is believed that the Stationmaster and his staff were fully aware of the required procedure if any of the patients made individual enquiries about rail travel!

Banff became a popular destination for Sunday School picnics and other excursions and its cramped lay-out with limited stabling resulted in strict timetabling (literally down to the last minute) in order to service trains. In September 1876 the *Banffshire Journal* noted that Banff afforded "*….the smallest accommodation of any station in the Great North system*" and that the local community was "*waiting patiently*" to see if the Great North would make improvements. Ever mindful of costs, it did not.

Ladysbridge looking east on 22nd June 1960. By then goods traffic had declined but the station retained staff to operate the level crossing. The block bells between Tillynaught and Banff were repeated in the station to warn of an approaching train; their sound was even heard on a radio programme for railway enthusiasts. After the closure of Banff signal box and the introduction of 'One Engine in Steam' in May 1960 the Signalman at Tillynaught would have been solely responsible for notifying Ladysbridge (and the other crossings) of approaching trains.

(Roy Hamilton/Strathspey Railway)

Difficult Years and Fishing Developments 1866-1881

The constant operational and cost reviews and the delay in making further progress along the Moray Firth coast was undoubtedly due to severe financial pressures which had been building on the Great North by 1866. The rapid expansion of the system had stretched the Company's resources, traffic was not yet up to anticipated volumes, most of the subsidiary companies required additional funding and the Company was committed to the costly Denburn Valley Line in order to connect to the main line south at, what was to become, the Joint Station in Aberdeen. The Highland Railway's direct and shorter line south over Druimuachdar to Perth, opened in 1863, had caused a major reduction in Great North revenue including the partial loss of mail hitherto passing through Aberdeen. The value of the shares in the Deeside Railway, in which the Great North had invested, was below its purchase cost. And, to compound matters, another national financial crisis caused by over-speculation, mainly by railway contractors, was besetting the United Kingdom. The failure of a major bank, Overend & Gurney, sparked panic and the collapse of other financial institutions. In modern parlance it was, for the Great North, a perfect storm. Dividends on ordinary shares were suspended from 1865.

The Board, fearing shareholder disquiet, set up a Committee to investigate the Company's financial affairs and a recommendation in the subsequent report confirmed the cancellation of the Banffshire Railway's extension from Portsoy to Portgordon. There was a complete change of Directors in 1867 with Sir James Elphinstone being replaced by John Duncan as Chairman. As matters failed to improve the Board initiated a policy of strict economy throughout the Company. That included a complete moratorium on proposals to develop the network. Progress was slow but the policy of austerity led to the resumption of dividends from April 1874 by which time most of the extraordinary debts were paid off. On 1st August 1875 the Great North and the Deeside Railway merged which left just the 18¼ miles of the Morayshire Railway as worked mileage.

Despite the progress there were still issues. No new locomotives and few passenger coaches or goods wagons had been obtained since 1866; there had been minimal maintenance of stations and, indeed, some locomotives and much of the Company's plant required renewal. Train services had remained largely unaltered. The Company Chairman from 1872 to 1879 was William Leslie but it was under the direction of his successor William Ferguson of Kinmundy and of William Moffatt, appointed Company Secretary and General Manager in 1880, that the Company made significant progress. Doubling of the main line commenced reflecting increased traffic; 2¾ miles of track from Ferryhill Junction to Cults on the Deeside Line were doubled; much track was upgraded; and signalling was modernised. There were hiccups along the way including the suspension of ordinary share dividend payments again in 1881, 1882 and 1883. However, gradually the Company moved forward with efficiencies leading to all-round improvement throughout that decade.

Despite its economic difficulties the Great North was keeping a close eye on the situation along the Moray Firth coast. There was still the gap in its rail network between Portsoy and Elgin and the fishing industry was developing rapidly. And the Company was aware that its bitter rival, the Highland Railway Company, was also evaluating associated potential opportunities. The Great North was already hauling fish out of Fraserburgh, Peterhead and Macduff and, of course, south from Aberdeen along with the North British and Caledonian Companies. Railways not only helped to develop fishing itself but also to increase the value of the catch by providing ready access to new markets. White fish was to become important from the 1880s, but the volume potential lay with the "*silver darlings*" – the herring – which could be transported away quickly in a fresh state thereby reducing the amounts cured locally for sale at a later date. There was a herring boom in the 1850s, 1860s and 1870s. More powerful and faster steam powered vessels appeared in the last two decades of the century adding trawl to traditional methods of line and drift net fishing. They could return more quickly to port to gain the highest prices. By 1880 there were 7,000 Scottish boats fishing for herring. The Great North recognised the potential although there was a downside. Herring are migratory and the fishing seasonal. The fish were landed in Stornoway in May, Lerwick in June, Wick and the Moray Firth ports from July to September, and Yarmouth from October to December. The larger boats started to follow the herring. For the Great North the seasonality was costly in terms of locomotives, rolling stock and people. The Company had to react at short notice to sudden heavy landings. Often predicted landings failed to materialise, whether due to the volatility of stocks or the weather. And, with transport charges being controlled by the Government, the returns were modest as well as seasonal.

Throughout the 1860s, 1870s and early 1880s there was continual lobbying from the Moray Firth coastal communities, especially Buckie, for rail connection. Local fishermen on the Coast looked enviously at developments in Peterhead and Fraserburgh with their rail connections which were attracting many of the Coast skippers. Ports like Cullen, Portessie, Buckie and Portgordon with no railway were watching the herring boom passing them by. The Coast fishermen were slow to embrace change and continued to beach their sailing dinghies on the shoreline. A stone-built harbour had been constructed at Buckpool in the 1840s but was prone to silting to the extent that there was a constant battle to keep it operational.

Matters, however, took a turn from 1876. The population of Buckie was approaching 5,000 and fishing was at last developing with the increasing use of the new, larger and more stable "Zulu" herring drifters. Cluny Estates commenced construction of a massive new harbour in Buckie over an area of nine acres with outer and inner basins providing a quayside of nearly half a mile. It opened in 1880 at a cost of £65,000 and, with a low water depth of 10 feet, access for the Zulus was straightforward. Suddenly, the profile of the Moray Firth Coast herring fishery changed. In 1879 an average of 28 vessels landed 6,714 crans from July to September spread between Portgordon, Buckie, Findochty, Portknockie and Cullen. The following year the total volume had increased to 75 boats landing a total of 18,816 crans; and by 1882 the number of vessels landing had increased to 95. And the landings were becoming centred on Buckie and Cullen with the number of boats increasing from 46 to 62 and from 9 to 19 respectively in the two years from 1880. A further two years on saw the smaller ports more or less squeezed out altogether with 91 and 24 boats landing at Buckie and Cullen respectively. There was also a modest trade in haddock, cod and ling from line fishing by small sailing boats. The value of crabs and lobsters was increasing. Steam powered trawlers were on the horizon. Associated boat-building was developing in Buckie. Coal, largely from Fife, and oil was required for the new steam drifters. Ice was brought in from Aberdeen and salt, general stores and materials were needed for the vessels, processors and employees. Many fishermen and factory employees had to travel to and from Buckie and the infamous fisher lassies embarked on long train journeys as the larger boats started to follow the herring shoals. As most of the catch was still exported by sea, it was time for the Great North to act.

Taken not long after the opening of the line, this photograph shows the extent of Cluny Harbour at Buckie. The passenger lines are in the foreground. Rows of open wagons wait for their loads of fish in barrels.
(George Washington Wilson/Aberdeen University Creative Commons Licence, CC BY 4.0)

The Building of the Coast Line 1881 - 1886

In 1876 the Great North secured powers to enable it to settle the outstanding debts of the Morayshire Railway and this allowed amalgamation negotiations to resume. It took 14 years to resolve the company's financial issues, but an agreement on 1st October 1880 sealed the union. Royal Assent was confirmed retrospectively in the Great North of Scotland Railway Act of 11th August 1881 and this heralded the final consolidation of the Great North's railway system. Alexander Watt, Secretary of the Morayshire Railway, was accorded great credit for the success of the amalgamation and he was appointed Superintendent of the Northern Section of the Great North until his retirement in 1906. That brought continuity and a bonus was that any potential conflict of interest over the proposed Coast Line linking with the Morayshire's line to Lossiemouth and operating into Elgin was removed.

The Great North Board discussed the Coast Line project at regular intervals throughout the 1870s and continued to engage with the landowners, not least Lord Seafield, but its financial difficulties held it back. Finally, on 14th October 1880, it resolved to promote a Bill for the railway from Portsoy to Buckie and Portgordon and, on 20th October 1881, the Board agreed to draw up plans for the full line between Portsoy and Elgin. This time it would be slightly longer and pass the back of Cullen as opposed to below the cliffs. However, when it decided again to terminate the line at Portgordon rather than push on to Elgin with its westward connections, there was fierce criticism in the coastal towns. The Highland Railway, sensing another threat from the east, opposed the scheme and, supported by Keith business interests, counter-proposed a new line from Keith to Buckie and onwards to Cullen and possibly further. It argued that a direct line from Buckie to Keith would provide the fastest route to the south via its connection to Forres and its main line. The Great North, on the other hand, contended that its line would serve a larger number of communities with direct access south via Aberdeen. A suggested compromise from some coastal residents was for the Great North to extend from Portsoy to Portknockie and for the Highland to construct a new line onwards to join their Keith to Elgin line at Lhanbryde. William Ferguson was in optimistic mood and in late 1881 he even assured a shareholders' meeting that, as soon as the new Coast Line was completed, a link would be built between Banff and Macduff as well as an east-west link from New Maud to Turriff. However, the Great North's Bill was rejected.

The following year, 1882, both companies outlined fresh proposals. The Great North convened an EGM on 9th February. It now planned to build a line of 25¼ miles from Portsoy to Portgordon and, crucially, on to meet the Morayshire's Elgin – Lossiemouth branch at a junction near Elgin. William Ferguson and his Board canvassed the support of both local residents and major landowners. Public meetings were held in Buckie, Portessie, Portgordon, Rothes and Macduff. At the Buckie meeting on Saturday 18th February 1882 supporters of the Great North's Coast Line pointed out that the Highland's proposed line from Keith to Buckie extended to Cullen would detract from Buckie being promoted as the main trading centre for the local area and that, by proposing the extension towards Cullen, the Highland had effectively confirmed that the Coast Line was required; but not just "*half a one*"! A local solicitor, Mr Mair, produced a petition of 1,000 names supporting the Highland scheme. There were allegations that some local Buckie folk had signed petitions in support of both projects in the hope that one of them would be passed and that, if both were, so much the better!

William Ferguson enlisted the help of the Earl of Kintore to influence the Duke of Richmond and Gordon on the merits of the new line and, initially, he was supportive but only if the Company continued the line through to Orton on the Highland and re-opened the Orton – Rothes link of the former Morayshire Railway which had been abandoned in 1866. The Duke's suggestions were met with little enthusiasm by the Great North and he withdrew his support completely. The new Earl of Seafield,

William Ferguson of Kinmundy, chairman of the GNSR 1879-1904

who had just inherited Cullen House and Policies, opposed the proposals as the grounds of his new home would be adversely affected. The Great North sought to placate him by proposing a 1,280 yard tunnel but to no avail. He and his family had close connections to the Highland Railway and he chose to support its direct line from Buckie to Keith. (When the Coast Line opened the family refused to use the local station preferring to travel to Rathven on the Highland line and they encouraged their visitors to do likewise). William Ferguson also courted the Duke of Fife, who was another large local landowner, but he preferred to remain neutral despite Ferguson offering him a seat on the Great North Board. The Duke, in fact, responded rather drily that *"such a step would be incompatible with my duty to the Highland Railway Company"*!!

The Highland Railway simply resubmitted its proposal from the previous year for a line from Keith to Buckie and Cullen. By early 1882 the Great North was becoming impatient with the Highland who refused point blank to discuss a joint line instead of pushing on with their own plans. William Ferguson fell out with Buckie Harbour Trustees over the provision of land for his new station and accused the Trustees of strangling his Company. There was another issue with Lord Seafield over access to his land for survey work. However, both proposals received full parliamentary approval although the Highland's line from Keith to Buckie was only authorised as far as a junction with the Great North at Portessie. The Great North of Scotland (Buckie Extension) Railway Act of 12th July 1882 authorised the line from Portsoy to Elgin to be completed within five years with new capital of £165,000 in shares and with borrowing powers of £55,000. The Company was given an obligation to replace the Coastguard station at Buckie but was granted the use of *"any rails"* at Buckie Harbour. There was provision for the Highland to connect at Portessie and for its traffic to be worked to Buckie Harbour. The Highland was granted running powers east to Portsoy and the Great North similarly from Elgin to Forres. There was a caveat, however, that these powers could only be exercised by both Companies together at the same time. Given that both jealously guarded their own territories that was highly unlikely and over time that particular clause in the subsequent Act turned out to be impotent!

The Highland built its Buckie station inland on the site of the old Hammond's Meal Mill and it faced one small but nonetheless important issue. The Trustees of Cluny Estates opposed its scheme and that meant tricky negotiations lay ahead on the issue of rail access to the new Buckie harbour. In practice it transpired that the Great North worked Highland goods traffic between the junction at Portessie and its Buckie station

William Moffatt, General Manager 1880-1906

where a Highland Railway booking clerk and inspector were employed. The Great North was granted access to the quays at Buckie Harbour. The new venture was named the "Buckie Extension Railway" and was greeted with great enthusiasm in towns and villages along the coast. In Buckie and Portgordon folk were out on the streets and lights were hung from houses and buildings in the evening. The church bells of Cullen were rung at intervals from late afternoon until 10.00pm. Flags were hoisted, the Volunteer Band paraded and over 1,000 people joined the Magistrates and Town Council at a huge bonfire of tar barrels. Such was the strength of local support for the new railway line.

Four separate contracts were awarded in January 1883 for the construction. The "Portsoy Contract" and the "Buckie Contract" were awarded to William and Thomas Adams of Callander underpinned by "Cautioners sureties" from a retired local coal merchant James Ferguson and a merchant of Fairlie and Glasgow, Andrew Clark-Imrie. The agreed price for the Portsoy Contract was £52,286.19.7d and this section commenced, rather bizarrely, *"....in the Garden attached to Roseacre Cottage, Portsoy...."* and terminated near Portknockie, a distance of eight miles, two furlongs and 180 yards. The contract included a comprehensive set of specifications and conditions for the line's construction covering excavations, embankments, earthwork, masonry of bridges, culverts, drains, retaining walls, water-falls, masonry, diversions of roads and streams, fencing of roads, service fencing of the line, station platforms, loading banks, accesses, oak keys, ballasting, laying of permanent way and station sidings (including rails, chairs, fish-plates, sleepers, spikes, iron dog keys, switches and crossings, carriages and cartages) and, just to be on the safe side *"....all other works whatever required to complete the same...."*. There was a whole raft of specific design details not least concerning the main viaduct at Cullen. The Great North did not waste a penny as the contract stipulated that the material excavated from all the Cullen viaduct foundations were to be deposited in the railway's embankments *"....or where pointed out by the Engineer or Assistant Engineer"*. Ultimately, Adams claimed £77,742.2.7d for this contract but the Great North submitted a counter claim for unreasonable delays amounting to £16,740 (837 days @ £20/day). The dispute ended up in the House of Lords and was not fully resolved until December 1891. The Lords had dismissed Adams' claim the previous year but it is unclear whether he ever settled, although his guarantor did so with a payment of £500!

A similar but separate contract, at a price of £39,063.17.9d, covered the Buckie Section of eight miles, five furlongs and 20 yards from Portknockie to the River Spey. The contractor

The viaducts at Cullen often featured in postcards of the town, such as this one looking east from the Links. This emphasises the massive embankments constructed here. (GNSRA collection)

was paid in monthly instalments with a 10% retention which was payable one month after the line opened less any further retention deemed necessary by the Company Engineer to cover maintenance issues arising during the first 12 months of operation. Interestingly, Fochabers (later Spey Bay) is referred to as "Tugnet Station" in the Contract, another twist in that station's identity issues.

The third (identical) contract was the "Elgin Contract" which covered the eight miles and 133 yards from the River Spey to Elgin. It was awarded to John & William Granger, Contractors of Coupar Angus, for the sum of £25,069.2.8d. The fourth and final contract was the "Spey Bridge Contract" for the construction of the Viaduct between Fochabers and Garmouth. It was awarded to Blaikie Brothers of Aberdeen at a cost of £25,483.3.4d. A separate

BR&CW Type 2 (later Class 26) D5346 accelerates off the level eight span Cullen viaduct with the 08.58 Elgin to Aberdeen on 15th July 1967. The viaduct carried a 20mph speed restriction and the train is about to tackle the 1 in 60 gradient up to Cullen station. It has been coasting downhill on the 1 in 80 from Portknockie and had to brake for the 20mph restriction which, with a heavy train and a strong spray of salty sea water on a stormy day, could make the 1 in 60 climb ahead challenging. Note that there are two parcels vehicles at the front of the train and a Brake Second at the rear. (Roy Hamilton/Strathspey Railway)

One of the piers of the west viaduct, taken from the A98 in June 2016. The track under the arch leads to the links. (Keith Fenwick)

chapter covers the construction of the Viaduct. An additional contract was awarded in February 1884 to builders Messrs Watt & Clark of Princes Street, Aberdeen for the construction of all the stations between Portsoy and Elgin. The cost of building the line was estimated at around £150,000 with the Great North to raise £200,000 on the Stock Market. In the event it cost £305,000, mainly due to the issues with the Spey and Cullen Viaducts. The project was managed by the Great North's Chief Engineer Patrick Barnett.

The undulating gradients between Portsoy and Elgin presented some notable engineering challenges, not least skirting the sea-town of Cullen on a series of high embankments and three brick and masonry viaducts and the crossing of the Spey at Garmouth. The major engineering structures at Cullen were due to a significant diversion to avoid a corner of the Cullen House estate on the south west side of the village and also involved a fairly lengthy cutting 48 feet deep near the house itself. Excavation through rock, clay and gravel sand proved difficult and costly. Lord Seafield did ask for the tunnel plan to be revisited, but the Great North declined. The Great North Chairman, William Ferguson, was not impressed and in 1885 he described the *"two expensive and unsightly viaducts"* as a *"blot on the fair face of nature in a lovely locality"* which would result in future generations accusing the *"company's engineering skills in laying out the line as sadly deficient"*. He hadn't calmed down by the following year, as the booklet produced for the line's opening ceremony ranted: *"Owing to opposition of the proprietor to the railway entering a corner of the Cullen House policies as was intended, the Company was forced to construct an immense viaduct and to throw up a large embankment to give the line a detour seawards. In any case, a viaduct or embankment would have been necessary, but had the first proposition been acted upon, they would have been of much smaller dimensions."* Interestingly, Cullen Town Council added their tuppence worth by requesting something *"ornamental as well as useful"* for the Seafield Viaduct. This led to the south side of the main arch being modelled on Fleet Street's Temple Bar in London which was designed by Sir Christopher Wren. It also had concerns over the proposed width of this viaduct's arch over the town's main thoroughfare as it would reduce the street width from 62½ to 36½ feet. A compromise led to the construction of the two small arches over the pavements.

The West "Seatown" viaduct of eight arches each of 62½ feet span is 613 feet long and 78 feet high and it crosses the public road (today's A98) and the Cullen Burn. The middle viaduct over Lower Castle Street originally had six arches each of 45 feet span and was over 400 feet in length and 41 feet high. The East viaduct over Seafield Street has four arches and is 213 feet long and 29 feet high. It is built of freestone with blue limestone from Glassaugh quarry. Fifty men were employed on the construction of the viaducts and large crowds monitored progress each day. Ferguson noted that from the East viaduct just after departing from Cullen station: *"the passengers could almost drop an apple into the chimneys of some of the houses below"*. Despite his previous rather testy comments Ferguson did concede that: *"sweeping along over the viaducts and embankments a magnificent view is got over the crescent-shaped Bay"*. Despite his misgivings over the Great North's architectural legacy the viaducts did become regarded as some of the finest masonry works in the north of Scotland. They remain so today.

The piers of the main viaduct over the A98 are built of limestone blocks and are hollow but infilled with rubble. The arches are three feet thick and consist of six layers of large red brick set in cement. A 225mm deep layer of clay was placed over the arches as a water barrier. A belting course of freestone runs along the whole length of the structure directly above the arches on which sit the parapet walls which are built with blue limestone. The contractors had problems finding firm foundations for the piers and, in some cases, had to excavate to below sea level to a depth of 20 feet. Stone was brought to the site from the contractor's quarry in Stirling by sea to Burghead and thence by traction engines. A stone-dressing machine shaped them on site. Two steam cranes and hoisting apparatus worked by horse from below lifted the stones into position. Fine shingle from the local beach was conveyed by carts brought from Aberdeen to make cement.

Ferguson's troubles were not limited to the Seafield Estates.

When the Cluny Trustees proposed that the railway be built further into the hill at Buckie his frustration manifested itself in a grumpy letter: *"you prefer to follow the advice of your Harbour Engineer, rather than listen to the experience of our Railway Engineer and Managers. You thereby shut us up to heavy additional expense....I place this on record that I may keep myself and the Railway Coy free from all blame in the future for whatever may be the result of your short-sighted policy"*. Despite this tiff, Ferguson did have an ally in Cluny Estates as it welcomed the railway to serve its new harbour and was at odds on the issue with its landowner neighbour the Earl of Seafield.

Lady Gordon Cathcart of Cluny cut the first turf at a ceremony in Buckie on Tuesday 24th April 1883. A special train departed Aberdeen at 8.30am and arrived in Portsoy at 10.30am from where *"conveyances"* departed at 10.45am for arrival in Buckie at 12.45pm. The cutting ceremony at 1.00pm was followed by luncheon at 2.00pm and the guests departed at 4.00pm for return to Aberdeen via Keith. An arrival time of 7.45pm in Aberdeen ensured that it was a long day. A general holiday was declared by most of the towns on the line. There were celebratory parades through Buckie with bonfires in the evening and the firing of two field guns.

Tillynaught Junction was rebuilt with a crossing loop on the new main line and a separate platform and loop for the shuttle service on the "new" branch to Banff. A new wooden station was built at Portsoy immediately south of the original terminus which was retained for goods traffic. The original engine shed was also retained for the branch engine. It was removed two years later on the line's completion. Rails were laid to the harbour at Buckie. Construction commenced from both ends and the first 4¼ miles from Portsoy to Tochieneal, which included 15 bridges, opened on 1st April 1884 with one intermediate station at Glassaugh. A temporary locomotive and coaching stock stabling point was established at Tochieneal and closed when the line opened in full two years later.

On Tuesday 29th July 1884 Major Marindin of the Board of Trade undertook a comprehensive inspection of the Elgin to Garmouth line which included rigorous testing of all the bridges by passing three locomotives over them at various speeds. He refused to grant approval. One of his concerns was the single-span iron lattice girder bridge over the River Lossie on the outskirts of Elgin which had been built by the Morayshire Railway in 1851. It was showing signs of wear and was about to experience a significant increase in use. To rub salt into the Great North's wounds, he did approve the Highland Railway's line from Keith to Portessie over the Enzie Braes the following day and it duly opened on 1st August. However, the Major relented and on 9th August he approved the Elgin to Garmouth section subject to compliance with "One Engine in Steam" working, improvements to Elgin station and an assurance that the bridge over the Lossie would be replaced as a matter of urgency. The 7¾ mile section from Lossie Junction (one mile from Elgin) to Garmouth opened three days later with two intermediate

Tochieneal was an unlikely place to have a station. After its busy period as the terminus, it served a scattering of houses and provided a passing place. The main building, on the Down platform, dated from 1884. The centre portion facing the platform was originally open to provide a sheltered area for waiting passengers. There was also a small shelter on the opposite platform and a wooden footbridge at one time. Photographed on 15th July 1966, just before the signal box closed on 24th July.
(Roy Hamilton/Strathspey Railway)

stations at Calcots and Urquhart. A temporary servicing point was established at Garmouth for operations over the following couple of years. The annual holiday for Garmouth and Kingston occurred on 12th August and many excursionists took advantage of cheap fares to Aberdeen, Elgin and Lossiemouth. Around 200 children were treated to a trip to Elgin for a picnic on Lady Hill on the 10.30am departure funded from within the two villages. They returned on the 2.30pm train. A company of gentlemen enjoyed a salmon dinner in Mrs Grant's Hotel washed down by several toasts pledging success to the Coast Railway. A further inspection on 22nd August confirmed Board of Trade approval. The original Banffshire's services to Portsoy were extended to Tochieneal while a new local service of six trains each way ran between Elgin and Garmouth on weekdays only. Immediately fish began to be carted from Buckie to Tochieneal.

The Great North now found itself in a bit of a tangle of their own making. Mr W. Caird of Cullen had for several years operated a horse bus service connecting Buckie and Cullen with the railway station at Portsoy. The Great North announced that it would provide three daily bus services from the Commercial Hotel in Buckie to Tochieneal returning after connecting with their trains. The bus was named *Earl of Fife*. On the opening day Mr Caird duly arrived at Tochieneal to meet the first train but was ordered to remove his vehicle from the Company's land by a railway inspector. He was forced to deposit and pick up passengers some 200 yards from Tochieneal station with his customers having to carry their luggage past the *Earl of Fife*. The local press published letters asking the public to boycott the Great North's bus service and, on 17th April, Mr Caird advertised his "*boycotted*" service adjacent to the Great North's bus timetable. It proved, however, to be an unequal fight and he shortly withdrew his service. The Great North immediately increased its fares between Tochieneal and Buckie and within a month Mr Caird was back undercutting the Great North and operating a viable service. The two parties slugged it out for a further nine months until, on 2nd March 1885, the Great North conceded and operated its coach between Tochieneal and Cullen only and allowed Mr Caird back into Tochieneal station. The issue certainly caused a good degree of local animosity and was a public relations disaster for the Great North, especially as the Highland was now actively competing for passengers in Buckie for their line from Keith.

In October 1884 the Great North and Highland met to discuss a new joint station at Elgin. The respective Company engineers, Patrick Barnett and Murdoch Paterson, were tasked with drawing up plans on ground owned by the Highland. Agreement was reached that passenger and parcel traffic would be handled by Highland staff with revenue split in line with the proportion sent by each line. Subsequently, the Great North decided to use its own staff and, as David Ross concludes in his Great North of Scotland History: "*....like other initiatives with the Highland the project languished in a climate of suspicion and hostility*".

The Great North had another problem at the Elgin end. Complaints had been made over the danger caused by the proximity of the new line to the road between Elgin and Pitgaveny at a point to the east of the underbridge of the Lossiemouth branch on the curve leading from Lossie Junction. The Board of Trade was involved and, on 26th January 1885, Major Marindin met the County Road Clerk, Captain Dunbar Brander, and representatives of the Great North. Major Marindin agreed that danger existed and requested that the Company erect 7-foot high boarded screens at the points where railway and road converged. In June the Great North suspended services to Lossiemouth and Garmouth on Friday 5th and Saturday 6th in order to replace the bridge over the Lossie outside Elgin and to comply with their previous undertaking to Major Marindin. The original cast iron structure was superseded by a more durable one of malleable iron similar to that being used on the Spey Viaduct.

An early and very poor image of Portessie which nevertheless shows some useful detail. The building on the Up platform is in its original condition with an open frontage, angled at the top. The wooden footbridge was a standard GNSR design.
(Ross Kerby collection)

The Highland Railway built its own locomotive shed at Portessie at the east end of the passenger platforms. A two-road shed, far bigger than would ever be needed, was provided together with turntable and substantial water tower. Beyond are houses for staff. In May 1936 it was becoming overgrown.
(E W Hannar, Highland Railway Society collection)

The Major returned on 21st September to inspect the alterations at Elgin station, particularly the improvements to platforms and associated lines and sidings. The signals and points were now interlocked and worked from a new raised signal box of 42 levers. Apart from a couple of minor adjustments, he was generally happy with what he saw, and he added that, while not a first class station, it was fit to receive new traffic from the Coast and he approved it for use. However, he expressed his disappointment that the Great North and Highland had failed to agree on a joint station and that the public were still to be inconvenienced by having to walk between stations to change trains. As there was no engineering difficulty to construct a joint station, "....*the existence of two single line stations within 200 yards of each other at a place like Elgin was not to be tolerated*"!

Progress on the remaining 13¼ mile gap between Tochieneal and Garmouth was slow and it took nearly two more years to complete mainly because of the major engineering works at Cullen and Garmouth. Most of the heavy work on the Cullen Viaducts was completed by October 1884 but the contractor Adams had to be advanced £5,000 that month and, in the following year, more men had to be employed on the line. There were high jinks on Hogmanay 1884 when some Cullen youths "borrowed" a traction engine being used on the new viaducts and drove it up and down Seafield Street and performed manoeuvres in the town square. Construction was also disrupted in 1885 when four ancient urns (three broken and one intact) were found near Buckie and several rare coins, including a Queen Elizabeth I sixpence dated 1572 and in perfect condition, were unearthed. Ironically, the contractors found it more convenient to bring in materials for the Buckie and Portessie areas over the new Highland line from Keith rather than to transport them from the temporary railhead at Tochieneal. That must have stuck in the craw! The Highland line was already attracting both passenger and freight business with fish, particularly herring (and kippers),

dispatched to the south. And there was yet another issue at Buckie where the Royal National Lifeboat Institution station stood in the way of the new line. That led to lengthy negotiations between the Great North and RNLI before the latter agreed to sell it for £121.10.2d which allowed the Great North to demolish it. The Great North then had to fork out £447.15s to build a new lifeboat station on the quayside.

Apart from the major engineering works and tracks, station buildings, station houses, goods sheds, engine sheds, platforms, overbridges, signalling, etc. had to be constructed. For the Coast Line, the Great North adopted a new design of plain wooden building with horizontal boards, as illustrated at Portessie. The layout was based on the stone ones on the Speyside and Buchan lines with a central booking hall flanked by a booking office with screened area for the station master on one side and a waiting room on the other. An inset on the platform side provided token shelter for those waiting on the platform, although in many places this was later enclosed. Portsoy and Cullen were provided with larger buildings in a more ornate style. North American redwood was being harvested at the time and proved a most durable building material.

The entire Moray Firth Coast Line opened to freight on 5th April 1886 and Major Marindin inspected the line on 24th April. That allowed the official opening for passenger services to take place in Elgin on Saturday 1st May 1886 which was declared a local holiday. The first train departed Aberdeen at 8.10am and called at nearly all the Coast stations to arrive in Elgin at 11.55am. This was followed by the 9.35am double-headed train which omitted some of the smaller stations and consisted of nine new first class carriages and two brake vans. With George Clark of Keith driving the leading engine, it conveyed the official party of guests led by Great North Chairman William Ferguson and his Directors and it was greeted all along the route. Addresses of welcome were extended at both Portsoy and Cullen before

Provost James Black welcomed the arrival into Elgin station at 12.30pm and led the invited party through the decorated streets to a celebratory lunch in the Town and County Hall. A total of four special return trains were run from Aberdeen to Elgin over the new line and there were two return trips (morning and afternoon) from Elgin to Portsoy. The Highland Railway joined in by operating a return from Keith to Elgin via the Coast. Over 10,000 people gathered to greet the trains. There were enthusiastic celebrations in Cullen too but, rather strangely, the response in Buckie was rather muted. The official party's train left Elgin for Aberdeen at 4.25pm returning via the Glen Line.

To complete the new route the link between Grange South Junction (later Cairnie Junction) and Grange North Junction was opened with a single line on 5th April on land donated by the Duke of Richmond and Gordon to allow direct running from the main line from Aberdeen. Parliamentary approval was sought and granted retrospectively in the Great North of Scotland Railway (Further Powers) Act of 19th July 1887, no doubt to the relief of the Company who could thereafter legally charge for its use! A new signal box at Grange North controlled the junction with the loop from Grange South, although trains continued to split at Huntly. Trains originating in Keith used the original Banffshire Railway single-track curve between Grange station and Grange North Junction signal box to access the Coast Line. The box also controlled the two separate level crossing gates on each of these spur lines over the minor road immediately to the south of the box. Over the years steam locomotives from Keith engine shed requiring a test run used the "triangle" at Grange for turning – running to Grange North Junction via Grange station, then reversing to Grange South (Cairnie) before returning to Keith Junction. The local hostelry at Grange, known as Ma Dows', was no doubt an added attraction!

There were intermediate stations at Cullen, Portknockie,

Free ticket issued to invited guests for the opening of the line.

Grange North Junction taken on 21st May 1960 shortly after the connection towards Grange was officially closed on 7th March. The original line from Grange station goes straight ahead and the double track curve from Grange South Junction (later Cairnie Junction), which was constructed for the opening of the Coast Line, is on the left. Note that the signal arms for the closed connection have already been removed; all that remained to be done was the removal of the track and small level crossing gates. The carriages in the background are stored in the siding beside the main line. (Roy Hamilton/Strathspey Railway)

Buckie looking west from the bank on the south side of the line. The coaches on the right carry roofboards showing Elgin via Buckie. It is likely that the photograph was taken shortly after completion of the line as the train in the distance appears to be involved with engineering works. There is some equipment in the wagons, along with six men. Buckie West signal cabin can be seen at the far end of the Up platform. The original Buckie East survived to the end as a shunting frame. The man in the foreground on the left was the photographer's assistant who will help with the development of the glass plates; this had to take place immediately after exposure.
(George Washington Wilson/Aberdeen University Creative Commons Licence (CC BY 4.0)

Findochty, Portessie, Buckie, Nether Buckie (Buckpool from 1887), Portgordon and Fochabers (Spey Bay from 1918). The main points for ticket examination and/or collection for Down trains were Aberdeen, Cairnie Junction (for trains from Aberdeen), Grange (for trains starting for the Coast Line), Keith, Garmouth (for express trains) and Calcots (for stopping trains); and for Up trains at Elgin, Tillynaught (for express trains), Knock (for stopping trains with Grange tickets collected) and Keith. Schoolhill in Aberdeen was added from 4th September 1893. The line was single track throughout with passing loops at Tochieneal, Portknockie, Spey Bay, Garmouth and Calcots, although there was a short 1¼ mile stretch of double track between Buckie and Portessie to allow the movement of fish vans from the former's harbour to the sidings at Portessie.

Signalling was an issue for the Coast Line. On 23rd July 1885 the Great North received a letter from the Board of Trade refusing to sanction the use of the same system of signalling as used on the Company's other lines. At that time the Board of Trade could only insist on the latest secure signalling systems for new lines. This was a blow as it had already purchased block signalling instruments but, fortunately, the supplier agreed to take them back. Consequently, the Company resolved to use the Electric Train Tablet System and ordered eight sets of Tyer's No. 1 Train Tablet Apparatus (as subsequently authorised by a formal undertaking signed on 23rd April 1886). From May 1889, the automatic tablet-exchange system designed by the Great North's locomotive superintendent James Manson was introduced on the Coast Line (following trials on the Buchan Line to Fraserburgh). Telegraph signalling was installed on the Banff branch from 1st July 1887. New tablet instruments of Tyer's more modern No. 6 type were installed on the Coast Line between Portsoy and Lossie Junction on 1st January 1893, delivered by special train from Kittybrewster. The Portsoy–Tillynaught section received new instruments on 12th January 1894 and the section from Tillynaught to Grange North on Monday 31st December 1894. Rather oddly, the remaining one-mile section from Lossie Junction to Elgin East had to wait until Monday 2nd May 1904 to be equipped with the new tablet working. The Great North immediately announced that it would operate special trains for fish when necessary. The Highland responded to the new competition by advertising a comprehensive timetable on the front page of the local newspaper.

The viaduct at Cullen in 1887 after part of the embankment collapsed. (Ross Kerby collection)

The Great North faced another problem over the Cullen Viaduct. There had been a minor collapse of an arch in high winds during construction but, on 15th January 1887, a crack of about five to six feet appeared in the centre of the east abutments over Castle Street. The issue dogged the company for the next 12 months as, despite the installation of a tie rod to hold the masonry together, the east abutment began to slip northwards by December. Even with further repairs the embankment collapsed and some shops and houses below were badly damaged but fortunately no one was killed. The Great North did, however, fork out another £600 to purchase the properties for subsequent demolition. And the local golf club was not happy at damage to their turf but mutterings that *"this wouldn't have happened at St. Andrews"* appear to have been ignored by the company.

Traffic was halted on Thursday 5th January 1888 to allow two spans to be replaced by an extension of the embankment, a mixture of gravel and cinders, while a third was filled in with concrete. The remedial work was a remarkable operation involving 15,000 tonnes of infill delivered by both Great North and Highland ballast wagons supplemented by 80 from the Caledonian Railway Company. One source of ballast was on the Coast Line at Meft Siding which was half a mile west of Urquhart. It was brought into use on 14th January 1888 specifically for ballast for the repair work and it was tablet operated without loop or home signals but with Up and Down distants. The siding was rather unique as it had a life of only five days! Similarly, Tillynaught Ballast Siding, 200 yards north of the station house, was brought into operation on the same date. And Gillyfurry Cutting Siding, just east of Cullen station within the distant signal and facing Down trains, also opened that day, possibly to hold back-up ballast wagons. It was still in existence 10 years later by which time it was spelt Gellyfurry. Initially, 300 men laboured around the clock to effect repairs but the number grew to nearly 500 after several days. Two provision vans were positioned in Cullen goods shed and five men were tasked with cutting bread and making coffee. Soup was supplied by the Seafield Arms. The Coast Line reopened to freight 15 days later on Friday 20th January, with two trains in each direction, and to passengers on Monday 23rd January. The cost of the remedial work was £2,408.

The Coast Line took its toll on the Great North's finances, with expenditure standing at £305,000 by 1887. This was largely due to the cost of the Spey Viaduct and the additional works at Cullen including the greater than anticipated cost of land from both the Seafield and Fife estates. The estimated final cost of the Cullen Viaducts was £34,000. The new spur from Grange South to Grange North was an additional cost. However, the Company was satisfied that the Coast Line receipts were ahead of budget largely due to increased mail revenue and the fish traffic.

The Spey Viaduct

The Spey Viaduct, originally and for many years known locally as the Fochabers Viaduct, merits further consideration. It linked Fochabers (later Spey Bay) and Garmouth over the River Spey. Often referred to as "Barnett's Monument" after Patrick Barnett, the Great North's Civil Engineer who designed it in conjunction with Messrs Blyth and Cunningham Consulting Engineers, its construction was not straightforward.

The Great North considered an alternative river crossing further upstream between Fochabers and Boat O'Brig with the railway swinging inland from Buckie and joining with the Morayshire's old route from Orton to Rothes to allow access to the south via the Strathspey Line to Boat of Garten. However, that would have led to further conflict with the Highland and indeed with the Great North's own preferred route south via Aberdeen. Barnett turned his attention to the mouth of the Spey where the total width between embankments was 2,270 feet. There was a problem, however. Although the river ordinarily flowed through one main channel it split into three channels during periods of heavy flood. When the floods subsided any of the three became the river's course. Barnett and his consultants proposed bridges of five spans over (at that time) the main channel on the east side; of two spans over the mid-channel; and of four spans on the west side. The spans were 100 feet each. Steel was considered but the Board of Trade, nervous after the recent Tay Bridge disaster in 1879, demanded that every piece would require full testing. The cost was prohibitive and high quality iron was the chosen material.

The Duke of Richmond and Gordon threw a spanner in the works. He owned the salmon fishing rights, objected to the three bridges, and demanded a complete redesign. He wanted a central span of 350 feet with the main course of the river to be diverted through the channel underneath. A uniform number of lengths of viaducts on either side of this central span would cater for flood water giving a total crossing length of 947½ feet. Barnett agreed and designed a bowstring girder bridge of 368 feet in length, 40 feet 8 inches at its highest point, and connected at either side by three double lattice girder spans 107 feet in length and 10 feet high. The width ranged from 19 to 22 feet. The track was 30 feet above ground level and the bridge was designed to take a rolling load of 354 tons distributed over its whole length with the centre

Postcard view of the bridge from the east bank, showing the south side. The quantity and size of granite blocks placed to protect the bridge from the river are prominent.
(GNSRA collection)

section able to withstand an additional 56 tons. The entire bridge had an estimated weight of 588 tons and Barnett claimed it to be the largest single span bridge in Scotland and possibly the U.K. Thankfully the Duke approved, the tender from Blaikie Brothers of Aberdeen was accepted and construction commenced on the foundations in June 1883.

As main contractor, Blaikie Brothers were responsible for forming the new river channel from a point 450 yards south of the bridge to one 450 yards north of it. The new "trench" was to average 15 feet in width by 5 feet in depth with a uniform fall. The new river course was to be used on completion, with the inflow of water regulated by temporary damming upstream to allow it to "*scour and widen*". And the contractor was bound to maintain these works "*….until the whole body of the water in the River has been diverted into the new channel thus formed*". The River Spey, however, was in no mood to be messed about and problems lay ahead for the railway company and its associates!

The Contractor was paid in four instalments. The first was on completion of certain concrete works in the piers, abutments and walls; the second on completion of the masonry work ready to receive the ironwork and on delivery of the ironwork to the site; the third was one month after total completion and the bridge opened for public traffic; and the fourth and final following the usual 12 month maintenance period subject to the Railway Company's Engineer certifying that the terms of the maintenance had been complied with. There was the usual 10% retention and a penalty for late completion of £20 per day after 31st July 1884 if the bridge was unfinished and not in use for public traffic.

There was an immediate delay due to problems bringing material to the site but by mid-August a contractor's railway from Garmouth allowed steam cranes and plant to access the west bank. The riverbed of shingle ranging from 10 to 25 feet in depth on top of red sandstone also caused problems and a flood in September required the use of additional pumps to keep the pier foundation workings dry. The shingle was acting like a giant sieve causing the builders great difficulty with groundwater. Over the 1883/84 winter there was a major problem with the main west pier as the sandstone was found to dip sharply away making it unsuitable for the foundation. Heavy rain and melting snow caused flooding and consequent increased pumping. When digging recommenced it took to a depth of 30 feet to find rock suitable for the foundation. On a more positive note, communication over the river was improved for engineers with the construction of a 500 foot steel cableway which enabled a two-person carriage to cross in under a minute.

In May 1884 the contractor for the stone masonry W. George Hind announced it could not continue to build the bridge due to the fragmentation and even absence of the sandstone rock for the pier foundations. Although Hind was contractually bound to resolve the issue, the Great North sought a new masonry company; two declined immediately but John Fyfe of Kemnay stepped up to the mark. Fyfe undertook his own surveys and resolved the foundation issue by using cast iron cylinders which

The main centre span begins to take shape. On the right, the approach viaduct is supported by temporary piling as is the main structure. (Aberdeen Art Gallery and Museum collection)

Construction of the main centre span nears completion.　　(Aberdeen Art Gallery and Museum collection)

were sunk on top of each other (by heavy blocks of metal) to allow teams of men to enter the inside to remove the soil with pick and shovel. Powerful steam pumps worked around the clock to keep the workings dry. Some suitable rock foundation was found at 24 feet but, where nothing was found, the cylinders were sunk to 50 feet. The piers were constructed in pairs side by side to form the bridge supports. Those of the central span were 15 feet in diameter and those of the approach spans 9 feet 3 inches. This solution was not entirely free of problems. Cracks in one of the cylinders led to water ingress which was solved by the use of high quality quick-setting lime plugging from Blackhillock quarries near Keith. The cylinder was also found to be off its level by half an inch, but Barnett was happy to continue as the water ingress had ceased.

For the delivery of the ironwork the Great North had to swallow its pride and ask its great competitor to assist. On 12th June 50 tons of iron was delivered to the Highland's Orbliston station from the south and transported to the Spey Bridge site by teams of horses and carts. A further 100 tons followed later. On Monday 28th July 1884 the foundation of the main span was laid in the presence of Garmouth dignitaries. A copy of the *Banffshire Advertiser* and various coins of the realm were sent 50 feet to the bottom of the workings before the cylinders were filled with concrete. This operation was carried out in a novel way by making use of the Spey itself. Each cylinder was filled with river water to a height of 5-6 feet before a mixture of sand, gravel and Portland cement was added and allowed to stand for a few days. Remaining water was then pumped out and the rest of the cylinder was filled up with normal concrete mix.

The stonework to protect the metal foundation cylinders progressed well with the smaller piers clad in local quality Spynie freestone and the main piers, expected to bear the full force of the Spey, clad by 9-ton Corennie granite blocks from quarries near Kemnay. Work was also undertaken to protect the railway embankments and to direct the river to the new channel under the main span by the construction of walls three feet thick and 21 feet high on both river banks. The stonework and masonry work was completed by early February 1885.

The erection of the girders commenced on 19th February on the west side. There was no prefabrication, with six steam cranes used to aid the fitting of individual plates and bars. Only 40 men were employed on the ironwork as technology had arrived, including a patented machine which could fix 900 rivets in a working day. By the end of April nearly 300 feet of ironwork was in place over the three piers on the west side and that allowed the construction of timber scaffolding for the main centre span to proceed. Good spring weather helped and encouraged large numbers of sightseers. At this stage it was decided that high quality steel should be used for the centre span. Blaikie Brothers assembled the end girder sections at their Footdee Works in Aberdeen and these were installed onto the bridge piers on sheets of "*best English lead*" secured by "*holding-down bolts*" three inches in diameter and 10 feet long. A nine inch gap between the bolt and the stonework allowed for expansion of the girders in hot weather. Work had also started on the upright pillars which would eventually rise to 40 feet above the structure's deck. The west end of the bridge was complete by the end of June apart from painting. On 18th June the Company Directors and various VIPs, led by Chairman William Ferguson, travelled over the line from Elgin to review progress. They inspected the site of the new Fochabers station before travelling in a contractor's train (an engine and two trucks fitted with seats) on to Portgordon.

There was a setback on 12th August. From the afternoon strong winds and heavy rain persisted through the night and by the following morning the worksite resembled a loch. Barrows, shovels and picks and other plant had been swept away and the staging for the main span was in imminent danger of collapse. On a more positive note, the new concrete wall protecting the west side foundations had done its job although it had forced the river onto a course it had never taken before which resulted in damage to a local farmer's potato crop. When calmer conditions prevailed later that month Fyfe's men started to cut the new channel for the river. By late September the bridge's building work was almost complete and painting was underway. All ironwork had been dipped in boiled linseed oil during manufacture to help prevent rusting and three layers of paint were applied. All the Board of Trade tests required to withstand the effects of wind pressure had been met. Work had still not been started on the rail link between the western embankment and Garmouth, partly because the Contractor, Mr Granger, had been preoccupied up north building the Highland's Strathpeffer branch! Nevertheless, the final rivet was driven home by Barnett on the centre span in front of a large local crowd on Thursday 22nd October 1885. The metalwork of the Spey Viaduct had been completed in a record 10 months.

Fyfe was discovering that construction of the new river channel was not quite as straightforward as he had anticipated. Machinery struggled with the variable conditions of the shingle beds of the Spey and he had to resort to manual labour, shovels and wheel barrows to persuade the river into its new course. The autumn weather was not particularly helpful and 300 navvies went on strike on 16th November when he refused to pay the diggers an additional 4d per hour. One of Mr Fyfe's timekeepers and a foreman were attacked and general disorder ensued in Garmouth, the resulting injuries ranging from bruising to broken limbs. The Chief Constable of Elgin and one of his Sergeants were summoned and, although the rioters scattered, a number of the ringleaders were *"rounded up, arrested and sent to jail in Elgin to await trial"*. The incident resulted in a depleted workforce of 150 men and no increase in pay!

Fyfe was now in a race against time. If the new river channel was not complete by the start of the new salmon fishing season on 1st February 1886 the Great North was contractually due to pay a penalty of £21,000 to the Duke of Richmond and Gordon. Although helped by farm workers and general labourers, who were unemployed during the winter months, filling the void caused by the rioting navvies, a thaw on 14th January sent thousands of gallons pouring into the digging operations. The spoil from the excavation work, some 50,000 cubic yards of earth and gravel, was used to build up the flood dykes on either side of the new course and to keep the river flow to its new line. On 26th January the new river course was complete and the gravel barrier was demolished to allow the water to flow into the new channel. At first all went well but gradually the river penetrated the gravel-filled jute bags which had been built to check the river from returning to its original course. Many were washed away. A temporary barrier upstream slowed the flow to allow repairs downstream and eventually 10,000 jute bags supplemented by high quality grain bags owned by the Great North and brought in from Garmouth station attempted to manage the river flow.

Despite these issues the bridge and its initial embankments on both sides were ready for operation from April 1886. Load-bearing tests were conducted by easing a train pulled by two of the Great North's heaviest locomotives coupled to 20 open filled ballast wagons weighing 400 tons onto the centre span. The dead weight test on Friday 18th March 1886 complemented a second test of running the train over the viaduct at 40 mph. (In BR days the normal operating speed over the bridge was 45mph). The results were highly satisfactory and the Great North was confident for the Board of Trade inspection which was arranged with Major Marindin for 24th April.

Local folk were sceptical that the jute bags to channel the river would last especially when it was in spate. Many believed that only a thick concrete wall would hold the river, but the Great North was unwilling to meet that cost.

Looking west across the viaduct, showing the substantial stonework at the end of the parapet.
(Graham Maxtone collection)

Possibly the Company came to regret that decision later that year when, by 25th November although the flow had deepened in the new channel, the jute bags on the east bank were mostly washed away. It was only the low water level which prevented the river from returning to its original course. Rumours began to spread that the east embankment approaching the railway was in danger of collapse due to instability caused by the river and that the bridge itself would fail when the Spey flooded. Some locals were concerned for their properties and lives from future floods. The Great North made reassuring noises but in December the Company decided to build new protective embankments on the east side. Two trains each of 20 wagons brought in granite blocks and 50 men worked through the night to place them. A siding was constructed and more material brought in. By mid-January 1887 5,500 cubic yards of material, mainly from Kemnay, had been built into the embankment which by now was 12 feet in width at its top.

A spate in early February tested the reinforced defence and the embankment required further remedial work. More trains arrived with granite rubble from Kemnay. By now the Great North was in trouble as it could no longer afford further expenditure on keeping the river to the central channel. Furthermore, it was in danger of reneging on its contractual undertaking to the Duke of Richmond and Gordon. Moffat wrote to the Duke to suggest arbitration. There was no immediate response and the contractors continued to shore up the defences of the viaduct and embankments throughout 1887. By January 1888 the granite rubble had been washed away and 6,000 tons of granite blocks were brought in as replacement. The contractor Tawse had by now given up the struggle and was replaced by Alex Riach who was convinced that he *"could tame the Spey"* within four months. Mr Barnett and Mr Moffat nervously watched the recommencement of the work.

Needless to say Riach's optimism was unfounded and, despite the Great North throwing all the material and effort against it, by March 1889 water was not flowing under the central span, but water to a depth of 30 feet was passing under the eastern end. Moreover, the west side was now under assault and track was laid to assist the unloading of granite boulders. This was even more concerning for the residents of Garmouth who feared flooding of the Garmouth – Kingston road and the surrounding arable land. The Great North was becoming increasingly nervous as it faced digging out local ditches and clearing burns. The press sided with the locals and hinted that the railway company would be liable to compensate any pecuniary loss. The Company also feared disruption to the operation of the Coast Line. Matters took a turn for the worse when the Duke of Richmond and Gordon finally responded to

An aerial view of the Spey Viaduct from the north, taken in October 2008, showing how the river has steadfastly refused to flow through the main span. The normal channel is to the left (Spey Bay) side while any excess flows on the right (Garmouth) side. It is not often that the latter sees water.
(Paul Warrener)

Moffat's letter, stating that he *"would consult with the Railway Company in the near future at the Court of Session"*. The *Banffshire Advertiser* anticipated the Great North being legally enforced to give up their *"indifference to life and property so long as the railway is kept safe and be ordered to confine the river into one stream"*.

The action by the Duke of Richmond and Gordon against the Great North was called for Tuesday 22nd October 1889 in front of Lord Kinnear. The Duke's sole concern over the next two days was the damage to and loss of revenue from his salmon fishing rights as testified by his fishing managers. He claimed damages of £21,000 for loss of fishing income due to construction delays. The Fisheries Board also complained that the viaduct had impacted negatively on catches. There was no reference to the concerns of the residents of Garmouth. A number of witnesses claimed that the work undertaken by the Great North was insufficient to contain the flow in the new channel under the centre span of the bridge. The Great North contended that the work to alter the Spey had been performed to suit the wishes of the Duke's commissioner and that it was not the business of the Company to maintain the river banks. Barnett and Benjamin Hall Blyth both gave evidence, the latter claiming that the embankments built after the construction of the bridge were only intended as "temporary" and that their main purpose was a means of disposal from cuttings built on other sections of the Coast Line. This was at best being economical with the truth!

Lord Kinnear published his ruling on 19th November. He confirmed that the original agreement bound the Great North to build up the embankments to force the river to flow under the centre span. However, to contain the required line of flow, the construction of sills of a considerable height under the smaller spans at each side of the bridge was necessary. There was no guarantee that this remedy (or any other for that matter) would work to the satisfaction of the Duke and would be burdensome for the Great North to maintain. The sills built up under the bridge could cause flooding to the detriment of local residents. Lord Kinnear dismissed the case and one suspects that he was as flummoxed as all the others involved in *"fighting"* the Spey!

The Duke of Richmond and Gordon was, not surprisingly, deeply unimpressed and on 5th December 1889 he attempted to have the judgement over-ruled. However, further costly court action was avoided when the two parties reached a final private agreement in July 1890. The Great North concentrated on operating its new Coast Line and undertook no further work on the banks of the River Spey which continued to refuse to flow under the centre span. No doubt there was a huge sigh of relief in Aberdeen, although it did come at a cost of £2,766 16/- to the company to free itself from its obligations on diverting the course of the river. The company also paid an *"annuit"* of £120 a year to the Duke which was eventually compounded in June 1918 for a one-off payment of £3,012.1.8d. The estate scooped out a new channel and deposited 400 tons of stones into and removed large quantities of materials from the river in 1902, but the river's course remained unchanged. In 1933 a new channel was cut from the mouth of the river back under the centre span of the viaduct but that did not work either. Wisely, both the LNER and BR did not allow themselves to be drawn into river diversion schemes and after 1933 the estate left it well alone too. The local authorities made comment on various risks down the years but, apart from some local flood protection measures, they avoided any involvement.

The initial contract to the main contractor Blaikie Brothers had been awarded in the sum of £25,483.3.4d on 10th January 1883. In the event the actual cost was £40,204.13.9d, made up of payments to Fyfe £20,412.4.5d, to Blaikie £19,261.18.8d, and for Sundries £530.10.8d. On top of these was the £2,766.16s plus the company's legal costs to settle with the Duke of Richmond and Gordon. Overspend on capital projects is nothing new! And the river had the last laugh. The Spey Viaduct still stands in 2024 but, apart from periods of severe flood, no water ever passes under its centre span!

With all its metal, maintenance was a constant task. This is the bridge squad in 1927. (GNSRA collection)

Coast Line Stations

When the line opened services were recast so that the whole route between Grange South Junction ("Cairnie Platform" from 1898 and "Cairnie Junction" from 1919, hereafter referred to as "Cairnie Junction") and Elgin was regarded as the Moray Firth Coast Line. There were four services in each direction. The original "main line" section from Tillynaught to Banff became a small branch operated as a shuttle. By 1887 the number of trains in each direction had increased to 11 as it had to connect with all the new Coast services at Tillynaught. The six mile journey now took anything between 13 and 20 minutes. Freight, mainly on mixed trains, continued to be carried, although sheep moving to the Highland area were sometimes conveyed in specials. Some passenger specials conveyed local folk to Aberdeen, especially in summer.

There were 16 stations between Tillynaught Junction and Elgin inclusive. Tillynaught had South and North signal boxes controlling the lines to Banff and the Coast respectively. A new footbridge provided a connection for the Banff branch passengers to access the Down platform for the Coast. There were now two freight sidings off the Banff branch line and the station work involved transferring parcels, mail bags, goods and luggage which had originated from or were destined for Ladysbridge and Banff. One minor change reflected the new status of the Banff branch. On arrival passengers were greeted with a new sign below "Tillynaught" proclaiming "Change For Ladysbridge and Banff".

The new station at Portsoy had opened on 1st April 1884 when the line was extended to Tochieneal with the original station retained for goods and, in 1885, the latter was altered to accommodate the storage of 15 carriages. The South box controlled the east entry to

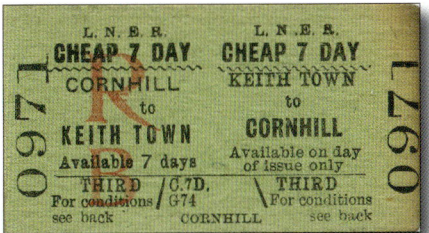

Cornhill looking towards Knock on 20th June 1964. The goods yard remained in use until 1968, latterly dealing with domestic coal traffic and continued to be used for coal distribution for many years after closure. Note what appears to be the porter's motor bike on the platform. The station building has been very tastefully renovated in recent years. (Roy Hamilton/Strathspey Railway)

Tillynaught in 1937 looking north. A Banff train can be seen in the branch platform behind the signal box. The main building has its original roof with large awnings. The signal box is a Type 2b, also found at Tillynaught North, Calcots and Knock. (H R Norman)

A general view of Portsoy looking north west taken in November 1964. The original terminus can be seen in the distance on the right with the goods yard to the left. The harbour line branched off the to the right of the old terminal building at the beginning of its steep descent to the shore. The 'new' line to Elgin curves away to the left past the station building and the Type 1 signal box. The signals and crossing loop were removed in August 1959 and the connection to the yard was worked by a ground frame released by the section token.

(Norris Forrest)

This group photograph of railwaymen at Portsoy shows the 1884 station in its original condition with the large building on the Up platform and a GNSR wooden footbridge. The verandah on the Down platform was a standard design with open front. (Ross Kerby collection)

the loop and the short spur to the original station. The North box controlled the other loop entry. The station was built on a sharp curve with two platforms connected by footbridge. The main (timber and fairly large) station building was on the Up side and there was a small wooden shelter on the Down platform. The harbour branch was out of use by the time the Coast Line opened. The port had experienced a sharp decline in the first 20 years of the harbour branch's existence due mainly to the development of the major harbours at Buckie and Macduff, but also, ironically, in some measure due to the arrival of the railway itself. The branch fell into disuse about 1880 and, in November 1886, the Company responded to a letter asking whether it intended to discontinue its working: *"at present the Company are not to work the branch"*. And that was the end of it although the rails survived for 30 years until lifted in the Spring of 1910. The harbour continued to handle modest fish catches and provided traffic for the railway.

Glassaugh station, with its original signal box dating from opening in 1884, served a rural community including the nearby villages of Sandend and Fordyce. The box was closed in 1896 but re-opened with a new crossing loop only two years later before finally closing on 14th November 1921 when the Down line and sleeper-and-ash-constructed platform were removed. The main

A postcard by Alex Roberston, Fordyce, showing Glassaugh looking east, complete with the loop which was installed in 1898 and taken out of use in 1921. The main building on the left had an open front which was later enclosed while the verandah on the Down platform and the Type 1 signal box were to later designs than at other stations on the line.
(GNSRA collection)

Cullen was situated on a tight curve and did not have a passing loop. There was little traffic in the goods yard when photographed in June 1937. (H R Norman)

wooden station building was on the Up side with small shelter opposite. The goods yard with loading bank on the north side served the nearby Glenglassaugh distillery.

Tochieneal, the temporary terminus from April 1884 to April 1886, is illustrated on page 31. It had its main station building on the Down platform and its East signal box (1884) and West box (1886) controlled the crossing loop and large goods yard (with shed) and several sidings. It had a large water tank at the side of the main Up line. It also served Deskford and Lintmill.

Cullen, catering for a relatively significant population including those of Old Cullen, Seafield and Farskane, boasted a substantial main wooden building, similar to Portsoy, on its sharply curved single platform on the Down side, signal box, and significant freight handling facilities. Coal was delivered and taken by horse and cart down to the gasworks. On Thursdays a special train carried up to 200 tons of cattle to Cornhill mart and the local butcher, Mr Shearer, purchased cattle there to bring back to the Cullen slaughterhouse. Throughout the life of the

The building at Cullen followed the same style as those on the Coast Line but was larger and similar to that at Portsoy. This view was taken not long after closure, when the nameboards had been removed. The yard layout had been simplified before closure with the removal of some of the sidings.
(Norris Forrest/ GNSRA)

Portknockie in Great North days. An east-bound train consisting of six-wheeled carriages hauled by Class T No. 105 enters the station. That locomotive was built in 1897 which suggests the photograph was taken around the turn of the twentieth century.

(GNSRA collection)

Coast Line, Cullen was a popular holiday resort mainly due to its crescent-shaped sandy bay which afforded safe sea bathing. The striking rocks on the beach known as "The Three Kings of Cullen" (reputedly so named after three kings killed in a battle against Vikings on the beach) became a familiar landmark to rail passengers crossing the viaducts.

Portknockie and its East and West signal boxes dated from 1886. It had staggered platforms and footbridge. Portknockie and Findochty had very similar wooden station buildings on the Up side but the former boasted a passing loop while the latter was single track with signal box. Both had small goods yards with loading docks and both were above the villages they served. The population of Portknockie increased significantly towards the end of the 19th century due to the railway and harbour improvements and the town became a burgh in 1912. Cattle and fish from the new Findochty harbour, built in 1880, were handled at the local station. Not all passenger trains stopped there and this was often a bone of contention.

A similar view of Portknockie to the one above in the 1950s before BR standard signs were installed shows that the building had not altered. The footbridge had been replaced by an LNER one built of old rails but in the same location and with the same 'Z' formation to match the staggered platforms.

(H A Vallance)

Findochty was perched on the hillside above the village. It had a single platform on the north side of the line and a small goods yard at the east end. Photographed in summer 1962 when, like most other stations on the line, it retained its LNER green paint. Reflecting light on the front makes it appear blue. (Bob Florence)

Just east of Portessie the line reached the junction where the Highland's line from Keith connected with the Great North's Coast Line, although the Highland line opened 2 years before that of the Great North. The two companies shared the Great North station at Portessie with the Highland using the outer face of the Great North's Down island platform. The Highland employed its own station staff when its line opened on 1st August 1884 but when the Coast Line was completed 20 months later the Great North supplied all station staff and the two companies shared the wooden station building on the island platform. And, surprise surprise, the two Companies were unable to agree on the terms of payment by the Highland for the use of the Great North's facilities. It took the Railway Commissioners five years to settle this one but, from March 1891, the Highland finally agreed to pay an annual fee of £153 10/- in perpetuity plus one half of Great North staff salaries, wages and clothing, and one half of rates, taxes and insurance. And, again in true Highland/Great North tradition, there was never any real attempt to organise meaningful connections between the two lines. From the start the Highland treated its line as a minor branch with an initial service of four daily mixed and very slow trains. The Great North ignored it in its timetables and maps. It wanted passengers for Buckie and

A general view of Portessie looking west in GNSR days. The station is in the centre with the double track continuing to Buckie. On the right is the small GNSR goods yard while the Highland station is on the left. The signalman is holding the handle to the auto tablet exchanger. The arm would be moved forward to enable the tablet to be picked up by the passing locomotive. There would be a similar exchanger on the opposite side for westbound trains. Because Portessie was at the start of the short double line section to Buckie the exchanger in this view was for uplifting the tablet (to Portknockie) only whilst the one out of view collected only.
(GNSRA collection)

Portessie looking east from the footbridge in the 1930s. The Highland station is on the right with the disused engine shed in the distance. The Highland line was still in use as far as its Buckie station. Today the far road bridge continues to carry the minor road linking Strathlene to the A98 over the old trackbed.

(GNSRA collection)

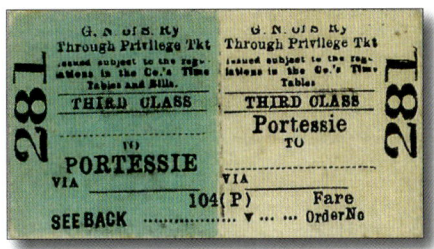

Portessie to use the Coast Line and it hoped to attract business from nearby Rathven and Loanhead. Interestingly, when the two Companies were holding talks on possible amalgamation in 1906, Buckie Town Council unanimously supported the union as it believed improved services would accrue!

Portessie was originally called Rottenslough (and is still known locally as Sloch and Porteasy) and was a separate town joined to Buckie (as were Ianstown, Gordonsburgh and Buckpool). The Great North had a 28-lever signal box at the east end of the double track, a loading bank and two sidings and a pedestrian overbridge. There were station buildings on both Up and island platforms. The Highland had a two-road engine shed (the only Highland shed built in brick), turntable, water tower, two "exchange" sidings and general goods sidings. It had its own 15-lever signal box about 350 yards to the west at the Buckie end of the island platform and its own loop, but the box closed when passenger services were withdrawn. The engine shed closed in March 1909 and was then used as a concrete block factory. There was a slight slope down to the Highland platform which, initially at least, was not finished with the normal Great North concrete blocks, but with wooden blocks and rough stone edging. The porters moved wooden "boxes" along the platform to help passengers alight. The station was built up the hill from the main road and was accessed by a quarter-mile hill-road or, from Chapel Street, a steep footpath of 102 concrete steps and nine concrete flights lit by three gas lamps. A major attraction was the nearby

As the largest town on the route, Buckie deserved a larger station. With the platforms part way up the bank, the result was unique on the Great North. A substantial stone building was constructed with entrance at road level and access to the platforms on the first floor. The harbour was behind the photographer and the goods yard to the left. The station was still presentable when photographed on the last day of service, 2nd May 1968.

(Keith Fenwick)

Buckie looking west in June 1937. The signal box on the Up platform was brought into use on 30th March 1903 and replaced separate East and West boxes. There is a weighing machine on the platform near the box. There was no footbridge linking the two platforms. Rather unusually, the Great North built an underpass. The overbridge in the photograph provided a convenient link from Buckie town centre to the station square. Being at the opposite end of the double line from Portessie the Manson 'collect only' exchanger for the single line section onwards to Spey Bay can be seen in the left foreground. The exchanger head is not in situ, the mechanism being protected from the elements by an easily removable wooden box. The head could be quickly fitted. Auto exchanges could work up to 50 mph whereas hand exchanges were restricted to between 10 and 15mph. The benefits to punctuality and adherence to the working timetable were clear. (H R Norman)

hotel, golf links and open-air swimming pool at Strathlene. Day excursionists and holidaymakers visited from Aberdeen by train.

The short 1¼ mile section from Portessie to Buckie was double throughout the life of the Coast Line. Buckie was the main intermediate station on the line. It was situated in the heart of the town's industrial area and docks and served the largest population catchment. It was a two-platform station, with the impressive main stone-built building on the Up (eastbound) platform a two-storey construction with the upper level at platform height complete with bookstall. The Booking Office was on the ground floor. Buckie's status was confirmed when it (and Fochabers) were awarded linoleum for the Gentlemen's and Brussels Carpeting for the Ladies' Waiting Rooms. There was a typical Great North timber building on the Down platform and, rather unusually for the Great North, the two platforms were connected by a pedestrian subway. A lattice girder pedestrian bridge linked the station "square" on the north side of the station over the platforms and lines to a set of stairs leading up to the town centre. Buckie had a large goods yard to the east on the north side of the through lines and adjacent to the harbour. It was approached from the east and had a large goods shed and loading platform. As early as late 1886 the loading bank was raised 15 inches over a length of 40 feet at a cost of £11 to enable dung traffic to be properly loaded. Buckie boasted a crane of 4 ton capacity, matched by Buckie Highland. There were two signal boxes – Buckie West was at the west end of the Up platform while Buckie East was at the east end of the goods yard. In 1903 the two boxes were replaced by a central box on the Up platform just to the east of the main station building. A small subsidiary box controlled the goods yard.

One mile west of Buckie lay Buckpool (Nether Buckie for its first eight months) with its single platform and wooden station building on the north side of the line. There was a cattle loading dock on the south side, serving an adjacent livestock

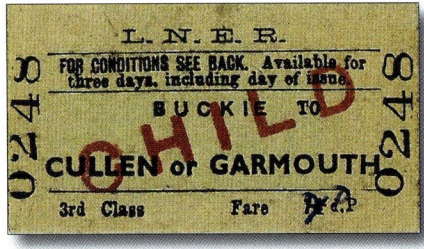

Buckpool on 21st October 1954 from the hillside. The base of the goods shed is by the siding near the centre of the image. The slaughterhouse was on the hillside to the left.
(J L Stevenson)

pen, with points at both ends which gave the illusion of a two-platform station. Other sidings were accessed from the west end and there was a small goods shed. The 1886 signal box at the west end was originally provided to protect the siding and loading bank but when the goods shed and pen were removed in 1896 the box closed, the signals were removed and the sidings became accessed by the single line token. In that year, however, a new centralised slaughterhouse was opened at the station at a cost of £800 which led to the closure of all the private ones in the district. The Buckie Stationmaster was thereafter empowered to use the locomotive from the 1.20pm Up goods to run a Special when required from Buckie to Buckpool "for Beef and Live Stock". The slaughterhouse expanded in the 1930s and Buckpool continued to handle some additional local traffic, but latterly the sidings were sometimes used to store vans to relieve congestion at Buckie.

In Buckpool itself a lattice girder footbridge crossed the line to connect the higher and lower levels of the village and survives today. The station also served Letterfourie and Gollachy.

The town of Portgordon was founded by the 4th Duke of Gordon in 1797 and the station was spelt "Port Gordon" in early timetables. Interestingly, the blue BR station board carried this version at closure in 1968. The single platform on the south side had a small wooden building and store and three two-siding yard and modest goods shed, approached from the east, was behind. The village marked the start of ten miles of valuable salmon fishing owned by the Duke of Richmond and Gordon. The station boasted attractive sea views and it served passengers throughout the life of the line. It was well used with an estimated 15,000 to 20,000 using it annually in the early 1900s. It attracted business from Enzie, Tynet, Mills of Tynet, Tannachy and Port

The station building at Buckpool on 5th March 1960, the last day that passenger trains called here. Goods services ceased on the same day.
(Norris Forrest/ GNSRA)

Port Gordon it states on the running in board but everywhere else it is usually referred to as Portgordon. This September 1967 shot is looking west towards Elgin. The former goods yard is behind the platform fence on the left and had been lifted after withdrawal of freight facilities. The station does seem to be still manned as the platform and immediate surroundings look well kept although the absence of platform seats may be a worrying development. A trio of milk churns sits outside the station building awaiting uplift which the guard would probably undertake himself if the station is unstaffed.

(G N Turnbull)

Tannachy. Beyond Portgordon the line crossed the Burn of Tynet into Morayshire.

Spey Bay was the station for Gordon Castle as well as Byres, Bogmoor, Auchinreath, Upper and Lower Dallachy and Tugnet. With its timber buildings on the Up side, it had a number of reincarnations throughout its life. It opened on 1st May 1886 as "Fochabers-on-Spey" and this was simplified to plain "Fochabers" in 1893. In 1897 W. J. Scott, writing in the *Railway Magazine*, decided to call it (unofficially) "Fochabers Road" due to its distance of four miles from the town. In 1916 it appeared as "Fochabers and Spey Bay" before being renamed as simple "Spey Bay" in 1918 for the rest of its working life. The changes were made to avoid confusion with the town of Fochabers which was over four miles distant; and with the original Fochabers station which was renamed Orbliston Junction when the Highland Railway opened its branch to the Fochabers Town half a mile from the actual village centre in October 1893. No doubt all the locals were confused, not least the inhabitants of Spey Bay and Fochabers, the latter effectively never having a station within its village boundaries. Spey Bay had staggered platforms and footbridge and served a scattered community, had a crossing loop originally controlled by East and West signal boxes, and modest freight facilities on the north side approached from the east. The station handled boxes of salmon from the

The road overbridge to the west of Spey Bay provided an ideal vantage point to see the whole station. In July 1963 it still had its loop and there is evidence of some goods traffic. The signal box is on the Down platform behind the footbridge while the small box in the foreground was one of the original two.

(Mike Stephen)

Garmouth on 11th August 1954 looking east. There was originally a second platform on the right with footbridge and signal box. The siding is behind the station building.
(J L Stevenson, courtesy Hamish Stevenson)

commercial netting business on the Spey estuary. The fish boxes were collected by a small lorry, taken to the ice-house at Tugnet to be repacked with ice for the rail journey south, and delivered to the station where usually at least one fish van was waiting in one of the three sidings.

Over the Spey Viaduct, Garmouth was next. It opened on 12th August 1884 and for 21 months it was the temporary line terminus for the section of the Coast Line from Elgin. During that intervening period connecting road coaches operated between Garmouth and Tochieneal. Garmouth was a significant community with sawmills which produced sleepers and pit-props and the station also served Kingston-on-Spey which was only a mile distant. It was a wooden shipbuilding centre which was, however, in decline and only lasted until 1914. The station sometimes had the name Kingston added in its early days and it also served Speymouth and Stynie. It had a wooden station building and small storage hut on the eastbound Up side, crossing loop, two platforms and three sidings. The West signal box was at the west end of the eastbound platform and the East box was at the east end of the westbound platform. The West box closed in 1917 with signalling concentrated at the East box. The rather limited goods yard with goods shed lay to the north side of the station approached from the east.

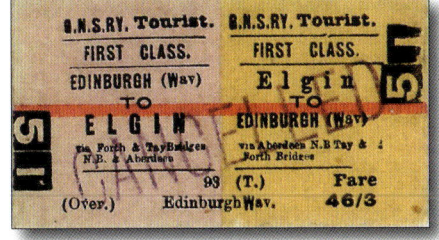

Urquhart targeted Innes and Viewfield for passengers and its single platform, wooden station

A good view of Urquhart was from the road overbridge at its east end. On 11th August 1954 the station still looked neat and tidy. Several milk churns are waiting on the platform; milk was a significant traffic at several stations on the line and was still being carried 10 years later.
(J L Stevenson, courtesy Hamish Stevenson)

Calcots on 11th August 1954 looking towards Elgin. The signal box was behind the photographer. The verandah on the left has its original open front while that on the main building has been enclosed. The footbridge is a standard LNER replacement for the original wooden GNSR one. Wooden ones rotted and were found to be unsafe in the 1930s. The LNER used old rails for the replacements.

(J L Stevenson, courtesy Hamish Stevenson)

building and small store were on the Down side. Behind the station was a goods yard and shed plus three sidings and loading bank accessed from the west with the usual goods handling equipment. The signal box closed in 1896 with access to the sidings thereafter controlled by ground frame.

Finally, dating from line opening in 1884, Calcots, close to Pitgaveny and Leuchars, was the last of the intermediate stations with its main wooden building on the Up side and a small wooden shelter opposite. It had East and West signal boxes, crossing loop and goods handling facilities. The West box closed in 1930.

After Calcots the line crossed the River Lossie by a viaduct to join the Elgin – Lossiemouth line at a new junction which, along with its associated 9-lever signal box, was constructed for line opening to Garmouth on 12th August 1884. This was Lossie Junction and the 1 mile 16 chains to the Great North station in Elgin was thereafter considered part of the new coast route with the branch to Lossiemouth commencing from the junction. The box also controlled Linksfield crossing gates on the Lossiemouth branch.

The isolated signal box at Lossie Junction. The Coast Line curves round in the background to the road overbridge on the right and the Lossiemouth branch continues straight on. The distant arm is for Linksfield level crossing. The photograph was taken in October during the "tattie holidays"; the pickers can be seen hard at work in the fields between the two lines.

(Roy Hamilton/ Strathspey Railway)

THE GREAT NORTH YEARS 1886-1922

From 1886 there were, therefore, three routes from Aberdeen to Elgin. The mileages between the two cities, Aberdeen and Inverness, were 108 via Mulben (Highland), 117¼ via the Glen Line (Great North) and 123¾ via the Coast Line (Great North). From Aberdeen to Elgin the new Coast Line had a mileage of 87¼ miles compared to 80¾ miles by its Glen Line, but the gradients on the former were easier and the line served a higher density of population. The distance over the third route from Aberdeen by the Great North to Keith and on over Highland metals via Mulben to Elgin was the shortest at 71¼ miles. However, the subsequent poor relationship between the two companies, reflected in the shenanigans which ensued over connections at Keith, did not mean that this was the fastest. The Great North still had its eye on access to Inverness and over subsequent years tried a number of wheezes to achieve this. If the Great North's strategy was offensive, the Highland was equally defensive, remained vigilant, and thwarted all attempts. To compound matters, the completion of the Coast Line brought the thorny issue of connections at Elgin to the fore.

The Parliamentary Act of 1884 which approved the Highland Railway's proposal to shorten its direct route south from Inverness to Perth via Slochd and Carrbridge, in preference to an alternative Great North proposal to build from near Nethy Bridge via a similar route, did recognise the need to improve through services between Aberdeen and Inverness. The Act provided for facilities to exchange traffic at both Keith and Elgin, unrestricted through bookings, provision of through coaches and wagons and, most importantly, that customers be prioritised. That did not stop the squabbling but did lead to some improvements. But as the Highland was still hellbent on retaining Keith as the exchange point for through traffic, the Great North petitioned the Board of Trade for provision of two connections in each direction at Elgin. Their motive was to develop the Coast Line as a route to Inverness. A rather indifferent Board of Trade did provide for traffic passing to and from the Great North at Elgin but left Keith as the point of exchange for the through coaches between the Granite City and the Highland Capital. Not surprisingly, the Great North was unhappy and its appeal for the case to be reheard was granted. However, in early 1886, the two companies forestalled this by entering a seven-year working agreement on through traffic.

As well as providing for the arrangement of services, the agreement covered the pooling of receipts from through traffic between Grange and Elgin, irrespective of route, with disputes referred to an independent arbiter. This led to an immediate improvement in train timings. Initially, the Coast Line was served by four trains in each direction. From mid-1886 a midday departure from Inverness connected with a fast train from Elgin to Aberdeen (introduced six months earlier and omitting some stops) covering the Elgin to Aberdeen route via the Coast in 2¾ hours. It departed Elgin at 1.35pm, arriving in Aberdeen at 4.20pm, and crucially it conveyed through coaches all the way. A separate train departed Elgin for Aberdeen via the Glen Line at 1.40pm. In the opposite direction this fast service with through coaches departed Aberdeen at 10.10am and arrived in Inverness at 2.15pm.

From 3rd May 1886, only two days after opening and in response to strong public demand for faster mail deliveries, the Company operated the Great North of Scotland Sorting Carriage which worked from Aberdeen to Elgin via the Coast on behalf of the Post Office. Initially it was introduced on 1st January 1886 by extending the Caledonian Railway's overnight Post Office Sorting Van from London to Aberdeen on to Keith by virtue of a hire arrangement. In April and May the Great North placed orders for two of its own vehicles at £325 each and these entered service on 15th November 1886 as P.O. Vans Nos 1 and 2. In the intervening period the Company hired a sorting carriage from the London & North Western Railway and on 1st September purchased it for £90 (plus interest accruing from date of first use) as Van No. 3. When Vans 1 and 2 appeared on 15th November this coach became a spare and was based for some of its time at Elgin. Apparatus was installed on the Down side to drop off mail bags and on the Up side to collect them at various stations south of Grange and later at Cornhill.

The daily pattern was to work northbound with mails from the south on the morning train departing Aberdeen at around 9.30am to 10.00am; with arrival back in Aberdeen at 4.20pm in time for evening connections south, particularly the Caledonian's 5.40pm departure. Accelerations further south meant that the morning departure from Aberdeen was brought forward in 1896 to around 8.00am and arrival put back to 5.10pm. The mail train called at Inverurie, Inveramsay, Insch, Huntly, Grange South/Cairnie Junction for dividing, Tillynaught, Portsoy, Cullen, Buckie, Fochabers and Garmouth. On-train sorting of both letters and parcels was undertaken by two sorters employed by the Post Office between Aberdeen and Buckie whereupon the mails were transferred in pouches to the guard's care for the rest of the journey to Fochabers, Garmouth and Elgin and onwards to Inverness (and vice versa on the Up journey). This allowed staff to take a full break at Buckie before the return leg. The Sorting Carriage ran empty to Elgin to be turned. There were

The interior of Elgin station before it was rebuilt in the early years of the twentieth century, with its low wooden platforms. The carriages are all early 4-wheeled ones. The roof was removed before 1897. (GNSRA collection)

The east end of the rebuilt Elgin station in the early years of the twentieth century. Two Aberdeen-bound trains wait for passengers, one going via Duifftown and the other via the Coast. They would join at Cairnie Junction. On the right is one of the GNSR Post Office sorting carriages.
(Sir Malcolm Barclay-Harvey)

An Aberdeen to Elgin train enters Cullen in GNSR days hauled by Manson-designed class O No. 18. The first vehicle is the Post Office sorting carriage.

(R K Blencowe collection)

timing variations and additional postal services over the years. Staff worked right through to Elgin from 1899 (possibly 1896). The official name "Great North of Scotland Sorting Carriage" was changed to "Aberdeen and Elgin Railway Sorting Carriage" on 21st November 1904. In May 1910 average weekly volumes were 17,551 letters and 707 parcels on the Down service and 37,569 letters and 1,514 parcels on the Up. The new Coast Line greatly speeded up the mail service from Banffshire and Moray to the south. Van No. 3 had deteriorated by the start of the new century to the extent that the Company authorised its breaking up on 3rd January 1901. Vans Nos 1 and 2 continued to provide sterling service and, following complaints from the Post Office, their oil lamps were replaced by Stone's electric lights in 1909. Steam heating was fitted by November 1911.

The fishing industry along the Coast embraced the new railway immediately. Each year from July to September thousands of tons of herring were landed and poured into farlins (troughs) from which teams of three herring lassies, comprising two gutters and one packer, filled the barrels for onward shipment. As the shoals began to migrate southwards down the UK coast, the teams of lassies, often family members or close friends, and menfolk would follow by train to ports such as Great Yarmouth (Yarmouth Beach station) and Lowestoft to continue their work. Some groups travelled by ordinary services, in which accommodation was reserved, although luggage was dispatched separately in vans, and others by special workings in through coaches. It is estimated that up to 4,000 fishworkers travelled annually by train to and from East Anglia for the herring. In Great North days the tickets, invariably third class, were printed "Fisherpeople" or "Fishworker" (no sex discrimination), but there are also examples of tickets printed "Fisherwoman". Their fares and accommodation were paid by their employers with a guarantee of minimum earnings and they would return to Portsoy, Cullen, Portknockie, Findochty, Buckie and the other ports by Christmas, again often in special trains and carrying presents for their relatives back in Scotland.

It was a gruelling journey in both directions and, on more than one occasion, Buckie Town Council appealed to the railway companies to tackle overcrowding and to improve on-board facilities. However, as late as November 1930, Provost Merson of Buckie was complaining to local M.P. Major MacKenzie Wood that returning fisherwomen had been locked out of their train at Yarmouth and had got soaked in the pouring rain. The Provost even travelled to Yarmouth himself to view the boarding arrangements and accused the railways of *"hopeless incompetence"*. This issue was raised in the House of Commons and the Minister of Transport asked the railways to respond. They met fire with fire and alleged that some fish curers were not giving the railway sufficient notice of the large numbers and that the behaviour of some Scottish passengers (not all girls) was *"unreasonable"*.

It was not just the land-based fish workers who used the trains. The fishermen also travelled to the fisheries by rail as this notice in the *Banffshire Advertiser* on 7th May 1896 announced: *"From 1st April to 30th May, Fishermen and their Assistants proceeding to the North and West Coast Herring fishing, will be conveyed from Peterhead, Fraserburgh, Macduff, Banff Bridge, Banff, Portsoy, Glassaugh, Cullen, Portknockie, Findochty, Portessie, Buckie, Buckpool, Portgordon, Elgin and Lossiemouth to Wick, Thurso, Stromeferry, Portree, Oban, Barra or Lochboisdale via Oban and Stornoway, at Cheap Third Class Fares."* These tickets were not valid for Express or Mail trains. And so, the Great North benefited from both fish and people, the latter in both directions.

Buckie flourished as a direct result of the new harbour and the rail links. The local Great North station claimed the bulk of the fish traffic:

Fish by rail (tons)	1888	1889	1890	1891	1892	1893
Buckie (GNS)	2,236	3,196	2,738	2,380	2,179	1,998
Buckie (Highland)	690	769	748	619	447	585
Peterhead (GNS)	4,172	5,679	6,731	5,981	6,465	6,782
Fraserburgh (GNS)	4,050	4,970	5,129	3,870	4,358	5,085

Source: David Ross, *The Great North of Scotland Railway: A New History*, 2015.

This pattern was followed until after the Second World War from which time there was more emphasis on white fish. Many workers living in coastal communities also used the trains to travel daily to and from the main processing centres, particularly Buckie. As the general fish trade and associated rail transport via both the Highland and Great North lines developed, fresh fish from Buckie was on sale in Billingsgate and Manchester Fish Markets within 14 hours of landing by the 1890s. The Great North had about 200 open box fish trucks many of which were seen in Buckie in the late 19th century. Although part of the Company's goods stock, these vehicles were fitted with Westinghouse air brakes or through pipes as they were designated to operate as passenger train traffic. As such they bore the chocolate-lake livery of the passenger carriages rather than the standard plain grey of goods vehicles. Interestingly, the Great North never had specialised fish vans and it was the LNER which introduced its design of covered van. The Great North used ordinary closed and meat vans as well as the open wagons; although it did hire covered fish vans from English-based companies during the local herring seasons.

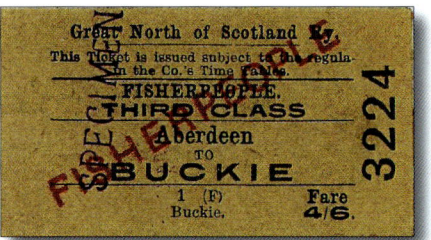

Other freight developed quickly. The railway handled significant volumes of livestock, mainly cattle and sheep, especially to and from Cornhill Mart, with the 1.20pm goods from Buckie delivering on a Wednesday and taking traffic away the following day. The Coast sent its share of beef annually to the London Christmas markets. Sheep were sent each Spring in special trains to pasture further west before returning to the north-east in Autumn. For example, on Sunday 1st April 1888 two locomotives, two brake vans and 38 cattle trucks departed Keith at 11.10pm and arrived in Portsoy at 11.50pm. There they were loaded overnight for a 5.30am departure along the Coast to Elgin (crossing the 6.30am ex Elgin Up goods at Calcots at 6.40am). Arriving in Elgin at 6.50am the cattle trucks were handed over to the Highland and the two engines and brake vans, along with goods wagons, returned to Keith via the Glen Line. On that same day another special sheep train, loaded at Banff, travelled the Coast Line to Elgin in the afternoon with four trucks for Beauly, eleven for Strathcarron and three for Stromeferry. Another destination from Banff was Newtonmore via Keith and the Strathspey Line. Other freight traffics were grain, oats, barley, draff, seed, fertiliser, potatoes, turnips, sugar beet (to Fife) and timber (especially during the two World Wars). Mr Barclay, a slate merchant in Buckie, was an early customer. Much of this traffic operated consistently down the years until the 1950s.

One group who were not entirely happy with developments were the good folk of Banff. They now found themselves at the end of a small branch rather than a terminus of a line from Aberdeen. There were no connections with either the 3.30am mail or the new 3.35pm express from Aberdeen and this led to a letter of complaint from Banff Town Council in 1887. When John Stuart, Assistant General Manager, visited the town he admitted that the timetable deliberately favoured the new Coast services. He did equalise the fares between Banff and Banff Bridge to Aberdeen, but nothing more was heard of Ferguson's proposed link between Banff and Macduff. The complaints grumbled on but a Town Council proposal in 1889 for an improved service was rebuffed by William Moffatt who stated it was too costly for the number of passengers. However, the Company finally relented in 1890 with timetable alterations. Passengers using the 10.55am service out of Banff could now reach Keith by changing at Rothiemay onto the 9.40am express from Aberdeen

Stations often attracted large groups of spectators to see passengers arriving or departing. Here a group of distinguished visitors await a train at Garmouth sometime before the First World War. The second platform and signal box can be seen on the right. (GNSRA collection)

to Keith. Additional trains were introduced to Tillynaught for connections for the Coast, Grange and Speyside. The Company hedged its bets, however, by making it clear that these services were experimental until the end of April 1891.

If the Great North thought that was the end of complaints from Banff, it was sadly deluded. It shot itself in the foot by withdrawing the 8.50pm train from Tillynaught in 1891 which so enraged the townsfolk that it led to allegations that the Great North was conducting a *"policy of revenge"* for the previous complaints. Moffatt's assertion that he failed to understand the reaction because so few people used that service provoked a fierce response from Banff spokesman and solicitor Francis George. He accused the Great North of building the Coast Line purely to antagonise the Highland Railway and that it would be better improving its local services than pursuing notions *"....of trying to push beyond Inverness"*. He urged the locals to use Highland services if the 8.50pm service was not restored. There was one small problem with this strategy. Banff was a long way from any Highland station!

To handle the increased traffic, Glenbarry was provided with a crossing loop in 1887. There was a footbridge with the main station building on the Up platform and a small wooden shelter on the Down side and a small goods yard. The signal box controlled interlocked points and signals but block working by telegraph continued until the introduction of electric tablet signalling in 1894. Being the summit of the line at 476 feet there were runaway trap points at both ends of the station and over time these became useful when crossing long goods trains in the rather short passing loop; and a water tank at the end of the Down platform and a water column at the end of the Up for the locomotives after their strenuous climbs from both directions.

Partly because of its construction on a steep gradient but in order to serve the new Knockdhu distillery, Knock station was moved northwards and rebuilt with double platform, loop, signal box, goods shed and four sidings in 1893.

In 1888 the Great North constructed a new four-road engine shed at Elgin at a cost of £4,019. It was built on the site of the Morayshire Sawmill and replaced the two-road shed which had been built by the Morayshire Railway in 1863 to accommodate the larger Great North engines following the completion of the Glen Line. A new turntable was installed at the same time. Signals were erected at Ladysbridge to protect the level crossing.

By 1888 relations between the Great North and the Highland were again on the slide and the number of cases being referred to arbitration was increasing. However, the fast train via the Coast had improved to 2 hours 35 minutes. The 10.10am and 7.00pm departures from Elgin and Aberdeen respectively ran via the Coast with through coaches to and from Glasgow via Aberdeen and Perth. The Highland refused to provide connecting services to and from Inverness at Elgin. In 1891 the Great North ran three Coast Line trains daily from Aberdeen via Cairnie Junction and a further three ran from Keith to Elgin via Grange where there were connections to and from Aberdeen. The Highland did relent in 1892 when improved timings were introduced on the Coast Line, but a year later the Highland withdrew from the traffic agreement and severed some of the connections at Elgin. The timing of this decision at the start of the 1893 summer season led to howls of protest from a long-suffering public fed up with the childish behaviour of the railway companies. By 1895 only three of six Up Highland services made connections at Elgin; and only one in the Down direction. Moreover, the Highland was refusing to take any through coaches from the Glen Line and only one set from the Coast.

The frustration of the Great North manifested in the promotion of a Bill in 1895 for running powers to Inverness. The Company maintained that negative policies in Inverness were adversely impacting on services; that poor Highland punctuality was delaying Great North trains; and that the Highland was

The second station at Knock, looking north from the adjacent road overbridge in the late 1950s. The Permanent Way Department have laid out sleepers and rails in the solum of the former down loop in preparation to relay the adjacent single line with flat-bottomed rail. Knockdhu distillery is in the background, on this occasion hosting the track workers' train and clerestory coach.

(Colin Brown)

An additional loop was installed at Glenbarry in 1887 but the original station building was retained, a rather ramshackle affair which survived until the 1960s.
(John Emslie/GNSRA)

being obstructive at Elgin on the issue of through coaches. The Great North believed that improved services would translate into increased traffic especially if connections to the south at Aberdeen were reliable. On the other hand, the Highland had always viewed the line from Forres to Keith as a branch and preferred to focus on promoting its main line south to Perth. The Great North did withdraw its Bill in order to avoid the expense and the two companies agreed to reach a new settlement. That was a case of pigs flying and the Board of Trade appointed the Railway & Canal Commissioners as arbiters.

Events took a turn in August 1895 as a consequence of the famous East Coast v West Coast "Race to the North". While the racing was stopped on safety grounds, the outcome was that both East and West services from London were timed to arrive in Aberdeen at 6.30am, a near-2½ hour improvement on journey time. This allowed passengers to catch the 6.50am Great North stopping train out of Aberdeen to connect with a Highland service from Keith to Inverness which arrived at 11.05am. As this train joined up at Forres with the "mail" from Perth, the Great North found itself able to compete for through traffic to the Highland Capital on equal terms timewise. In truth, not many used this service, but the Great North introduced a new faster service in September which departed Aberdeen at 6.45am and connected with the Highland service at Elgin via both Coast and Glen Lines. The train split at Huntly with the rear portion allowed 75 minutes for the 46½ miles to Elgin via the Coast with five stops. The front portion was allowed 80 minutes to cover the 40 miles via Craigellachie with five regular and four conditional stops. A corresponding Up train departed Elgin via the Coast at 7.30pm and via Craigellachie at 7.32pm arriving in Aberdeen at 10.00pm. A connecting Highland service departed Inverness at 6.00pm.

When, in 1896, an accelerated service from London was introduced, the Highland was able to bring forward the arrival of its mail train from Perth to 10.15am and its Keith and Elgin departures to 8.20am and 8.53am respectively to join at Forres.

Consequently, the Great North accelerated its 6.45am Aberdeen to Elgin service via the Coast by 27 minutes to 2 hours 3 minutes with only five stops at Huntly (which was reached non-stop, covering 40¾ miles in 45 minutes), Tillynaught, Portsoy, Cullen and Buckie. Five minutes was allowed at Huntly for dividing the train and taking water and smart station work along the Moray Firth Coast was mandatory to achieve a journey time of 73 minutes for the 46½ miles. It brought forward arrival in Elgin from 9.15am to 8.48am. The timings were helped by the relatively light load of up to 105 tons to Huntly and 75 tons along the Coast, but were short-lived, however, as the trains from London were slowed by around one hour and the Great North could no longer make the connection. It is likely that speeds were slowed as a measure of economy, but the 6.45am still covered the route in 2 hours 15 minutes and with additional stops at Fochabers and Garmouth. There are records of some extraordinarily short station stop timings – Tillynaught 44 seconds, Portsoy 20 seconds, Cullen 35 seconds, Buckie 33 seconds. Garmouth recorded 1 minute 13 seconds but undertook ticket collection! *Railway Magazine* recorded "*without hesitation*" that in 1897 "*….the 6.45am from Aberdeen is today the best train for speed anywhere except in the United States, but for one thing – its lightness of load*". A grand accolade, nonetheless!

There was further acrimony in the summer of 1896 over the issue of local Highland passengers using the Great North's through coaches from Inverness with the Great North proposing to position a uniformed inspector at Inverness station. The Highland objected and the matter headed for the courts. It was resolved by agreement for stronger management control, although the Great North did place a travelling attendant/conductor on certain trains to ensure the through coaches were not being abused. This was not the most pleasant of jobs as *Railway Magazine* recorded tongue-in-cheek the following year: "*Poor man! Despite his revolver and hidden mail shirt, we believe no insurance office will grant him a policy; they know well that he carries his life in his hands, plunging daily as he does into the heart of the enemy's country."*

But it was not long before the two companies were at each others' throats again. This time it was over the exchange of through coaches at Elgin. It had been agreed that the Great North could have one through service in each direction via the Coast Line and it proposed to speed up the 6.45am departure from Aberdeen over the route. However, with only a five-minute connection at Elgin, the Highland would not guarantee to accept the through coaches and proposed Keith as the alternative point of exchange. The Great North dug in its heels and started to prepare another application to Parliament for running powers from Elgin to Inverness, although on this occasion it offered to pay the cost of doubling the line in order to accommodate the extra trains.

Meanwhile the arbiters from two years previous, the Railway & Canal Commissioners, had been sitting on their hands hoping the whole sorry business would just go away. They now felt compelled to announce their findings. In fairness, they did attempt to achieve a final solution. From 1st April 1897 Keith and Elgin were both designated as points of exchange for an equal number of services (initially four) in both directions and Elgin was to exchange though coaches in both directions from both the Coast and Glen Lines if required to do so. Each company was required to maintain the average speed of the train following handover at Keith or Elgin. A timetable was to be drawn up by both companies for approval by the Commissioners. The Great North believed that the designation of Elgin as a point of exchange strengthened the case for running powers to Inverness, but when the Highland undertook that it would fully accept the arbitration, the Bill was rejected. And that finally ended the feud. The Great North had failed to gain direct access to Inverness and the Highland was secure from further attack. The Great North had secured Elgin in addition to Keith as a point of exchange.

There was a wee problem in November 1892 when Portknockie East box was destroyed by fire which resulted in a temporary electric block section between Tochieneal and Portessie, but the Company acted swiftly to rebuild and re-open it on 2nd January 1893.

A growing feature for the Great North staff in the 1890s was the annual party or "festival" with a financial contribution from the Company. In fact, staff from Banff and Macduff stations had held a joint event back in December 1882, although this was probably self-financed. In 1893 the Company locomotive department organised a trip to Elgin with 1,350 passengers (including "lady friends" – were wives excluded?) conveyed in two special trains which departed Aberdeen at 6.20am and 6.30am destined for the Coast Line. There was much merriment, music and dancing on arrival in Elgin. Such trips became annual.

In 1896 a new station was constructed at Tillynaught. The old *"discreditable building"* which had served since 1859 was demolished and was replaced with a *"handsome and commodious structure"* on the island platform which was covered over 150 feet. There were waiting rooms for both ladies and gentlemen, a general waiting/booking hall and lavatories. There was a grand innovation on the Coast Line in March of that year – the late express from Aberdeen to Elgin contained a carriage lit by the new system of electricity which was generated by the motion of the carriage. It is recorded that *".... this resulted in a marked improvement in light and cleanliness over the old oil lamps"*! However, all was not well at Findochty as, in April, local businessmen and traders complained about the last trains of the day from Aberdeen and Elgin not calling which restricted their time for business in these places unless they walked the 1¾ miles from Portknockie. The Great North largely ignored such complaints. At Glassaugh, Cullen, Findochty, Buckpool, Portgordon and Urquhart the signal boxes closed and were replaced by tablet-operated ground frames. However, the development of the fishing industry in Buckie led to the provision of a new dedicated booking office for fish traffic, adjoining the loading bank, in late 1897.

The new timetable, dubbed the "Commissioners' Service", came into force on 1st April 1897. It became the basis for train services and journey times right through to the 1950s. There were eight through services between Aberdeen and Inverness – four by each route – although these were soon reduced to six return journeys to match demand. Trains exchanged at Elgin proved to be faster and through coaches to and from Inverness ran over both routes. The Glen Line trains ran through Keith Junction and called at Keith Town (Earlsmill until 1897) which, as the name implies, better served the community.

Trains serving both routes continued to divide and join at Huntly until 1st June 1898 when the exchange platform, Cairnie Platform (Cairnie Junction from 1919), was opened at Grange South Junction. It had an island platform on the main line with normal station buildings including a tall signal box which leant rather curiously to one side. The layout was designed for splitting and combining trains. Up trains from the Coast Line ran past on an outside track onto the main line before reversing into the Up platform to connect onto the Glen Line portion from Elgin after its locomotive having had detached. There was no road access, indeed no public access, although there was a footpath for employees, some of whom lived in adjacent cottages. In practice some members of the public did join and alight from trains at Cairnie Junction as there is evidence of tickets having been issued over the years for that station. Another small curiosity from those days was the fogman's hut beside the signals when many hours of unpleasant work ensured that the signal indications were passed to the locomotive drivers correctly during fog or falling snow. Cairnie Junction often only appeared in timetables as a footnote or with the addition of "exchange only" (for the two routes to and from Elgin).

Five months earlier, from 17th January 1898, Grange signal box opened and the short section from Cairnie Junction to Grange North was doubled. These changes not only facilitated the handling of traffic but produced economies of locomotive

Trains combining at Cairnie Junction. The coaches via the Glen have already arrived and the locomotive has drawn forward and is sitting in the Down platform ready to return to Keith. Class B1 No. 61346 arrives with the 9.30am from Elgin via the Coast. It will run forward onto the Up Main line and then reverse onto the Glen Line coaches before setting off for Aberdeen. The layout was specifically designed for these moves.
(Douglas Hume)

mileage and allowed additional connections between Keith and the Moray Firth Coast. Some slower trains divided and joined up at Grange with local trains from Keith picking up coaches from the rear of Down trains from Aberdeen.

The new Cairnie Junction was soon making a name for itself for fast train breakage and remarshalling as the staff divided and reconnected its portions. One newspaper correspondent at the time described the procedures as *"one of the smartest bits of railway working in Britain"*. Four new passenger services were introduced from Keith to the Coast Line, three of which connected with Banff services at Tillynaught. A new crossing loop was installed at Glassaugh which led to some (unfounded) speculation that a "Coast suburban service" was to be launched. The Great North of Scotland Railway Act of 12th August 1898 authorised the doubling of four Great North sections including the one mile between Elgin and Lossie Junction. As the Great North hit another period of difficulty at the turn of the century with falling revenue and rising costs (especially coal) a new climate of austerity put paid to that.

Although the public did not at the time realise its significance, a small event in the first week of July 1898 heralded the start of slow, but nonetheless momentous, change. The first motor car ever seen in Buckie made its appearance. It was driven by Mr Barbour of Messrs R. J. Barbour & Co. Blacking and Boot Polish who used it as a novelty with his retail clients. Built by the Stirling Motor Carriage Company of Hamilton it had four seats and was powered by a 4hp Daimler engine. The petrol tank held four gallons which gave a range of 70 miles. Top speed was 12mph. A new car cost £350. Despite its early limitations, this was the first indication of trouble ahead for the Coast Line.

At the end of the century all Coast stations had a morning and evening pick-up goods in both directions and there was an additional working between Portgordon and Portsoy. The last decade of the 19th century saw a decline in Great North fish volumes and more changes within that industry. Larger vessels and deeper water operations led to further decline in the north-east's small ports as fish landings concentrated more and more on Aberdeen, Peterhead and Fraserburgh and, to a lesser extent, on Buckie which also had extensive curing yards mainly for kippers. The volatility of landings was noted in the Report to the Ordinary General Meeting of the Great North held on 29th March 1900: *"The failure of the herring fishing on the east coast of Scotland also adversely affected the revenue, but fortunately the excellent fishing which followed on the English coast helped to lessen what otherwise would have been for Aberdeen and Banff shires the most disastrous fishing season of recent times."* Of increasing importance was fish traffic from west of Elgin which was consigned via the Great North to the south; and large consignments from Stornoway and the west coast to Aberdeen and north-east fish merchants to supplement supplies, especially when the east coast fishing was poor. There was a trend towards fish traders using vans attached to passenger and general goods services, especially for white fish, rather than special trains which, however, continued to be used for herring. Often these were double-headed and special arrangements were put in place for those too long for certain passing loops. One bone of contention between the Company and fishermen along the Coast was the use of the lineside palings for the drying of fishing nets, which was not permitted. In 1900 this resulted in police involvement!

The layout of Banff station was altered in 1900 and this involved a Board of Trade inspection by Colonel von Donop on 5th February. A new signal box with interlocking became operational in December that year. Banff was one of the last stations to be interlocked – several years after it was a legal requirement! Additional siding and loading bank accommodation was provided at Grange in 1901.

In 1902 the antiquated station at Elgin was finally rebuilt. Vallance records a description of the original station as *"a miserable collection of dilapidated wooden sheds, bordering a large bare platform space completely open to the weather"*. W. J. Scott visited in 1897 and described the station as "scunnering" in the Railway Magazine and commented: *"Neither the long gravel platforms nor the cross space on to which they join have the slightest vestige of roof, and the 'station buildings' are some shanties seemingly knocked together out of odds and ends from a builder's yard."* Plans had been approved by the Board in 1895 and, encouraged by Elgin Town Council, a joint station with the Highland was proposed in 1897, but it subsequently pulled out of the scheme. In fact, both Companies rejected each others' proposal. The Great North proceeded on its own to a "baronial style" design by Patrick Barnett, not dissimilar to that of Aboyne, with the track layout unchanged. The four platforms, however, were raised and protected by a glass roof. The large and imposing buildings, which still stand today, incorporated spacious and well-lit booking hall with a circular glass roof, waiting rooms, a restaurant, ticket and other offices and newspaper kiosk. There were more offices and staff rooms on the first floor, as well as the Stationmaster's residence on the ground and first floors with access from the concourse. A superintendent and district officers of the traffic, signalling and telegraph, permanent way and other departments were now based in the new building. The station had the air of a "spacious layout" and there was a single long platform for through trains in both directions between Aberdeen and Inverness which provided an unprotected as a walkway to the adjoining Highland station. At the eastern end there were three terminal bays to serve Lossiemouth, Coast Line and Glen Line trains. As part of the project a new replacement goods shed was built at a cost of £595 with the old one transferred to Aberlour.

Despite the investments and improved services, traffic failed to meet expectations. Both the fishing and whisky industries were not matching the volumes of the 1890s. Calls were made to the Great North in 1901 to reduce the fares to Yarmouth for fish workers, but the Company declined as southern companies would not agree. The single fare remained at £1.10s. Boat building on the Moray Coast was declining and coastal steamers were undercutting the railway. In early 1905 the Board requested a report on the traffic lost to sea at Macduff, Buckie and Lossiemouth (as well as at Peterhead and Fraserburgh) and, later that year, its members were studying closely the prospectus of the Leith & East Coast Steam Shipping Company which was targeting the north-east ports for business to and from Leith. The outcome was an empowerment for the Goods Manager *"to continue to modify rates where necessary"*.

A revision of the main line timetable was made as early as 1899 and one casualty of the reduced service was the fast 9.45am Aberdeen – Inverness train which now ran only via Craigellachie. The 12noon departure was withdrawn and the 6.00am train now ran only via the Coast but was suspended for the winter. From 1902, however, it was reinstated in winter on Mondays only but via Keith where the Inverness coaches were exchanged. The 2.20pm departure from Aberdeen ran only via the Glen throughout the year; and the 6.45pm winter departure ran only via the Coast. In the opposite Up direction the fast through service from Inverness was replaced by a stopping train connecting with an existing Great North service at Keith. Express trains on the Coast Line did not stop at Knock, Glenbarry and Cornhill, except for the 9.30am morning "mail" from Cairnie Junction.

By 1902 the turntables at both Portsoy and Banff were too short at only 22 feet in length and were no longer in use. Locomotives were now hauling the "Banffie" tender-first from Tillynaught to Banff. A very important train ran the length of the Coast Line from Elgin to Cairnie Junction on Monday 8th September 1902. The Royal Train carried King Edward VII and Queen Alexandra on their way from Invergordon to Ballater, one of the longest possible journeys on the Great North system. The train was double-headed by a pair of 4-4-0s and included the Great North's Royal Saloon (No. 1) acting as a subsidiary vehicle to the larger of two saloons belonging to the Duke of Sutherland. As was normal security practice, it would have been preceded by a light engine and railway staff would have been placed at intervals in sight of each other along the Coast Line.

The relationship between the Great North and the Highland improved considerably following the settlement of 1897, although a new joint working agreement stalled mainly due to financial difficulties and the opposition of some Highland shareholders. Nonetheless, by 1905 discussions were turning towards full amalgamation but, although the Great North shareholders approved, the deal floundered on the opposition of Highland shareholders who feared the transfer of administration jobs to Aberdeen and of locomotive maintenance work to Inverurie. In addition, a large number of Highland shareholders displayed complete indifference by failing to vote. And so, amalgamation failed, never to be revived. However, by 1908 some trains running between Aberdeen and Inverness were being worked throughout by the locomotive of one company. Great North locomotives worked to or from Inverness via Mulben while Highland engines worked through via the Coast and, to a lesser extent, via the Glen Line which was subject to weight restrictions. Generally "Small Ben" or "Big Ben" classes of the Highland were seen on the Coast, but, for the Great North (and, from 1923, the LNER), the line was exclusively worked by their various types of 4-4-0 locomotives.

As traffic showed signs of recovery by 1905 the Great North pioneered a half-day excursion to Strathspey and it (and one on Deeside) proved so popular that, from the following year, the Company introduced a similar excursion from Aberdeen to Elgin via the Coast. The 58 miles from Aberdeen to Tillynaught Junction were covered non-stop in 75 minutes, with Elgin reached in 2 hours 10 minutes with only four stops after Tillynaught. None of the regular trains on the Coast matched these timings. These excursions were not entirely new as Bank Holiday excursions were operating in the late 19th century. For example, on the Spring Holiday of Monday 1st May 1899,

24,000 day-trippers passed through Aberdeen Station and that included 400 departing on the 6.40am "special" to Elgin and the Coast. These excursions ceased on the outbreak of War in 1914.

A new major attraction was the Spey Bay golf course which opened on Tuesday 10th September 1907. The station was busy that day as 3,000 people arrived to watch an exhibition match. To complement the new course the rather grand Gordon-Richmond Hotel was constructed that same year (and extended in 1908 and 1909) to cater for the "gentry" – golfers, fishermen (trout and salmon) and seasonal holiday visitors, many of whom arrived by train. The Great North did not usually take much notice of its customers' comments and complaints but, in response to a suggestion from the Spey Bay Golf Club, from 1st May 1909 it brought forward the 3.04pm departure from Buckie to 2.40pm to arrive in Fochabers (Spey Bay) at 2.55pm. This allowed golfers to complete one round and return on the 6.15pm service; while those wishing two rounds could return on the last train. The Company also believed the new timing would appeal to the general public. By October 1914 the hotel was being used as a convalescent home for Belgian soldiers. Although it revived between the Wars and was enlarged in the mid-1930s, it was requisitioned for troops to use during the Second World War with the local station serving its wartime "visitors". It gently declined in the 1950s and 1960s until it burned down in 1965. A replacement Spey Bay Hotel was built on the site of the coach houses of the original hotel but it subsequently closed in 2007 and was later demolished.

The Highland line from Keith was undoubtedly a thorn in the side of the Great North in respect of Buckie fish traffic, with some consignments such as kippers for London, Liverpool and Manchester being transported more directly over the Enzie Braes and onwards via Keith and Aberdeen, usually in vans attached to passenger services. The Great North held an advantage in that their station and sidings were at harbour level while, as John R. Gray wrote in his 1968 *Northern Scot* article The Passing of the Railways: *"it was a sore struggle carting fish up the brae....to the Highland station at Buckie"*. However, there was an element of co-operation between the Great North and Highland for a couple of years from 1907 to 1909 when George Pirie & Sons of Aberdeen secured the contract to construct a new reservoir and water treatment plant to serve the town of Buckie. The chosen site was at Rochomie adjacent to the Highland line and a dedicated siding was installed about a quarter of a mile on the Rathven side of Drybridge station to receive clay and pipes. Clay was transported along the Coast Line from Tochieneal in such large quantities that Portessie was soon full of wagons awaiting onward shipment to Pirie's Siding. Although additional workings were introduced between Portessie and Drybridge the ongoing congestion led the Highland Railway Company's solicitors to write to Piries suggesting that it regulated its loadings from Tochieneal to match the handling capacity at Drybridge. For once this was a positive problem for both Companies! By completion in March 1909 nearly 8,000 tons of clay had been transported by rail from Tochieneal to Drybridge. The siding was closed and lifted shortly afterwards. Meanwhile, at this time, the fishing industry was booming again and, in 1908, ownership of Buckie Harbour passed from the Cluny Trustees to the Town Council. That led to an expansion of landing facilities, although it took 20 years to complete them.

By 1911 the first train for Inverness out of Aberdeen was the 3.30am departure via Mulben and it was followed by the 6.00am "limited stop" via the Coast arriving in Inverness at 9.35am. The 8.05am departure split for both Coast and Glen while the 10.05am ran to Buckie only but had a connection at Keith for Inverness. The 2.20pm train ran via the Glen only and it was followed by a rather slow service at 3.40pm via both routes arriving in Inverness at 7.35pm. The last Inverness service departed Aberdeen at 6.35pm and ran via both Coast and Glen routes with relatively few stops to make Inverness at 10.14pm. In the opposite direction the first four departures from Inverness at 6.00am, 9.05am, 11.05am and 3.25pm all operated over both routes, but the last through train at 6.00pm ran via the Coast only and arrived in Aberdeen at 10.10pm. An interesting development in December 1911 was the introduction of steam heating in the passenger carriages, initially on the 8.05am Aberdeen – Elgin service and the return "mail" at 2.40pm. The Coast also had one daily "local" between Keith and Buckie and three daily freight services served the line, principally for fish traffic. Pre-war timekeeping on the Coast Line was reported by *Railway Magazine* in 1910 to be "poor" and that very often the two portions from Elgin for Aberdeen failed to re-join at Cairnie Junction and ran forward separately. That was a costly issue!

On 2nd January 1912 the main East signal box at Spey Bay burnt down while the signalman was away for his dinner leaving a large fire burning. It was assumed that hot cinders had fallen on the floor and the Great North hurriedly conducted a review of whether suitable fenders were required at all its boxes. The Board decided to close the West box and build a new single box on the Down platform to operate all points and signals. The cost was £300 of which £235 was charged to insurance.

Rather surprisingly, as early as 1910, the Great North management was questioning the future of Cairnie Junction which was then only 12 years old. Passenger Superintendent William Deuchar maintained that, if it closed, expenditure would be required to transfer facilities to Grange or Huntly with consequent unproductive light engine running. If Grange was used, a new turntable would be needed there unless engines ran light to Keith and that would adversely affect Highland Bens working the Coast due to delay in turning them. The postal sorting carriages would also need turning at Grange for the mail

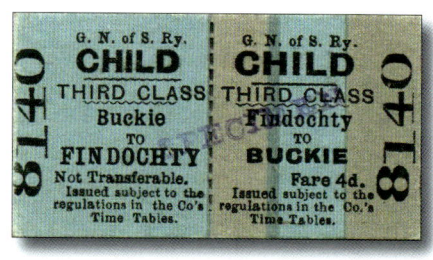

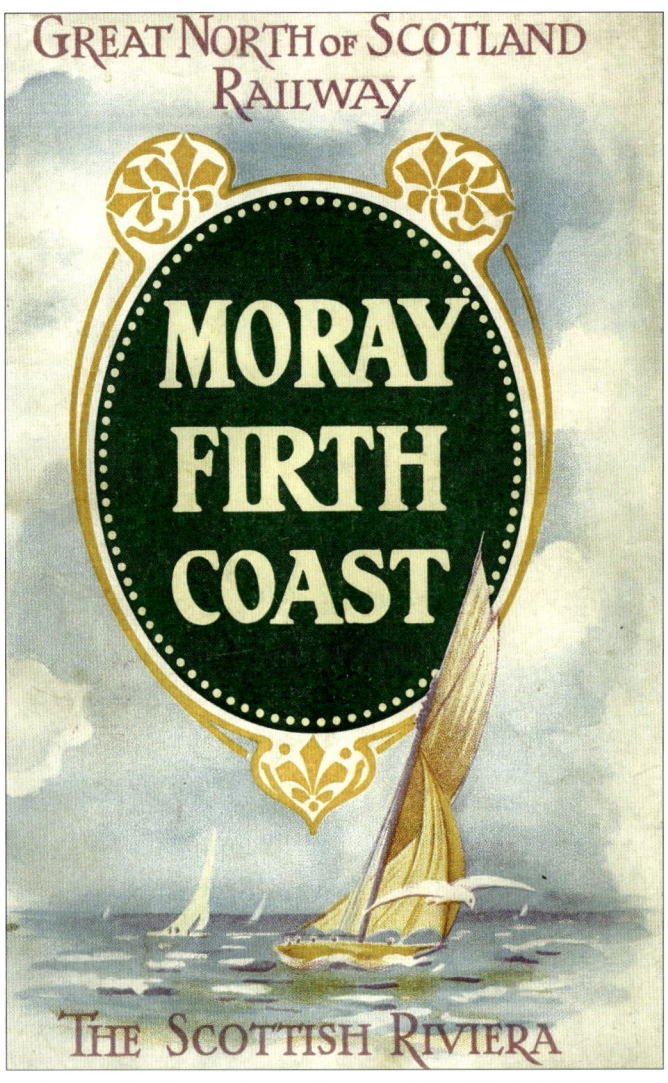
Cover of guide book issued to attract tourists to the line.

which was causing more delays as it had to be constantly cleared for passing trains. There was at least one instance of wagons being unable to be detached from an incoming train due to the congestion. In spite of what was a serious operational issue no progress appears to have been made to resolve it.

In 1912 the Traffic Agreement with the Highland was extended for a further 10 years to 31st October 1923 under the same terms, except for new pooling and division of receipts at exchange points: Elgin, Highland 77% Great North 23%; Keith, Highland 62% Great North 38%; Buckie and Portessie, Highland 35% Great North 65%.

Before the War the Banff branch locomotive departed Banff at 5.15am with a goods only train for Tillynaught returning at 6.15am. And it was the only train permitted to pick up wagons at Ladysbridge for Banff. Thereafter it worked the 10 return passenger services (some mixed) on weekdays only. Ordens Platform was *"worked in the charge of the guard"* and there were occasional calls at Boyndie Siding (1½ miles from Banff) which served Inverboyndie Distillery, taking in coal and grain and dispatching the whisky. This siding's points faced Up trains and so any traffic for the distillery arriving in Banff had to be propelled back by separate workings to the siding, which was operated by a ground frame unlocked by the section tablet.

On 1st October 1913, between Ladysbridge and Banff, wooden-constructed halts were opened at Bridgefoot, 4¾ miles from Tillynaught serving Inverboyndie and slightly closer to Whitehills than Ladysbridge; and Golf Club House, 5¼ miles from Tillynaught, serving Boyndie Links Golf Course. These halts with "wood and cinder" platforms cost £34 each and were unstaffed. They were totally unprotected, although later a small wooden hut was provided at Bridgefoot. They had special ticketing arrangements. Passengers travelling from Banff had to purchase a ticket at that station and immediately give it up to the "examiner" before the train departed; and it was the duty of the guard to collect tickets on the train for passengers travelling from the halts to Banff and to deliver them to the Banff Stationmaster for "snipping" and auditing. On 12th December 1913 automatic ticket-issuing machines were installed at both halts and the guard was tasked with directing passengers who did not hold a return ticket to buy one from the machine. For passengers travelling to or beyond Ladysbridge tickets were collected at Ladysbridge. 1d tickets were issued for Third Class travel to Banff or Ladysbridge only and First Class travellers had to purchase two! Return tickets cost 2d Third Class and 3d First. The machine tickets were valid on the day of issue only, but were not dated! A discounted "book" of tickets was available from Banff to both halts at 9d for 12 Third Class single journeys and 1/6d for 12 First Class. The Company urged staff at Banff station and the train guards to be "….careful to collect one of these tickets for each journey made." One can only speculate whether these ticketing arrangements were open to abuse.

exchange apparatus to work on both main line and Coast Line. And passenger connections would be broken. A simultaneous but coincidental request was made by Cairnie Junction's local Parish Council to open the station for public use. The Council even offered to provide materials for the upgrading of the employee footpath and provision of a small goods station. The cost including a footbridge was estimated at a modest £1,600. Another issue at Cairnie was the limited siding space which was causing delays to re-marshalling freight trains and, although some extension work was proposed, nothing materialised. While occasional review of facilities is good business practice, the consideration to close Cairnie Junction at this time seems odd; and the Great North fudged the issues of public opening and siding capacity sufficiently to be saved by the outbreak of the War in 1914. The matter of siding capacity was considered again in some detail in 1920, as often the lines were full of wagons and shunting was occasionally encroaching on the main line

An afternoon train to Tillynaught passes Golf Club House Halt in BR days. The platform looks neglected without even a nameboard. Banff can be seen in the distance. Bridgefoot had a similar wooden platform but with the advantage of a small shelter. The locomotive is a BR Standard Class 2; these provided the motive power on the branch in its final years. The girl watching on with interest is standing on the footpath which connects the Links up the hill to the A98 and which exists today.
(George Robin/GNSRA)

In 1913, in a bid to boost holiday business, the Great North published a visitor guide entitled "*Moray Firth Coast – The Scottish Riviera*". It appeared under the name of the Company's General Manager George Davidson and it extolled the attraction of the coast "*….to the tourist, holiday-maker, and the seeker after rest or health*". Of course, it was keen to point out that, while the area's relative remoteness from the major population centres meant that it was relatively undiscovered, "*….the accelerated speed and augmented facilities of present-day railway travelling have brought it within ready and easy reach from all parts of the United Kingdom…. the Great North of Scotland Railway affords the most direct route to the Moray Firth Coast….*". The booklet provided a potted history of the larger towns and villages, amongst others Elgin, Lossiemouth, Garmouth, Spey Bay, Portgordon, Buckie, Portessie, Findochty, Portknockie, Cullen, Portsoy, and Banff. Golf is highlighted as a major attraction with the courses at Banff, Duff House (also Banff), Cullen, Strathlene (Portessie), Spey Bay and Stotfield (Lossiemouth) all featured. The guide was distributed in the United Kingdom, on the Continent and in America and certainly stood the test of time as it was still being distributed in its original form by the LNER in the 1920s. It was complemented by 5,000 posters of the Moray Firth Coast which cost £200.

Incredibly, the issue of signal interlocking was still on the Board agenda in early 1914 with a number of Great North stations yet to comply fully with the Board of Trade rules. Tillynaught, Portsoy, Tochieneal, Portknockie, Garmouth and Calcots were amongst those agreed for action by the Board.

When the War broke out operation of the Great North was taken over by the Government from midnight on 4th August under the Regulation of Forces Act of 1871. At first there were no drastic changes although some local services were cut which resulted in the faster trains making additional calls with a consequent slowing of timings. Improvements were made to Portgordon station in 1915, with the platform extended. From late 1914 to the second half of 1916, Great North engines worked all the through trains between Aberdeen and Inverness to relieve pressure on the Highland's stock on account of the latter's crucial war effort.

An opportunity to increase freight business for the Great North manifested itself when, in 1915, the Highland's services from Buckie to Keith were withdrawn as a wartime economy measure. A restricted service continued to serve Crooksmill and Aultmore Distillery from Keith while the Great North served Buckie (Highland) and Rathven stations from Portessie. The last passenger train over the whole line ran on Saturday 7th August and already by that time the *Banffshire Advertiser* was describing the "*deserted appearance*" of Buckie (Highland) station with "*….not a single wagon being left in the vicinity*". However, some of the customers close to Buckie station had doubts. Mr Alex Gray operated a meal mill receiving 2,000 tons of grain per annum by rail and dispatching meal to London and Glasgow for which he paid the Highland around £800 annually. He calculated the closure would cost him an additional £200 per year. Mr John Johnstone owned the adjacent sawmill and manufactured dressed timber for house building, but he threatened to close due to the additional cost of bringing timber "up the hill" from the Great North station. Messrs Jones & Sons of Larbert and Buckie cancelled an order due to the extra carriage costs and were unhappy at having to "cart" some dressed trees and props from the Buckie (Highland) station to that of the Great North. Rathven station was beside the main turnpike road and served Inchgower distillery. Surprisingly, it handled over 3,000 tons of goods annually, mainly grain, meal, coals, potatoes and livestock, successfully competing with the Great North stations between Tochieneal and Portgordon. Petitions of protest at the closure were sent to the Railway Executive Committee, the Highland Railway and the Wartime Traffic Committee to no avail. The responses decreed that the Great North's service between Keith and Buckie via the Coast Line could handle all traffic. Presumably music to the ears of the Great North!

However, from 1st May 1917, the Great North service at the northern end of the line was regularised (initially on an experimental basis) with the 5.40am goods from Keith to Buckie extended on Tuesdays, Thursdays and Saturdays to Buckie (Highland). It was further extended to Rathven by July, with the Great North locomotive watered and turned in the Highland sidings at Portessie and propelling the Rathven wagons from the rear and hauling the Buckie wagons and brake van. The working procedure involved the Portessie signalman issuing the Annett's Key to the driver. This key released the siding points at Buckie and Rathven. This service only lasted until the end of the year when the government closed all distilleries, including Inchgower, and the remaining traffic was rendered unviable. By June 1918 the rails along most of the line were requisitioned by the Admiralty, lifted and transferred to the ports of Inverness and Invergordon.

In the following year the two stubs at each end of the line were re-laid. The Highland supplied the rails for the Great North to reconnect Portessie to Buckie (Highland) and recommence services from November 1919 as previously (although Wednesday replaced Saturday). Mr Gray and Mr Johnstone were happy again, as grain, meal and timber business recommenced and Inchgower distillery now received coal and grain at Buckie (Highland) instead of Rathven. Fish landings at Buckie recovered and, in the early years of the decade, train loadings were at times so heavy that the Highland's Buckie station was used to relieve pressure on the Great North's station. With "Grouping" on the horizon, the Highland dithered on the issue of rebuilding the entire line and it was left to the LMS to make the decision to do so in 1923.

As a wartime economy the Sorting Carriage or ran for the last time on Saturday 3rd June 1916 on the 8.05am Down and the 2.40pm Up Aberdeen – Elgin service via the Coast and was never restored. All the station exchange apparatus was removed in the summer of 1918 (Cornhill on 27th June) and the two Great North Sorting Carriages lay unused until April 1925 when the LNER converted them into passenger vans Nos. 76S and 77S. (76S was withdrawn and sold on 1st January 1939; 77S was withdrawn on 21st July 1943 and converted to a ballast carriage for use at Bellgrove in Glasgow.) Mail, along with parcels, was still carried in ordinary vans and additional ones were added as required, especially at Christmas. For example, for Christmas 1920, an extra van was required for the Coast to serve Cornhill, Portsoy, Cullen, Portknockie, Buckie, Portgordon, Spey Bay and Garmouth.

In 1917 all through trains between Aberdeen and Inverness were withdrawn. There was additional war traffic over the Great North's routes much of it non-time sensitive freight and special passenger traffic diverted from the heavily congested Highland Main Line which was prioritising the movement of servicemen to and from Scapa Flow. During the five-year duration of the War the Great North moved nearly 50,000 full and 10,000 empty wagons to and from Highland stations. The closure of the ports on the Coast Line to merchant shipping because of potential attack from enemy warships led to a compensatory increase in rail traffic. One exception at the Aberdeenshire and Banffshire ports was the landing of herring, considered as a staple food in wartime. The English East Coast ports were closed and the Great North handled an increase of over 46,000 tons per annum during the War with Buckie landing its share along with the major Buchan ports and Macduff. With the Russian and German markets closed a large proportion of the summer herring was transported to the Scottish and English domestic markets by rail. Much of this volume had been sent to the Continent by sea before the War.

There was also increased movements of agricultural goods from north-east farms. The huge demand for timber led to the Great North opening a siding at Shiel Wood on the Fife Estate, ¾ mile south of Knock, on Monday 15th May 1916 at a cost of £258. This was for Messrs Alexander Park & Co., timber merchants of Fraserburgh, and there was an official opening on Saturday 6th May by local parish councillor Mr G. H. Pritchard. The siding came under the control of Knock Stationmaster Mr Walker and wooden houses and horse stabling were erected nearby for the workmen. Having served its purpose, the siding and its tablet controlled ground frame were disconnected on 28th April 1921. Another timber siding was installed 1¼ miles west of Garmouth on 23rd March 1917 for Messrs James Jones & Sons, the Buckie timber merchant, at a cost of £280. It was also controlled by tablet operated ground frame and it was closed and disconnected on 21st June 1921. During the summer of 1916 a loading bank was constructed at Boyndie Siding at a cost of £14.12.10d for the Banff Distillery Company who thereafter paid an additional 3d per ton on top of the normal Banff goods rates for the new facility.

The spiralling cost of sea transport and lack of shipping resulted in additional mixed traffic for the Great North such as coal, oil, food, clothing and ammunition. In the late summer of 1917 a new wagon turntable was installed at Buckie to provide full access to the coal store. The cost of £625 was shared between the Great North and McWilliam the local coal merchant. One practical issue during the War, the general restriction of lighting and drawn blinds, led the Great North to emphasise that the "calling" of station names should be made loud and clear opposite each carriage of arriving trains on the network. More specifically, because of the difficulty of observing passengers at Ordens, Bridgefoot and Golf Club Halt, all trains running on the Banff branch during the hours of darkness were instructed to stop at these stations at all times from November 1916. A shortage of new footwarmers over the winter of 1916/17 led to the withdrawal of this "luxury" on some Coast services.

Inverboyndie Distillery was on the north side of the line, west of Bridgefoot Halt, and was served by a single siding facing Banff. The loading bank was constructed in 1916, not long before the government stopped all distilling for the duration of the War.
(J L Stevenson, courtesy Hamish Stevenson)

The First World War saw the financial deterioration of Britain's railways. Investment was restrained and post-war inflation led to spiralling costs of wages, coal and materials, not helped by heavier taxation and the introduction of the eight-hour working day. In 1918 the issue of a joint station at Elgin arose again. The Great North suggested a connection between the Highland line from Keith to its Glen Line to the east of Elgin in order to convert the Great North building into a joint station. The Highland declined because of the expense and "*the conditions obtaining at present*". On this occasion, at least, their response was understandable. In September 1919 the frustration of low pay and long hours throughout the War resulted in a National Rail Strike and most of the Great North network was closed. The public was generally against the strike and some car owners volunteered to provide transport. The Aberdeenshire mails were conveyed out of Aberdeen by road and the Ministry of Food organised sea transport to Peterhead, Fraserburgh, Macduff and Buckie. Although the strike ended in early October, none of this helped the Coast Line or the wider Company.

Pre-war service levels were gradually restored, although the 6.00am train from Aberdeen via the Coast did not reappear. Ordens disappeared from the timetable again in 1921. From July 1922 the Great North introduced a restaurant car (hired from the North British but built by the North Eastern Railway in 1904) on the morning 8.05am Aberdeen – Inverness service via the Glen Line; it returned via the Coast on the 12.50pm ex Inverness service which departed Elgin at 2.25pm and arrived in Aberdeen at 5.14pm. These timings remained unchanged until the 1950s. This car catered for up to 10 First and 15 Third Class passengers, had a kitchen/pantry and was well utilised. Breakfast and lunch cost 3/- and tea 1/-.

Volumes of fish dropped significantly as the UK industry returned to normal after the War and was not helped by the loss of many fishing vessels during the conflict. However, up to five daily special fish trains were still operating out of Lossiemouth and Buckie in 1920. Cod fishing was developing at Lossiemouth and Buckie in February, March and April and 1,432 tons were transported south in 1922. These movements, of course, were balanced by the return of empty rolling stock in the opposite direction. However, the goods-only train on the Banff branch disappeared and Bridgefoot and Golf Club House Halts became request stops. In fact, Golf Club House was now closed over the winter from October to April and many of the golfers switched to Duff House on the other side of Banff, especially following amalgamation in 1923. Thereafter the Golf Club House became more of a general leisure centre, in particular giving access to the grand beach. Ordens was back in the Working Time Table "*for passengers under the control of the guard*". Two lunchtime mixed trains from Tillynaught to Banff now had to convey two porters, one from each station, to assist with the dropping and collecting of wagons at Boyndie Siding. These trains were allocated an additional five minutes for this work. Glassaugh's signal box closed and its loop was removed on 21st November 1921 with the Up line of the loop becoming the single line. And Garmouth lost its remaining signal box on 14th March 1922 (the West box closed in 1917), with the Up line of the loop also becoming the single line. The sidings at both stations became accessed by tablet-controlled ground frame, but at Garmouth Messrs J. A. Rose, wood merchant, had been allowed to install a private siding over the Company's ground in 1920.

It became obvious that extensive re-organisation was required and the Railways Act of 1921 led to the "Grouping". The Great North was allocated to the LNER (London & North Eastern Railway) and, on 1st January 1923, the Company with its 336 route miles lost its identity. As the Highland Railway became part of the LMS (London, Midland & Scottish) full integration of the Aberdeen to Inverness services was as far away as ever!

The LNER Period 1923-1947

In terms of day-to-day operations little changed immediately under the LNER and that included the Moray Firth Coast Line. Diminishing freight traffic removed any incentive to extend siding capacity at Cairnie Junction or anywhere else for that matter. An interesting small change at Cullen in September 1923 saw tow-roping banned with all empty wagons and those containing non-perishable and non-urgent traffic for destinations to the west by Down train taken by Up trains via Portsoy. In an attempt to attract holidaymakers, the LNER revived a Great North pre-war initiative and ran a special northbound service from Edinburgh and Glasgow, which combined at Thornton Junction, to Boat of Garten and Lossiemouth, dividing at Craigellachie. It ran northwards on the first weekdays of July and August 1923 and returned on the last days of the same month, largely to cater for more affluent customers who rented a house for a month in the summer. Departing Edinburgh Waverley at 11.10am, the Lossiemouth portion arrived at 5.00pm. It operated in the following two years only as its market was declining.

A summer-only sleeping car from London Kings Cross to Elgin was also introduced in 1923 and extended to Lossiemouth the following year. Initially it was for First Class passengers only (return fare £10.14.2d) although it was catering for both First and Third Class by the 1930s. Later a pair of articulated sleeping cars from the overnight *Aberdonian* was attached to a new 7.45am seasonal express from Aberdeen to Inverness but via the Glen Line to Elgin. If there were passengers for Lossiemouth, the 9.56am service took it on to arrive at its final destination at 10.15am. A breakfast car was also added for the summer (reverting to the 8.05am ex Aberdeen service in winter). The return working departed Lossiemouth at 4.05pm to connect via the Glen Line with the night service out of Aberdeen. The through working of 610 miles was one of the longest in the UK, but was exceeded by the Elgin – Penzance service in 1984. The sleeper was a regular summer feature until the outbreak of the Second World War in September 1939.

The first through service to Aberdeen left Inverness at 7.40am and conveyed a through carriage from Elgin for Edinburgh which travelled via the Coast Line. The fastest Up service of the day was the 6.00pm departure from Inverness via the Coast which arrived in Aberdeen at 10.20pm. By now the Coast Line was served by seven passenger trains daily to the Glen Line's four. Each route had three daily freight trains and the Coast had an extra local to Buckie. One of the goods was the daily Monday to Friday 10.34am fish train departure from Buckie which arrived in Aberdeen at 12.51pm. On Saturdays it ran from Lossiemouth at 12.20pm running via the Coast Line to arrive in Aberdeen at 5.24pm. Fish vans were still being attached to passenger services. Special trains continued to carry the fish

In early LNER days, LNER No. 7866 class D38, formerly GNSR No. 77 class Q, at the head of an Aberdeen train at Portsoy. The locomotive is resplendent in its new lined-green LNER livery. The first vehicle is an NBR Fish Wagon while the 6-wheeled coaches behind are still in GNSR white and dark lake livery.
(GNSRA collection)

Great North 4-4-0s continued to be the main motive power in early LNER days, supplemented by a few ex-North British locomotives. Here class D42 No. 6810, originally GNSR Class O, leaves Elgin on a local service passing milepost 87 from Aberdeen via the coast. The view across the field that shows Elgin locomotive shed would be changed in 1930 when Elgin Town Council built the Pinefield Gas Works on this site.
(R D Stephen)

workers south to Yarmouth each year departing from both Elgin and Buckie throughout the 1920s and 1930s. On a more modest note, the LNER finally included Ordens into the public timetable on a permanent basis from 14th July 1924; in practice it had never closed, operating as an unadvertised conditional stop when not included. In 1928 Banff Harbour became plain Banff.

The Great North had steadfastly avoided the thorny issue of Cairnie Junction's future by claiming it could do nothing until it was out of the Government's hands. Immediately following Grouping the issue arose again at the behest of local farmer George Staples. He wrote to Mr J. M. Calder, the new LNER General Manager for Scotland, requesting a proper station. He claimed the lack of access to Cairnie Junction caused hardship to six local farms and he listed various pairs of horses and associated crofts and other issues such as egg traffic. The farmers had to send goods by road steam wagons whereas they hoped for a siding and a station open to passengers. The LNER responded that the amount of traffic did not warrant alterations at Cairnie, especially as the Stationmaster reported that the projected egg traffic only amounted to one box (½ cwt) per week, that no eggs had been dispatched over the past two years as they were all sold locally, and that Grange was only half a mile away anyway. Mr Staples appears to have shot himself in the foot!

With regard to the Highland line from Keith to Buckie, the passenger service was never restored by the LMS but local traders in both these towns had been lobbying for the return of freight services. The Buckie & District Traders Association and the Buckie & District Fishcurers Association promised to send some of their traffic directly to Keith rather than via the Coast Line. In May 1925 Mr Mathieson, Deputy General Manager for the LMS in Scotland, met representatives of Buckie and Keith Town Councils and of Rathven Parish Council. He was unable to make any commitment but asked if the traders and fishcurers could give a "definite assurance". In June Mr Singer, the Buckie LNER Stationmaster, reported at the request of William Johnston, the LNER Northern Scottish Area Traffic Superintendent, that he anticipated the re-opened line would take back all the traffic it had prior to closure, including building stones from Keith to Buckie, Gray's Mill traffic, Inchgower distillery coal (Rathven) and barley (Buckie). Timber and significant amounts of coal for the Gas Company were potential business for Buckie (Highland) which would undoubtedly compete aggressively with the Great North station. Mr Singer did not believe that Buckie (Highland) would be a major threat to the LNER's fish and passenger traffic.

Reinstatement work was effectively completed by mid-1925 but there was no indication as to the re-opening date. The months dragged on and in March 1926 the LMS informed Buckie Town Council that *"unforeseen difficulties had presented themselves"* but that re-opening was still being considered. Meanwhile the LNER continued the three days per week goods service to Buckie (Highland) by the 5.40am ex Keith which had reverted to the original Tuesdays, Thursdays and Saturdays. It occupied the LMS section from 10.05am to 10.35am on each operating day and, with the locomotive reversing back from Buckie, the speed limit was set at 15mph. There remained a strong working link between the Great North and the local fishing industry, however, and this was exemplified on Friday 10th September 1926 when a deputation of the local fish and other traders met the Aberdeen mail at Buckie station to present veteran locomotive driver Alex Davidson with a wallet of treasury notes for his retirement. Downie Flett, President of the Buckie Fishcurers Association, raised three cheers for Mr Davidson as his engine departed.

The Highland line was then dealt a hammer blow because, from 1st March that year, Miller's Coaches of Buckie introduced a regular return bus service between Buckie and Keith. A twice daily service over the Enzie Braes matched the former train journey time of 50 minutes and a third service routing via Fochabers took an hour. The bus also operated on Sundays. The farmers embraced the new service especially as the buses carried an assortment of calves, lambs, poultry and other livestock for Keith Mart. And the buses deposited their passengers at individual farms and road ends on the return trip. Buckie fishwives and their baskets were also keen to use the buses and, after their long morning walks, were collected at Clochan crossroads for return home. In May railwaymen throughout the UK joined the General Strike and the Government gave its full support to alternative means of traffic, especially road hauliers. This resulted in some permanent loss of rail traffic on their return to work and the LMS began to cast a critical eye over the economics of its operations and over branch lines in particular. Hopes of re-opening the Keith to Buckie route were fading.

The service on the two stubs continued into the early 1930s but the closure of Inchgower distillery in 1930 (it re-opened in 1937), increasing road haulage competition and the depressed economy all conspired against the line. The fish trade was now suffering and by 1933 the LNER had spare capacity at its Buckie station. From Monday 10th April it discontinued the service to Buckie (Highland), although it continued to use the former

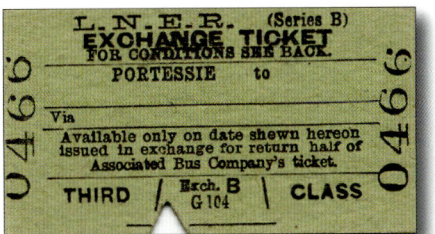

Highland turntable and watering facilities at Portessie for locomotives. The rails to Buckie (Highland) were used for storing empty wagons but the entire line was lifted for a second and final time in 1937. The section of line from Portessie to the east end of Buckie (Highland), which had been re-laid by the Great North in 1919, was retained. In 1939 the main station building was moved to nearby Strathlene Golf Club to act as a Clubhouse (until replaced in 1973) and the rest of the site was acquired by Buckie Town Council. When the LMS finally departed in December 1937 the former Highland sidings at Portessie passed to the LNER for storage of reserve rolling stock especially during the summer herring season. Although this is speculation, one cannot but conclude that the LNER and LMS both realised the commercial folly of re-opening an unnecessary competitive line and that the new competing bus service over the Enzie Braes did not help the case.

The Great North had remained the only Scottish company to refuse to break the Sabbath (apart from some mail trains prior to 1864 and permanent way trains), but 1928 heralded the LNER's introduction of two Sunday trains from 1st July in both directions between Aberdeen and Elgin via the Coast serving principal stations. Attitudes to Sunday observance were softening. One of these trains was then altered to operate to and from Inverness via Keith while the other was extended from Elgin to Lossiemouth. These services were withdrawn in 1939 and never restored. A modest programme of excursions also started during that summer and were developed during the 1930s.

Competing private bus enterprises became a growing threat to the railway after the First World War. Local services sprang up all over the north-east. For example, in Banff and Macduff Horne's was a long established business from horse-drawn days and in 1923 the Davidson brothers commenced a service between the two towns as well as a twice weekly service to Aberdeen. Buses also connected with trains at Banff Harbour (and Banff Bridge) to convey passengers to the centre of the town. The Great North had itself pioneered bus services in the first decade of the 20th century and the LNER inherited these along with the lorry fleet. From 1925 it slowly attempted to develop services. However, the LNER's attitude was rather half-hearted, as developing private competition was eroding returns. And the LNER was in danger of shooting itself in the foot as some of their own buses competed with the trains. On 1st June 1928 the Huntly–Aberchirder route was

1929 OS inch map of Buckie and Portessie showing the Highland line from Keith. The Highland station at Buckie was not close to the town.

Bus design improved greatly during the 1920s. No. 4 (YP4264) was a 1926 Thornycroft A2 seating 20 passengers. It was typical of the vehicles used to compete with the Coast Line trains. It was transferred to the Scottish General (Northern) Omnibus Company in 1930. With manual non-synchromesh gearboxes, these buses were slow to drive but their ability to take passengers close to home gave them a great advantage over rail services. (GNSRA collection)

extended to Banff via Alvah. By the following year the LNER was increasing its bus fleet significantly and, from 17th June 1929, a new bus service was introduced along the Moray Firth coast between Macduff and Banff to Elgin via Portsoy, Cullen, Buckie, Portgordon and Fochabers in direct competition with its own trains. An additional short service was begun between Cullen and Portgordon.

The changing interaction of road and rail transport throughout the UK was becoming a concern for the government and a requirement for regulation. The resultant Road Traffic Act of 1930 introduced a more comprehensive and rigorous system of bus licensing for vehicles, staff and services. Larger existing bus companies were in the driving seat (no pun intended!) and one of these, SMT (Scottish Motor Traction Co. Ltd.), offered LNER and LMS jointly a 50% financial stake in a newly structured SMT Company which would become a holding company for a significant number of bus companies, in many of which SMT already had a financial interest. In return the railway companies would transfer their bus services in Scotland to their new "partner". Both LNER and LMS agreed and from 16th February 1930 the LNER passed over the Elgin–Macduff service to Scottish General (Northern) Omnibus Ltd of Elgin which had been acquired by SMT. The rest of the LNER's bus services followed by August and, in addition to 34 buses and four lorries, the railway handed over 30 motormen and 12 conductresses. The nominal separate existence of the Moray Firth Coast bus services only lasted until the following year as SG(N)O Co. Ltd. was swallowed up by W. Alexander & Sons in 1931. The railways' road services for goods only lasted for a short time and from mid-1931 LNER lorries only operated to interact with rail conveyance of freight.

The depression of the late 1920s and 1930s, combined with growing road competition, resulted in reducing rail revenue. A prime example concerned Banff. By 1933 bus competition was forcing the railway to offer "mileage rates" to Aberdeen from Banff Bridge at only about half the normal rate; while full rates continued to apply from Banff station. While the train was about 30 minutes faster, there were only five services to and from each station. W. Alexander was providing an hourly service from 6.30am to 10.30pm. Wages were cut, stations were downgraded to halts, the post of Stationmaster was abolished at some stations and other stations were grouped under one manager. On the Coast Line there was a further, albeit rather piecemeal, rationalisation of signal boxes. Knock, Tillynaught North, Portsoy West, Tochieneal West, Portknockie West, and Calcots West all closed in the late 1920s and 1930s. Knock's crossing loop was removed at the same time with access to the sidings from September 1928 by a ground frame released by the Glenbarry – Grange North Junction tablet. Tillynaught South was renamed Tillynaught Junction. Calcots East Box then burnt down on 2nd March 1934 but was rebuilt and operational by 22nd August.

There was an interesting development at Elgin where, from July 1933, the LNER and LMS agreed, in the interests of economy and despite some local business concerns, to concentrate all passenger and parcel bookings at the former Great North station. A joint Stationmaster was appointed and six LMS positions, two clerks and four porters, were taken out. Through goods traffic from Keith to Elgin and stations beyond was to be routed via Mulben to minimise freight traffic on both Coast and Glen lines in order to reduce operating costs. It was envisaged that some staff at the smaller stations could be dispensed with. Some long section working between signal boxes was introduced. From 1936, for example, when the LNER closed the minor Portsoy North box, the South box controlled all operations in both directions and, until 1959, could be "switched out of circuit" during quiet periods to allow long section working between Tillynaught and Tochieneal. A king lever altered the lever locking system to allow the Up loop to be used in both directions. A ground frame released by the long section tablet allowed access to the yard when the box was switched out. Some services were reduced, and the first line closures on the old Great North system (Oldmeldrum and Boddam) were implemented. The LNER's bus strategy misfired as competing private bus and lorry services developed in the rural areas. Some bus routes intended to feed the railway were extended and resulted in more competition. The convenience and mobility of lorries impacted on the movement of agricultural produce, although the railway responded by encouraging larger traders to establish distribution railheads at the larger stations. Direct transfer of animals by floats from the farm to market increased. And lorries started to make inroads into the valuable fish traffic, although a decline in herring landings was offset by an increase in the domestic market for white fish. Whisky sales were down. The Coast Line was not exempt from the changing world, but for the present it remained largely unaltered.

More positively, despite overall passenger traffic being adversely affected by the depression, holiday and excursion traffic increased as more people enjoyed summer holidays with pay and the Moray Firth seaside resorts benefitted accordingly. From 1926 the LNER began to actively advertise holiday resorts by means of highly artistic posters by eminent artists. Bright colours were used to allure holidaymakers and *"Banff"* by Frank H. Mason, looking towards Blackpots (Whitehills) from above the town, was an early feature. Two authorities on Scottish railways, Charles Buchan from Aberdeen and Angus Shand from Fort William, were sent down to London to extol the many attractive features of holidays accessible by rail in Scotland. The LNER's famous "land cruise" train *Northern Belle*, introduced on Friday 16th June 1933 from London Kings Cross, travelled over the Coast Line. In the inaugural year the day portion undertook a day trip from Aberdeen to Lossiemouth and returned via Buckie and Cairnie Junction. And in June 1937, 1938 and 1939 both the day and night portions ran via the Coast Line on route to Inverness after the former had visited Ballater the previous day. The *Northern Belle* was withdrawn after the summer of 1939.

The LNER introduced the concept of holiday "camping coaches" in 1933 and within two years these were located at Portsoy (beside the original 1859 station), Glassaugh, Tochieneal, Portessie, Spey Bay, Garmouth and Calcots. Holiday-makers used the adjacent station building toilet and washing facilities and it was a condition of rental (£3 per week) that they travelled to and from their chosen location by train. The 1936 LNER *Camping Holidays* book listed all seven stations and gushed: *"The enchanting Moray Firth coast with salubrious sea and mountain breezes is an ideal holiday place where restfulness and recreation can be enjoyed."* The LNER also promoted rail travel to and from camp sites and provided basic details of those near the Coast Line stations of Grange, Banff, Glassaugh, Tochieneal, Portknockie and Portgordon. Glassaugh camp site was highlighted as *"very convenient near sea, rail or road [with] very fine beach [Sandend] and safe for bathers."* At Banff, Portknockie and Portgordon the Company made camping easier by offering a cartage service for camping equipment to be delivered to and collected from the camp site at a small charge. The Stationmaster was responsible for organising this. Portknockie was advertised as close to Cullen Golf Course and presumably the poor lad designated for carting duties had to struggle with the golf clubs along with the tents! The location of the nearest drinking water supply was given – at Banff it was *"close to tea rooms on links."* In 1932 the Banff branch boasted seven return trips per day with the ratio of passenger to mixed services

Although at Murtle on the Deeside Line, this photograph from July 1935 illustrates a typical camping coach and the basic pleasures which made them so successful. The enamel can bottom right would be used to bring water to the coach.

(Ian Sandison/GNSRA)

50/50. Although all trains stopped at Ordens, calls at Bridgefoot and Golf Club House halts were when required with the latter still closed from October to April inclusive.

The LNER introduced Sunday half-day and evening excursions to the Coast from the late 1920s. By 1937 the Sunday half-day excursion departed Aberdeen at 11.20am and picked up at Inverurie, Insch, and Huntly and set down at Portsoy, Cullen, Portknockie, Findochty, Buckie, Portgordon, and Spey Bay arriving in Elgin at 1.53pm. From Elgin there were optional connections at 2.00pm and 2.50pm to Lossiemouth. The Third Class Return from Aberdeen to any Coast station was 5/- and to Lossiemouth 5/6d. The return from Lossie at 7.15pm connected with the 7.35pm departure from Elgin which arrived in Aberdeen at 10.08pm. This train was made up from stock used on the Saturday Speyside excursion to Boat of Garten and included a Restaurant Car. It offered luncheon at 2/9d on the outward journey and high tea at 2/9d or plain tea at 1/1d (all including gratuities) on the return journey. Other refreshments, of course, were offered at *"popular prices"*. The evening excursion ran on Wednesday (local half-day closing) and departed Aberdeen at 4.00pm and arrived in Elgin at 6.30pm with the return departing at 9.00pm to arrive in Aberdeen at 11.23pm. This excursion was so popular that the Working Time Table instructed that it *"will be run in duplicate if necessary and Train set formed of 9 bogies controlled by Vacuum Brake and worked by Class B12 Engine to be in readiness at Kittybrewster"*. These trains took on water at Huntly on the outward leg and at Buckie on the return. There was also a well-used local Wednesday evening excursion from Portessie to Elgin. And Strathlene by Portessie, by now a popular resort with its open air swimming pool, hotel and golf course, attracted large numbers of Summer excursionists from Aberdeen. The swimming pool was upgraded in 1932 and re-opened with a grand gala on 20th July. It had become such an attractive holiday destination that Buckie Town Council petitioned the LNER to change the name of Portessie station to "Strathlene". The LNER refused, but following constant pressure from the Council, it did agree to add "For Strathlene" to the Portessie station boards in January 1936. It also suggested that the Council should erect a large "Strathlene" sign on the golf course which could be seen from the trains. Unfortunately, the War brought a premature end to these initiatives.

By 1938 the summer Coast service had increased to eight return workings with an additional Down service on peak dates. An extra Summer Saturday service departed Aberdeen at 7.45am for Elgin via the Coast; and in the opposite direction from Elgin at 9.10am and with a through coach for Edinburgh. On weekdays this coach was part of the 8.10am departure also via the Coast. The 2.20pm Aberdeen – Inverness service ran via the Coast on Saturdays only, reflecting weekend holiday and excursion traffic. During the rest of the week it ran via the Glen Line, although in the 1950s it operated on Friday and Saturday only but was well patronised. The 3.30pm departure from Inverness conveyed through coaches for Aberdeen via Mulben, but at Keith this train picked up portions from Elgin by both Glen and Coast Lines, plus the London Kings Cross sleeping car and through carriages for Aberdeen from Lossiemouth. The Glen Line was still considered as the historical "main line", but the Coast Line boasted an equal level of services particularly during the Summer. And, during that decade, there was investment in the line. For example, in 1930 the bow-string lattice girder bridge crossing the Isla at Grange North was replaced by a steel plate girder bridge with trough flooring.

The outbreak of hostilities in 1939 resulted in increasing pressure on the nation's railways again. The advisory Railway Executive Committee, established in September 1938 in anticipation of events, took control of the country's rail network. Some local train services were withdrawn with expresses making more stops. Many restaurant, sleeper and through coaches disappeared. The camping coaches at Glassaugh, Garmouth and Calcots were withdrawn in 1938, with the remainder in the Great North area disappearing the following year. Timber and military supply traffic increased. Traffic was switched from road and coastal shipping to rail. However, fishing was curtailed due

The swimming pool and golf course at Strathlene were developed in the 1930s to cater for a growing leisure market. The Highland Buckie station building was moved to the golf course to act as club house, as seen on 21st October 1954. (J L Stevenson, courtesy Hamish Stevenson)

In its early days, the LNER had to meet an urgent need for more powerful locomotives for the area. The GNSR had in fact prepared plans for additional and improved locomotives but had deferred any decision due to the pending Grouping. The best the LNER could provide was "hand-me-downs". Initially these proved to be little better than the existing stock, but the arrival of the ex-Great Eastern Railway B12s from 1931 onwards brought a great improvement. The B12s survived until 1954, although used on lesser services such as this Up freight at Tillynaught on 3rd June 1953 headed by No. 61502.

(Graham Maxtone collection)

to the danger from submarines and mines, to the conscription of many fishermen into the Royal Navy, and to the requisition of some trawlers for minesweeping and Patrol Service duties. However, landings did continue and even tiny Ladysbridge did its bit, handling over 1,000 tons of white fish in 1940. The Moray Firth coast was heavily fortified during the War and the Army conveyed men, equipment and vehicles along the line. Glassaugh distillery was used as a wartime Naafi depot served by the local station. Aircrew training took place along the Moray Firth Coast and Dallachy Airfield, just to the east of the Spey Viaduct, opened as a training school in 1943 and became an operational base for Beaufighter squadrons the following year.

In October 1943, as the railways were strained further and further, all rail movements were placed under closest control to ensure the optimum use of men, engines and vehicles. Aberdeen Control was part of a nationwide network and had responsibility for Keith to Elgin via Buckie with direct telephone communication with the Control Office. It was also responsible for Tillynaught to Banff but without telephone, so communication continued by telegraph. Troop trains were seen in Banff and another visitor was a camouflaged-livery train consisting of tank locomotive with heavily armoured steel plating and flat wagons mounted with light artillery field guns and Lewis guns for anti-aircraft defence. As D-Day approached in 1944 beach landing training was undertaken in the far north of Scotland. This involved tanks being transported by rail to the practice areas. A wooden bridge on the main Perth – Inverness line and the bridges over the Spey at both Craigellachie and Boat o'Brig were all incapable of taking the weight. However, the Spey Viaduct met all the requirements (and with a good margin to spare) and, therefore, trains of "warflats" hauled by double-headed B12 locomotives carried the tanks and armoured vehicles north via Aberdeen and the Coast Line.

The Great North served various air stations including Lossiemouth and Banff (at Boyndie, which was nearer Portsoy). Spey Bay served RAF Coastal Command at nearby Dallachy which was taken over by the Army and Territorial Army after hostilities ceased. Elgin handled goods and spare aircraft engines for the Navy with onward shipment by road to the airfields of Lossiemouth (HMS Fulmar from 1946) and Milltown (its diversion airfield HMS Fulmar II, operated by RAF Bomber Command to the north of Calcots). However, to avoid the danger of explosives in Elgin, Calcots received munitions and ammunition which were collected by local naval personnel during and immediately after the war. Coal for heating the Lossiemouth base was delivered by rail and, after the war, scrapped aircraft which were no longer required were taken out by train. Massive double-headed leave trains visited Lossiemouth; some of them had to be propelled from Elgin because they were too long for the loop there. Often such movements were for swapping personnel on aircraft carriers with the trains travelling as far as Plymouth or Portsmouth depending on where the carrier was anchored. The war led to an upsurge in passenger traffic and a further boost to passenger numbers resulted from petrol rationing which reduced private motoring, although the government discouraged unnecessary travel. In the final months of the war there were steady movements of freight to RAF Banff in the form of spares for the Mosquitos and Beaufighters of the famous Banff Strike Wing. Some of the Great North network suffered a relatively small degree of bomb damage but the Coast Line survived unscathed.

The allocation of class B1 locomotives to the ex-Great North lines from 1946 was the first brand new motive power for 25 years. The class proved to be masters of the job. Here No. 61308 waits to take the 2.12pm train from Elgin via the Coast to Cairnie where it will combine with the 2.14pm train via the Glen route.

(J L Stevenson)

Great North engines could still be seen on the Coast Line in the 1950s. An eastbound freight enters Portknockie hauled by 62267 of class D40. It was withdrawn in August 1956.

(Colin Brown)

British Railways: Death by a Thousand Cuts 1948-1968

The UK's railways were exhausted by the end of the War. Investment was desperately needed and Nationalisation lay ahead from 1st January 1948. The north-east saw few immediate changes apart from the introduction of Thompson B1 locomotives on the Coast Line for the first time and from some slight adjustments to services and timetables. In 1947, for example, the 4.30am departure from Aberdeen ran via Mulben but with portions for Elgin via Buckie and Craigellachie. The 8.05am train contained through coaches and a restored restaurant car for Inverness via the Glen Line, but also conveyed a portion for Elgin via the Coast. The 9.40am had through coaches or connections for all three routes. In the opposite direction the 6.00am train from Elgin via the Coast still operated. The 12.40pm train out of Inverness used both routes with the restaurant car returning via the Coast. There were five Down trains daily on both Glen and Coast routes and extra services on Saturdays; and seven Up trains via the Coast and five via the Glen.

The LNER lost the steady flow of servicemen using the trains, some people had become used to staying at home and car use started to increase. The Company did try to promote post-War traffic such as reintroducing cheap day return tickets (return for the price of the single journey) for parties of eight or more, a move targeted at organised groups such as football teams. Similarly, "guaranteed" excursion trains offered the same deal to groups of 300 or more – targeting works and club outings. Train times were slower than before the War and there were local calls for the Coast Line services in particular to be speeded up by omitting some stops. The Banff branch had six return trips plus an extra each way on Saturday evenings, although the service increased back to seven return trips plus the Saturday extra in 1949. These trains offered reasonable connections for Aberdeen, Keith and Elgin. Shortly after Nationalisation the former Highland section of track to the edge of the old Buckie (Highland) station was lifted.

From 1948 the Great North/LNER system came under the management of British Railways Scottish Region. There were still few service improvements as the post-War period of austerity dragged on. The through coaches from Edinburgh to Elgin were reinstated on a summer-only basis from 1949, similar to the 1930s service, but only lasted until 1952. A through seating coach for Elgin on the main overnight London–Aberdeen service, replacing the pre-war sleeping coach, was equally short-lived. It ran throughout the year from September 1957 but was withdrawn after only two years. However, a through coach from Glasgow Buchanan Street to Elgin via the Coast ran on Summer Saturdays from 1949 to 1962. It also conveyed an all-year through coach from Glasgow to Keith Town which was attached and detached at Cairnie Junction.

The post-war shortage of coal led to reduced passenger services from 1951. The 9.45am service from Aberdeen was withdrawn on 12th February and that resulted in a six-hour gap between the arrivals of the overnight London and mid-morning Edinburgh trains in Aberdeen and the onward connections to Elgin. That issue was not resolved until summer 1959, although it was June 1960 before the mid-morning Aberdeen–Elgin service was fully restored all-year round with the introduction

On 19th June 1951, D40 No. 62264 heads a westbound train at Spey Bay. This was originally Class V No. 115 and survived until March 1957. The passengers with the large type of pram which was the norm in those days still found the railway useful. Moreover, the railway route from Spey Bay to Elgin was the quickest.

(Graham Maxtone collection)

Ex-Caledonian Railway 0-4-4 tank No. 55221 waits at Banff in the 1950s for its next run to Tillynaught. The Caley tanks were one of several types of 'foreign' locomotives transferred to the north east in BR days.
(David Fraser)

of the fast Aberdeen–Inverness diesel service via Mulben. This was operated by new Diesel Multiple Units, one of the key cost-reducing and revenue-increasing measures promoted in BR's Modernisation Plan. For the first time it catered properly for through traffic between Aberdeen and Inverness. The increased Banff service did not last long and even the Summer service was reduced to four daily return trips plus two Saturday extras by the middle of the decade. Ticket prices were also uncompetitive with a monthly return from Banff to Aberdeen in 1951 costing 17/11d compared to 6/6d on the bus. There was, however, a modest increase in services in 1952 following the closure of the Inveramsay to Macduff line to passengers on 1st October the previous year. Also, an unadvertised service operated from Glenbarry to Keith Town for schoolchildren in the 1950s.

Freight was suffering too. For example, livestock volumes from Cornhill Mart did not pick up after the War and fell during the 1950s as road floats took over. However, the reduced wartime fishing effort had a beneficial effect on stocks which led to a temporary resurgence for the herring industry. Increasing quality standards and the development of frozen fish helped. An interesting initiative at Tillynaught was the opening of a Sub-Post Office within the station building in March 1949. It was run by the Stationmaster and dealt with telegrams, stamps, insurance stamps and parcels. Local stations soon started to use the facility, sending

Throughout the 1950s, the railway was operated much as it had been for decades. On 25th September 1959, a Standard Class 2 2-6-0 enters Banff with a train from Tillynaught. Coal was still a staple traffic in the goods yard.
(Robin C. Nelson, courtesy Museum of Scottish Railways)

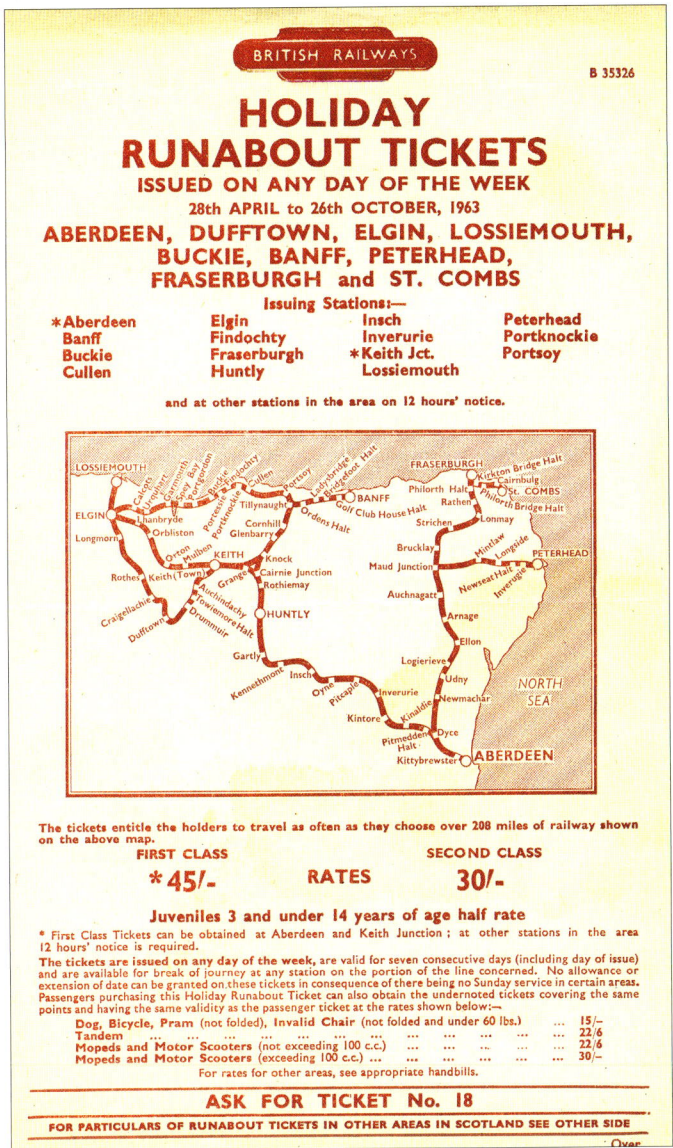

Runabout tickets, usually for seven days, were introduced in the 1930s and expanded by British Railways. They offered good value for money, especially for railway enthusiasts.

BR advertised their Cheap Day tickets with an extensive range of handbills for groups of stations such as above. Timetable flyers were issued separately.

cash for weekly insurance stamps. It closed on 31st January 1957.

During this period, as holiday traffic began to recover, the Scottish Region did boost passenger revenue by promoting cheap fares and day excursions, such as Sunday School outings from Keith to Golf Club House. The annual Keith Show in August was a regular attraction for rail passengers along the Coast. On Monday 13th June 1949 BR operated an excursion to Aberdeen from Spey Bay calling at Portgordon, Buckie, Findochty, Portknockie, Cullen, Portsoy and Cornhill. It departed Spey Bay at 9.31am and arrived in Aberdeen at 12.11pm; and departed back from Aberdeen at 7.15pm. On the same day, in the opposite direction, excursion trains departed Portsoy at 9.58am and 1.44pm for Elgin, calling at Cullen, Portknockie, Findochty, Buckie, Portgordon and Spey Bay. A third train departed Portsoy at 11.48am, but did not stop at Portknockie, Findochty or Portgordon and took only 56 minutes from end to end. Everyone returned on a 6.00pm departure. The Third Class day return from Spey Bay to Aberdeen cost 8/6d and from Portsoy to Elgin 3/3d. Aberdonians were not left out as they could enjoy Third Class monthly return fares to any station between Tochieneal and Buckie inclusive for 17/11d. That was more expensive than the bus, but the train was quicker.

In April 1950 BR advertised *"Springtime Cheap Tickets By Any Train Every Day"* from Cullen, Glassaugh, Portsoy and Tochieneal to a variety of stations on the Coast Line and including Lossiemouth and Banff as well as Keith Junction, Keith Town and Huntly. During this decade special trains ran from Glasgow to the Moray Firth Coast every Summer for the Glasgow Fair Fortnight and the coaches filled the sidings at Buckie for the two weeks in readiness to take the holidaymakers home. BR ran additional trains and specials over the Christmas/New Year holiday period. Although these were mainly to Edinburgh and

Portessie from a Down train in the late 1950s, looking east with the signal box in the distance. A solitary wagon sits at the loading dock while on the left is a camping coach, complete with washing line tied to the buffer stop. The coach had been built by the London & North Western Railway in 1906. (John Emslie)

Glasgow for shoppers, there was a weekday excursion from Elgin to Aberdeen via both Glen and Coast routes which departed Elgin at 9.13am. There was a choice of returns from Aberdeen at 3.40pm and 6.50pm, the latter allowing football supporters to attend Pittodrie on New Year's Day. The Coast portion picked up at Garmouth, Spey Bay, Portgordon, Buckie, Findochty, Portknockie, Cullen, Portsoy, Tillynaught (with a connection from Ladysbridge and Banff) and Cornhill. And on Christmas Eve a relief service departed Aberdeen at 2.30pm calling at all the Coast stations from and including Tillynaught, except Buckpool and Urquhart, to ensure last-minute shoppers and trawlermen made it home for the festivities. It was also common practice at busy times such as public holidays to strengthen the trains from Elgin and run then separately south of Cairnie to Aberdeen.

Camping coaches with six berths returned to Portessie in 1952 and to Portsoy in 1958, although they did not survive past the 1963 season. They were available for hire from late March to mid-October and by 1962 the weekly rental had increased to £7, £10, and £12.10s for low, mid and high season respectively. The station staff undertook the cleaning and linen duties with the dirty laundry sent to Aberdeen by passenger train. Weekly Runabout Tickets, which had been introduced before the War, also reappeared. From May to the end of October the Area 18 ticket was issued at Banff, Buckie, Cullen, Elgin and Keith for unlimited travel over the three former Great North routes from Cairnie Junction to Elgin and the Banff and Lossiemouth branches. At 113 miles of railway track this represented a third of the Great North's network and for only 15/- (7/6d if under 14 years of age). And dogs and bicycles were not forgotten, with corresponding charges of 4/10d and 9/6d respectively. Rather

The LMS Class 2P 4-4-0 design owed its origins to the Midland Railway, which followed a 'small engine' policy. By the 1950s work for this class was drying up so nine of them were transferred to the GNS section. No. 40663 came north in May 1954 and was seen on 21st October that year at work in Buckie goods yard.
(J L Stevenson, courtesy Hamish Stevenson)

reassuringly, BR added clarity that *"these tickets cover the same points and have the same validity as the Passenger Ticket"*. No doubt the train guards were relieved!

The significant increase in summer holiday traffic led in the early 1950s to an operational change. The long-standing 8.08am (previously 8.05am) departure from Aberdeen, connecting with the overnight Aberdonian from London Kings Cross, did not divide at Cairnie Junction but continued to Elgin via the Glen Line. A following train departed at 8.15am for Elgin via the Coast. A single coach train from Keith connected with this service at Cairnie Junction. A similar procedure was adopted in summer for the 2.15pm departure from Aberdeen with the Coast portion following at 2.30pm. At this time Class B1s based at Kittybrewster were hauling these trains. The Spring of 1951 saw a small boost to Spey Bay station as the Army started to prepare a Summer Camp at Dallachy Aerodrome. In addition to the regular salmon dispatches, large quantities of general freight arrived in vans for the camp. Tanks and Bren gun carriers also arrived on special wagons. The camp became very busy and Friday evening dances attracted many local young people by train. Unfortunately, the camp closed after the summer and the facilities were dismantled and sent south from the station. That coincided with the end of the salmon net fishing season. It would be a quiet winter in comparison.

There were, by now, early signs of trouble ahead for the former Great North network. The Alford and Macduff branches lost their passenger services on 2nd January 1950 and 1st October 1951 respectively. And Tochieneal closed to passengers on the latter date; some freight facilities were also removed. The reduction in services over both routes, however, led to complaints in the local press in 1953 about slow and infrequent services as well as dirty trains and stations. Glassaugh station closed to passengers and its goods services became unstaffed on 21st September 1953. The Lossiemouth branch which at one time had boasted 14 daily return services had suffered previous cuts and by 1954 was down to only three daily returns. Tillynaught lost its platform canopies by 1956 but one consolation was that the unusually ornate architecture of the station building was fully revealed. The Coast Line had six daily services in each direction which was one more than the Glen Line. The Coast also had a local Elgin – Buckie evening train departing at 6.00pm and there were still some additional trains on Saturdays.

Further complaints were led by Buckie Town Council who convened a meeting of affected neighbouring burghs along the Banffshire coast in November 1954 and demanded the restoration of the withdrawn "Trawler Train" and through portions to the Coast on later trains. The "Trawler Train" was the Coast portion of the 2.15pm ex-Aberdeen which was regularly used by Moray Firth fishermen employed in the large Aberdeen deep-sea trawler fleet to travel home. This service was indeed restored from February 1955 on Fridays and Saturdays only (via both Glen and Coast) but on a trial basis and its continuation

Elgin East station on the evening of 7th July 1959. In preparation for the evening 'rush hour' a pair of north east commuter services await departure. On the right in Platform 2 is No. 80004 with the 5.50pm to Dufftown and on the left in Platform 1 is No. 78054 working the 6pm to Buckie. The 6pm would reach Buckie at 6.32pm and return empty coaches at 7.10pm. No. 78054 and sister locomotive 78045 saw out their days on the Banff branch as steam lingered on that line. (Roy Hamilton/Strathspey Railway)

was dependent on the numbers using it. It did last until 1960. Throughout the 1950s Banff Sheriff Court heard several cases of drunkenness on Buckie trains!

The Buckie herring fleet was in decline as it was replaced by seine net boats and some local fishermen moved from the inshore fleet to deep-sea trawling based in Aberdeen. Many of the crews travelled to and from Aberdeen by train. Fish traffic from Lossiemouth, Buckie and Portsoy was by now mostly conveyed in vans attached to passenger trains. The Working Time Table allowed six minutes at Buckie and four minutes at Portsoy on certain trains, but there were no such allowances at other stations. Significant quantities of lobsters, crabs, whelks and salmon were dispatched from Portsoy, some destined for Billingsgate. A Saturday Only fish train from Lossiemouth to Aberdeen still operated in 1956, picking up consignments at Buckie and Portsoy. It was brought to Elgin by the Lossiemouth branch engine, a D40 or Caledonian 0-4-4 Tank, and D34 4-4-0 No. 62469 *Glen Douglas* was a regular on the branch after it was transferred to Elgin in the early 1950s. A B1 then took charge for the Coast. It departed Elgin at 1.00pm, stopped additionally at Cairnie to change train crew and at Huntly for water, and arrived in Aberdeen at 4.48pm. There it was consolidated at Clayhills with two fish trains from Peterhead and Fraserburgh for an overnight run south. There was now, however, only one daily freight in each direction over the whole length of the line. Portsoy saw an operational change to the goods sidings from 24th January 1953. The ground frame operated by the long-section tablet was removed and the points became operated from the signal box. Nevertheless, freight volumes were holding up mainly from fish, oatmeal and oat flakes dispatched by William Ewing's mill in vans to Goole and Robertsbridge (East Sussex) and from whisky to Glasgow and Markinch.

In 1955 Keith Junction took over from Cairnie Junction as the transfer point for goods to and from Aberdeen. Freight trains were now being worked by K2 Class 2-6-0s and D40s and, on passenger services, B1 Class 4-6-0s and Standard Class 4 2-6-4 tank engines had replaced the old Great North and B12 locomotives. LMS Class 5MT 4-6-0s and former Caledonian or LMS engines occasionally appeared. Carriage stock from the LNER period was gradually replaced by LMS stock and by BR Mark 1 coaches by the early 1960s. Following closure on 22nd August 1959, the signal box and crossing loop at Portsoy were removed and replaced by a two-lever ground frame released by the section tablet to the goods yard. Calcots became unstaffed for

Cairnie Junction at around 3.20pm on 21st May 1960 as Black Five No. 44921 accelerates away from the exchange platform under the watchful eye of the Signalman with the three coach Coast portion of the 2.15pm Aberdeen to Elgin. The front portion via Craigellachie has already departed. Both trains will arrive in Elgin within 4 minutes of each other. (Roy Hamilton/Strathspey Railway)

Diesel multiple units operated many of the trains after 1960, although several remained locomotive hauled. Bus-type seating may not have suited everyone, but the views out of the large windows and the simple saloon interiors were a strong selling point. This is Cairnie Junction looking north in the mid-1960s after combining and splitting had ceased. The unit on the right will be waiting its next turn of duty.
(Graham Maxtone colln)

both passenger and freight traffic from Monday 2nd November 1959 although the signal box remained operational. Thereafter parcels, general merchandise and less than truck loads were handled by "Elgin (for Calcots)" and truck loads were booked to and administered by Spey Bay. Buckpool closed on Monday 7th March 1960. This came as no real surprise as no freight had been handled in the previous five years, Buckie was under a mile away handling passenger, freight and parcel business, and a bus service operated between the two locations. Until 1955 Buckpool continued to handle cattle for the nearby Buckie slaughterhouse, but that traffic ceased after Government wartime controls on meat were abolished. The sidings were lifted in June 1961. The short chord between Grange and Grange North Junction, the original line out of Grange station to Banff, was also closed on that date. Banff signal box closed on 29th May 1960 with all signalling removed and the branch thereafter worked under the "One Engine in Steam with Train Staff" Regulations, the ground frames being released by the train crew.

Diesel locomotives appeared on the Coast Line on trial in 1958 and within three years had almost completely replaced steam on former Great North metals. Elgin shed (by now a sub-shed of Keith and reduced to three roads) closed to steam in June

Grange North Junction on 15th July 1967 and four Mark 1 coaches hauled by a Type 2, Class 24 D5670 uplifts the token for Tillynaught from the signalman as it passes the signal box with the 10.15 Aberdeen to Elgin via Buckie. With no exchange 'pulpit' to assist, the signalman is at full stretch from ground level with the hoop and of course the driver is leaning out downwards as far as he can. Only the BG at the rear is in the new British Rail corporate blue/grey with the remaining stock in British Railways maroon and the diesel engine in Brunswick green.
(Roy Hamilton/Strathspey Railway)

A busy time at Tillynaught as the branch engine draws forward from its train to go through the facing crossover to the left, clear of the main line, in order to set back again and round its coaches sitting in the branch platform. Note that the branch engine already has it Class 2 head lamp in place on the tender for the 11.55 return trip to the terminus having connected with the main line passenger train, likely the 10.20 Aberdeen to Elgin due at 11.48, already signalled on the down line. (Bob Florence)

1961 and the turntable was decommissioned, although the shed functioned until 1969 as a store for five withdrawn North British Type 2 diesel locomotives before it became a transport depot for Grampian Regional Council. Keith shed was fully dieselised by September 1961, apart from occasional light maintenance visits by the Banff locomotive. Type 2 diesel locomotives, including the notoriously unreliable North British locomotives, hauled the "main line" trains, and in 1960 two experimental return express services operated by Swindon Cross Country DMUs were introduced on the Aberdeen – Inverness service via Mulben. They called at only six intermediate stops and cut the end-to-end journey time to 2½ hours, with some services overtaking the slower trains using the Glen and Coast routes. These trains proved popular with the public and were increased to four each way and made permanent in 1961, but a knock-on effect was that, as the service developed, it tended to marginalise the services running over both Glen and Coast routes which were further reduced to only four daily services in each direction. They were now largely serving local traffic.

One notable exception to diesel was the retention of steam, in the form of BR Standard 2MT 2-6-0s Nos 78045 and 78054, along with BR Standard Class 4MT 2-6-0 No. 76104, on the Banff branch until it closed. The service had increased to 10 return trips in summer and five plus two more on Saturdays in winter. There was an issue with Type 1 diesel locomotives being unable to provide steam heat to the coaches and independent heating equipment was not justified because of its cost and the uncertain future of the line. The use of a Type 2 diesel was considered uneconomic. Public freight services at Grange ceased on 4th December 1961 and the signal box closed on 18th March 1963. By 1962 the only crossing loop between Cairnie Junction and Tillynaught was at Glenbarry. BR did make attempts to promote local travel with "Special Cheap Day Tickets" by any train from Elgin to a variety of destinations including all the Coast

The introduction of the Swindon DMUs on a fast schedule between Inverness and Aberdeen in 1960 led to a revolution in travel in the area and a reorganisation of services. The units were also employed on Coast Line services as seen on the right at Portessie on the last day. (Norris Forrest)

NBL Class 21 D6145 shunts what is left of the goods yard at Cullen in July 1965 under the watchful eye of a young lad sitting at the end of the old loading dock. Not that it seems to be a particularly complex manoeuvre as it is essentially one unfitted mineral wagon of domestic coal being positioned for unloading by the local merchant. This particular service did not appear in the standard Goods Train Working Timetable but in the Trip Notice and was worked by a set of Keith men who left at 9.30am, went to Buckie (via Banff) and back shunting the various yards en-route, arriving back home at 4.57pm.
(David MacLeod)

stations in 1961. Rather oddly, First and Second class returns to Tillynaught were 11/9d and 7/9d respectively but you could travel further to Knock for only 7/3d and 4/9d respectively; and BR made it clear that on any journey "*Passengers may alight at a station short of destination in either direction….*" While BR may have been catering for the passenger totally hacked off with their journey, it does appear they were opening themselves up to a level of ticket abuse.

And then came the Beeching Report in March 1963. It included an analysis of passenger receipts by station and, while Forres and Elgin both recorded income of over £25,000 per annum, Inverurie, Huntly, Keith Junction, Nairn, Lossiemouth and Buckie earned between £5,000 and £25,000. All other stations took in less than £5,000. The Banff and Lossiemouth branches were specifically mentioned in the Beeching Report's table of 10 case study routes, illustrating the claimed financial argument for closure. Both branches had high operating costs per mile, as services were not DMU-operated, with the steam-operated Banff branch being the worst of the 10 examples. Freight income generally followed the same pattern. It was a bleak picture. On the former Great North, all lines and stations were designated for closure apart from the main line from Aberdeen to Keith with only one intermediate station, Huntly, remaining. In due course Inverurie and Insch remained open.

On the Coast the Lossiemouth branch passenger services were the first to be withdrawn on 6th April 1964 quickly followed by the Banff branch (and its engine shed) on 6th July, although the last train ran on Saturday 4th July. The station was busy all day as locals came to say their farewells and the last Up and Down services were crewed by driver Tom Ross who was approaching 45 years of railway service and fireman Jimmy Fraser. As Class 2MT 2-6-0 locomotive No. 78045 pulled its train out of Banff for the last time, the two coaches were packed to the rafters and crowds thronged the platform. There were similar scenes at Ladysbridge and Ordens, many people waved from the lineside and several detonators exploded. The final Down train departed Tillynaught Junction at 8.15pm to the sound of more detonators and the blaring horn of the connecting Inverness-bound diesel preparing to depart along the Coast Line. The locomotive sounded its whistle all the way back to Banff where a huge crowd cheered and waved the train into the station for the final time.

In the pre-closure financial analysis the Banff branch had annual passenger earnings of £800 on the branch itself but through fares contributed £6,130 to the wider BR system, of

Early afternoon departures shown at Elgin in the early 1960s, before the Lossiemouth service was withdrawn in 1964. The traditional departures via Coast and Glen to Aberdeen just before 2pm are shown, but passengers via the Glen route have to change at Cairnie. The dilapidated state of the departure board was typical of stations at that time. (Norris Forrest)

Portsoy after removal of loop in 1959. Even although the old westbound platform was out of use it was still maintained by the station staff to a high standard, being weed free with tidy flower beds and neat whitened edges to the coping stones. (Norris Forrest)

which £4,000 (plus the £800) was anticipated to be lost if the branch closed. The annual operational cost of the six miles was £14,150 plus £950 for terminal expenses and £600 for signalling costs, and so an annual saving of £10,900 was expected. The 1961 figures equated to loadings of only two passengers per train, but the Beeching Report was widely criticised for using a single week in April to analyse traffic flows, thereby excluding most holiday traffic! Both lines closed completely when freight services ceased; Lossiemouth on 28th March 1966, with the redundant Lossie Junction signal box closing on 11th June, and Banff on 6th May 1968. Although Banff is recorded as handling between 5,000 and 25,000 tonnes of freight per annum, it could not survive the Coast Line closure. It had struggled on for nearly four years with a daily return freight worked by Type 2 diesels as part of the ongoing Keith to Buckie working. The signalling on the branch had been removed in July 1965.

Glassaugh, Tochieneal, Portessie, Portgordon, Spey Bay, Garmouth, Urquhart and Calcots lost their freight services on 20th April 1964 with Tillynaught following on 10th August and Glenbarry on 2nd November. The sidings at Glassaugh,

Glenbarry signal box and station sometime in the latter part of 1964. The GNS Type 2a box was still operational at this time, not closing until 25th June 1966. The goods yard had been lifted as it had been closed in the April of that year. Note the small building between the box and the footbridge which doubled as a waiting room and small booking office after the original Banffshire Railway buildings, which were beyond the footbridge, had been demolished. (Ian Johnstone)

An unidentified Type 2 diesel (later Class 24) waits at Portknockie for station business to be completed in the 1960s. The three coaches are now all BR Standard vehicles.
(Graham Maxtone collection)

Tochieneal, Findochty, Portgordon, Garmouth and Urquhart were lifted on 2nd and 3rd June 1964. By mid-1965, between Elgin and Portsoy, Buckie had retained its sidings, Cullen still had two, and Portknockie one operational. All the others had gone. Portsoy sidings were still unaltered but, with the closure of the Banff branch, Tillynaught became a rather ghostly wayside halt and it had lost its siding on the Down side. Ladysbridge and Blairshinnoch level crossings lost their home (but not distant) signals on 7th July 1964. The Coast Line saw a small change as timetable references to "exchange" for the now-unstaffed Cairnie Junction were removed from 14th June 1965 and, rather bizarrely, it gained public status despite still not having any public access! The single track chord from Grange to Grange North was lifted in 1965 and Spey Bay signal box and loop closed on 18th June 1966. Then, on 24th July, Portknockie and Tochieneal boxes and loops were closed, creating a very long block section of just over 13 miles from Tillynaught to Portessie. That left just five boxes on each Great North route between Cairnie Junction and Elgin. The remaining operational sections were now Cairnie to Grange North; Grange North to Tillynaught; Tillynaught to Portessie; Portessie to Buckie (which was still double track); Buckie to Calcots; Calcots to Elgin East. Portknockie had freight facilities

A Banff bound train calls at Ladysbridge with the 4.10pm from Tillynaught on 22nd June 1960. The track patrolmen (note keying hammer held by the man on the right) are exchanging pleasantries with the Driver and Guard who are patiently waiting the advertised time to depart. Non-corridor stock was standard on the branch until closure.
(Roy Hamilton/ Strathspey Railway)

withdrawn on that same date, although some equipment had been removed in the 1950s. Sidings at Cairnie were removed in August and the station building at Ladysbridge was relocated to Whitehills for use as a changing room for the local football club.

BR announced the introduction of 11 Area Managers in the north and north-east to replace Stationmasters in October 1965 and two were based at Buckie and Elgin. They were empowered with a high degree of decision-making in a bid to attract more business to the railway. In retrospect this was an interesting development in the context of what was about to take place. The stations at Cullen, Portessie, Cornhill, Findochty, Garmouth, Glenbarry, Portgordon, Portknockie, Spey Bay, Tillynaught and Urquhart became unstaffed from Monday 24th April 1967 with tickets being issued on the trains. It became necessary to re-book tickets for destinations beyond Aberdeen and Elgin and parcel traffic ceased at these stations as a result of the destaffing. Grange had become an unstaffed halt from 16th January 1967 and, although the freight siding at Knock was unstaffed from 21st February 1967, it remained in use. The Lossiemouth line was lifted by 1967.

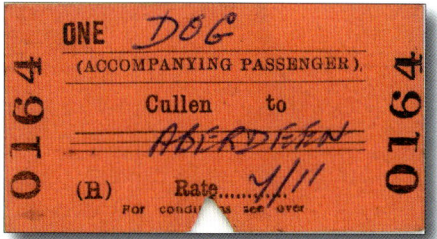

The road to closure was a tortuous one for the Coast Line. The British Railways Board gave notice in September 1963 of their proposal to discontinue all local railway passenger train services between Aberdeen, Keith and Elgin via all three routes i.e. via Mulben, Buckie and Dufftown. That meant the closure of all stations on both the Coast and Glen lines and of intermediate stations (apart from Huntly) on the main line. At this time there were six trains daily to Elgin by the Coast Line – three from Aberdeen, one from Cairnie Junction, one from Keith Junction and one from Keith Town. There was an additional lunchtime Saturday only service to and from Buckie. In the opposite direction there were seven trains from Elgin – four to Aberdeen, one to Cairnie Junction, one to Keith Junction, and one to Buckie plus the Saturday only to Buckie. An analysis of passenger numbers was undertaken during weeks ending Saturday 3rd July (summer) and Saturday 11th

Spey Bay on a sunny morning in April 1968. It is 09.14 as the 08.58 Elgin to Aberdeen calls hauled by an unidentified Class 26 in BR corporate blue livery. The majority of coaching stock is maroon BR Mark 1 with an LMS brake at the rear. Only the BG next to the engine carries the then new blue/grey livery. The clock is ticking towards final closure the following month but even at this time Spey Bay had already been rationalised with the closure of signal box and the almost complete lifting of the crossing loop. The footbridge and derelict signal box are still there but the former small waiting room on the Up platform has gone. In this view looking towards Buckie, the North Sea can just be seen on the left and the Bin Hill is visible in the distance on the right. (Graham Maxtone colln)

Buckie goods yard seen from a departing eastbound train about 1960. The former East signal box, which was retained as an elevated Ground Frame electrically released by the main signal box to operate the east end connection to the yard, is near the centre of the photograph. It was of a non-standard design with vertical boarding, although the window frames are recognisable as of GNS origin. The fish loading platform is to its left while the main sidings are to the right. (Colin Brown)

December 1965 (winter). It demonstrated that on Mondays to Fridays in both summer and winter passengers travelling from Aberdeen to Elgin via the Coast Line numbered around 250, of whom only 102 used Coast Line stations. Numbers increased on Saturdays and were slightly higher in summer, especially on the 2.10pm departure from Aberdeen when 183 departed as many headed for the coastal resorts of Portsoy (29), Cullen (59) and Portknockie (15) as well as to Buckie (33). In winter 149 passengers clambered aboard the 6.25pm departure from Aberdeen, presumably a combination of shoppers and football supporters, out of a daily total of 443. In the opposite direction the daily numbers using the Elgin to Aberdeen service were steady at around 350 in summer and 250 in winter. Some Coast stations saw no passengers joining or alighting and, of particular concern, was the local Saturday only service between Elgin and Buckie. In both summer and winter only about 12 passengers used the westbound train and no one joined at Buckie! Numbers were slightly higher in the opposite direction.

A public inquiry into the proposed closure was held in Elgin Town Hall on 27th May 1966. Buckie was still a busy station with more passengers using it than any station north of Inverness. And a high proportion of journeys both arriving and departing were long-distance high value tickets. However, the case of the objectors was ill-prepared. The main opposition to closure was from the Town Clerks of the larger coastal communities but they were unable to put forward strong reasons for the line's retention. The only really persuasive argument came from a local Buckie seafood producer who lambasted British Rail after turning up straight from the factory floor resplendent in white overalls and Wellington boots! As the Minister of Transport recognised the *"complexity of services provided by no less than ten bus operators"* in the area and the potential for "hardship", he requested that the BR Board consult with the relevant bus operators and present alternative co-ordinated service proposals to the Transport Users' Consultative Committee for Scotland. That resulted in a combined rail/road strategy of, firstly, a fast Aberdeen – Inverness diesel rail service with four trains per day from Aberdeen and five from Inverness plus three fast diesel trains from Aberdeen to Elgin and two from Elgin to Aberdeen, all trains calling at Inverurie, Huntly, Keith Junction, Elgin, Forres and Nairn; secondly, the continuation of existing bus services throughout the area; and, thirdly, additional bus services. A greater degree of rail/road timetable coordination was envisaged. A caveat

Spey Bay signal box was on the east end of the Down platform. It had opened in 1912 to replace separate boxes at each end of the station. (Graham Maxtone colln)

for this was "as far as practicable" because, with the proposed closures, the scope was limited. An analysis of comparative fares was also undertaken with the bus only slightly cheaper than the train. For example, a cheap day rail return from Huntly to Portsoy at 6/6d compared to a bus return of 5/9d. Huntly to and from Cullen was 7/3d by train and 7/- by bus. However, on some routes cheap day returns were not available by rail and ordinary returns were significantly higher.

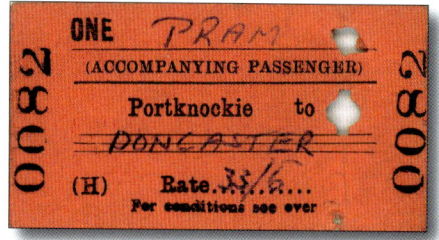

In March 1967 British Rail undertook a detailed economic review of the remaining freight traffic on the Coast Line including the Banff branch. Five freight services in 1955 had reduced to four by 1960, to only two by 1964 (Keith to Buckie return and Keith to Banff and Portsoy return) and to just one by the end – and the proposal to withdraw passenger services had been announced. Only Knock, Cornhill, Banff, Portsoy, Cullen and Buckie retained freight facilities at this time and indeed until final closure. An analysis of full wagon load traffic (freight "sundries" had already been concentrated at Huntly for onward road distribution and collection) during the 12 months to June 1966 was undertaken for the Coast Line and Banff branch: coal 26,238 tons; grain 7,366 tons; miscellaneous 6,184 tons, oatmeal 1,914 tons: total 41,702 tons. Gross revenue was £128,000. Looking forward, BR adjusted for future projections and assumed that, in the event of passenger closure, the Coast Line would be worked by "One Train Working" arrangements with no signalling. Three options – retaining all freight depots to Banff and Buckie, to Banff only, and to Portsoy only – were examined. The conclusion was the fourth option – complete closure. There would have also been operational complications at Cairnie Junction due to the installation of a ground frame and tokenless block signalling on the main line. However, the 1967 study does demonstrate that, contrary to the common misconception, BR was not prepared to lose business without proper and professional analysis.

Further BR reports decreed that there should be no duplication of rail routes. The 23 miles of direct line between Cairnie Junction and Elgin via Mulben was duplicated by the 32½ miles via the Glen Line and the 39 miles via the Coast. Despite arguments that the Glen and Coast routes served completely different geographical areas, clearly the writing was on the wall. There was a short lull in closures as the bus services were finally sorted out. Spey Bay was a particular problem but a new morning and teatime service on Mondays and Saturdays to and from Elgin calling at Garmouth for those working and shopping in Elgin was to be introduced. It would be a long journey via Fochabers. The sting in the tail was an increase to 5/6d for a return in the new bus from 3/6d for the rail cheap day return. A new afternoon feeder service on Fridays and Saturdays only would connect with Alexander's buses into and out of both Elgin and Buckie for shoppers. There were to be new services: Huntly–Rothiemay–Knock, Keith–Glenbarry and Huntly–Cullen. And there would be a new Monday–Friday service of four buses in each direction (five on Saturdays and two on Sundays) from Buckie to Aberdeen via Findochty, Portknockie, Cullen, Portsoy, Ordens and Cornhill to Aberchirder, and thence by the B9001 to Rothienorman and Inverurie; this was a re-routing of the existing Aberdeen–Macduff via Aberchirder service.

BR&CW Class 26 D5335 shunts the busy looking yard at Buckie on 3rd May 1968, the penultimate day of goods train operation around the Banff and Moray Coast. A further train would run the following Wednesday to mop up the empties and take away any loaded traffic due to be despatched. Note the McGruther & Marshall coal lorry, once a common site around towns and villages, being loaded in the distance, almost jockeying for position with the locomotive. Today D5335 operates on the Caledonian Railway in Brechin. (David Spaven)

The final crossing at Tillynaught as the last Down and Up trains pass each other on 4th May 1968. The day had been wet, raining steadily until the early evening, but it was still gloomy. The hardship that the closure would bring was exemplified later on the train when an elderly lady worried about how she would get to Aberdeen to buy her hats. (Keith Fenwick)

There was some delay over the alternative bus services, but the axe became inevitable in 1967 when Minister of Transport, Mrs Barbara Castle, approved closure of both Glen and Coast lines. The remaining intermediate stations were confirmed for closure as were Cairnie Junction and Grange on the main line. Despite the usual mobilisation of community protest groups, meetings, letter writing and Questions in the House of Commons, the Coast Line closed on 6th May 1968. All freight services were withdrawn on that same date. The Minister of Transport did offer a glimmer of future hope by stipulating: *"….as a safeguard against the possibility of future need it would be prudent to retain for the time being the formation of the lines from Keith Junction and from Cairnie Junction to Elgin and the sites of the stations proposed for closure"*. That statement turned out to be rather hollow as, over subsequent years, parts were sold off or disappeared within road improvements. The demise of the Coast Line was part of the overall decimation of the Great North system. Within 15 years from 1964 the route mileage reduced from 303 to 53¼.

By the time of closure the Coast Line was underused and indeed largely ignored by many of the public who either owned a car or who preferred to use the bus which was perceived as offering a more convenient and reasonably-priced service. Some of the route's stations located at the top of the coastal escarpment, such as Findochty and Portessie, were not convenient for the town and village centres closer to the sea-shore in contrast to the flexibility of the bus. The trains were considered slow and requests for faster "express" trains with fewer stops had fallen largely on deaf ears. One Up and three Down services no longer called at Portessie by 1967, but generally, the more populated central section of the line with its necessary stops precluded such a move. In 1897 several trains covered Aberdeen – Buckie in under two hours; in 1951 and 1968 none matched that! The Coast Line became a virtual local branch as through passengers were diverted onto the faster and more direct line via Mulben. This all led to a general feeling of pessimism over the future of the Coast railway in the years prior to closure. Freight charges were also perceived to be high, even being seen as a barrier to new investment. The 1967 inquiry had concluded that there was no future for freight in the event of passenger closure. The Transport Users' Consultative Committee inquiry did concede that a degree of "hardship" would accrue to some passengers, but it noted that there was an hourly bus service along the coast generally running through to both Elgin and Aberdeen.

Could the Moray Firth Coast Line have survived through rationalisation? The concept of a "basic railway" with most crossing loops removed, the smallest stations closed and other cost cutting measures could possibly have worked. By the mid-1960s there were just six crossings a day – one at Portessie, two at Tillynaught and three at Buckie. It is conceivable that, with various timetable adjustments, just one signal box and crossing loop at Buckie, rather than the five boxes extant at closure, could have been workable, albeit that a 24½ mile single track section from Cairnie Junction would have exceeded Britain's longest (Helmsdale to Forsinard). And Buckie freight might have lasted at least until the demise of the traditional vacuum-braked domestic coal service around 1983, although this would undoubtedly have necessitated a second loop at Tillynaught to allow flexibility of train movement and shunting at Knock, Cornhill and Portsoy (and possibly Banff). There was, at one point, a plan mooted to install a physical junction at Huntly in order to operate

two separate parallel lines to Cairnie (using the existing double track which still existed in the 1960s), one for the main line and the other for the Coast. The lines would simply have parted at Cairnie which would have allowed Grange North box to be replaced by an automatic half barrier; otherwise it would have had to be retained to control the level crossing over the local road. This would have resulted in a block section from Huntly to Tillynaught of 18 miles or to Buckie of a rather restrictive 32 miles. However, there was little strategic consideration of longer-term transport and environmental requirements let alone any allowance for future growth of train services which would materialise from the 1980s. The die was cast.

The last official freight train ran on the Coast Line on Friday 3rd May 1968. Saturday 4th May was the final day for passenger services. Most trains were DMUs but Class 24 locomotive D5132 hauled the last Elgin–Buckie local at 12.45pm, returning from Buckie at 1.30pm with the guard collecting passenger names on a card as a lasting memento. Locomotives also hauled the 4.00pm departure from Aberdeen and the 4.39pm and 7.09pm departures from Elgin, that last by Class 26 D5331. These services were not full by any means, but the last train departing Aberdeen at 6.25pm was a twin DMU packed to the rafters, especially onwards from Tillynaught where it crossed the 7.09pm train from Elgin. There were some crowds along the way and detonators marked the final passing between Cullen station and the viaduct and at Buckie. Only a small group greeted the train at Elgin, but quickly dispersed.

All the remaining Coast Line signal boxes (Cairnie Junction, Grange North, Tillynaught, Portessie, Buckie and Calcots) continued to be operational until they officially closed on 29th September 1968. This was, in part, to allow redundant signalmen to work out their notice and to operate some "mop up" goods. The final signal box registers from Cairnie Junction and Grange North Junction were completed by Keith men Jimmy Forsyth and Willie Ewan respectively on the morning of Wednesday 8th May showing the very last revenue service. Thereafter there is only one more entry….completed by Elgin Relief man William Armstrong at Grange North Box on 23rd September 1968 to allow track lifting gear to pass over the level crossing. Elgin East signal box, which controlled the junction for Coast and Glen lines, closed on 15th December 1968. The ticket office in the Great North station at Elgin remained open until Saturday 23rd August 1969, with a new one opening on the following Monday at the former Highland station. The Area Manager remained based at Elgin East as it continued to deal with parcels, sundries and full-load freight traffic. Staff continued to use the connecting platform to the replacement Highland station to push a barrow full of parcels to meet incoming diesel multiple units.

However, the Moray Firth Coast Line was consigned to history!

The last entries at Grange North Junction Signal box in May 1968. Keith Relief Signalman Eddie Pearson signs on duty on 4th May at 06.20 and perhaps appropriately, it's raining – as it did for the entire day. Eddies' turn of duty finishes at 12.15 as Huntly Relief Signalman Roddy Gordon from Gartly has signed on. The very last passenger train passes through at 20.32 and heads round the corner to Cairnie Junction and on to Aberdeen. Tillynaught closes at 20.33, Grange North closes to Cairnie at 20.34 and Roddy heads home. One more day's revenue earning operation starts at 09.00 on Wednesday 8th May when Billy Ewan from Keith signs on to signal the last goods trains to and from the Coast. The final service heading for Keith passes through at 12.44, Billy signs off at 13.00, and that's it. There is one further single entry on 23rd September as Relief Signalman William Armstrong, all the way from Elgin, signs the book. He was presumably a travelling Signalman rostered to operate each signal box en-route as a demolition train passes round the coast, burning the rust off the soon to be lifted rails.

Post Closure 1968....

After the closure of both Glen and Coast routes BR singled the double track between Aberdeen and Keith, apart from a short 5¼ mile section between Insch and Kennethmont, at the end of the decade. The buildings and platforms at Cairnie Junction were dismantled and the main line track was eventually realigned to increase line speed. By 1973 there was practically no trace of this rather unique junction. The Coast Line tracks were lifted in the months following closure and in 1970 Banffshire County Council undertook part-demolition and tidying up at Grange, Knock, Cornhill, Portsoy and Tochieneal. The station houses and buildings were spared as BR undertook to seek alternative use, but signal boxes and sheds were demolished. Tillynaught Junction station, however, was completely demolished and burned on Thursday 1st October 1970 as, due to its remote location, it was deemed of no sale value or possible future use. The site was levelled and only the road overbridge survived as evidence of a once-busy rail junction.

By 1972 many of the stations had been vandalised with graffiti, broken glass and boarded-up windows all too evident. Calcots had become a refuge for tramps, although Urquhart was still in good condition, being used as a store. The footbridge at Buckie was closed but an alternative concrete slab path was laid over the trackbed. Following minor fire incidents at Portgordon and Portknockie, Findochty station building was destroyed by fire on 6th September 1972 despite the efforts of the Buckie and Cullen firemen. The Garmouth station site was leased by local hauliers Baillie Brothers who allowed the Garmouth and Kingston Youth Club free use of the station building. And at Spey Bay the blackboard noticeboard still optimistically proclaimed the train departure times!

The future of the Spey Viaduct, Barnett's Monument, remained uncertain. BR continued to maintain it and looked to either demolish it (with anticipated difficulty) or sell it for £6,000 to Moray and Nairn County Council. The Council was concerned over the estimated annual maintenance cost of £1,000, although this figure was challenged by at least one Councillor. A public meeting in Garmouth in 1975 considered two alternative proposals. One was to convert it into a new and shorter road link between Elgin and Buckie to alleviate pressure on the A96 at Fochabers and to serve industrial development at Dallachy, although the projected cost of £180,000 was considered prohibitive; and the other that it be used as a footbridge and scenic walkway at an estimated cost of £15,000. Eventually the Council concluded that the Viaduct was an historical part of the County of Moray and that its costly removal would leave a legacy of unsightly granite pillars sticking out of the river. Moreover, it conceded that a link of a few hundred yards between two communities would be replaced by a 12-mile road detour. It was officially opened in August 1978 as a public footpath to link Garmouth and Spey Bay but, ultimately, it passed in 1980

Portsoy, seen in May 2008, is the great survivor. The station building is in community use while the surrounding area has been attractively landscaped and levelled. Even the original train shed survives.

(Keith Fenwick)

Spey Bay in August 1988 shows how quickly trees grow up on former railway lines. The station building remains in private use but the overbridge from which this photograph was taken has since gone.
(Keith Fenwick)

into the control of Moray District Council who replaced the wooden decking and re-painted it. The viaduct now forms part of the Speyside Way long distance walking trail which officially opened on 3rd July 1981. Additional work in the 1990s improved wheelchair and disabled access. Barnett's Monument is today listed in Category B.

By 1973 rumours abounded that the main viaduct at Cullen above Seatown was unsafe and that it was scheduled for demolition. There were further concerns that its demolition was required to realign the A98 "S" bend running underneath it due to a plan to build a nuclear power station at Whitehills by Banff which would involve equipment being delivered by sea to Buckie and thence along the coast by road. However, in 1975 the Secretary of State for Scotland, William Ross, ruled against such a project. Happily, the viaduct not only celebrated its centenary in May 1986, but also it survives today and is used as part of a cycle route and walkway. All the viaducts remain and are listed, three in Category B. The arch in the viaduct over Lower Castle Street which was filled in is still clearly visible today.

In late 1974 Garmouth, Urquhart and Calcots were offered for sale by BR for light industrial use. Calcots station buildings were demolished shortly afterwards and there is now no trace of the station. Urquhart was adapted to service a caravan park for a short spell and was later replaced by a private house. Garmouth

One of the sections which is now a footpath is that to the west of Cullen, seen here in March 2008, ¾ mile from Cullen. It includes the two main viaducts, although not the one over Seafield Street, and continues towards Portknockie.
(Keith Fenwick)

The viaduct at Spey Bay on 7th August 2014. The centre has a hard surface for the footpath. Maintenance is a constant problem; the metal barrier on the right protects a section of the parapet under repair.

(Mike Cooper)

station was demolished. The original terminal building at Portsoy was used as a builder's warehouse and subsequently by a potato merchant. In 1977 the "new" station building was taken over by the local scouts and guides for conversion to a meeting hall. After several years of deterioration and vandalism at both stations, Portessie was demolished in 1979 and Buckie in April 1980. The flight of 102 steps up to Portessie station from Chapel Street is still functional with care, along with its three redundant metal gas lamp standards.

Significant freight continued to be handled at both Elgin and Keith with associated investment. At Elgin the old Great North yards were used for Freightliner and Speedlink traffic. However, British Rail vacated the Elgin East station building in 1988 and by early 1990 the old Great North station was refurbished by the Scottish Development Agency and Grampian Regional Council as an enterprise centre for small businesses at a cost of £420,000. There are ten studio units on the ground floor and nine first floor offices. The interior booking hall area remains largely intact today, mothballed in Marie Celeste-style as a wonderful timepiece of local railway history. It is now B-listed. The four-road engine shed at the east end of Elgin East goods yard, which lost its original role on the demise of steam in 1961 but continued as a diesel stabling facility until closure in 1968, remains today as a C-listed structure but is no longer in railway use.

When the present station building at Elgin opened on 7th March 1990 the parcel business, by now trading as Red Star, was relocated to it from the old Great North building. The connecting platform between the two stations finally fell into disuse and removed, although a path was retained but via a locked gate.

On the Banff branch, Ladysbridge station building survived for about 40 years as a changing facility at Whitehills for the

Banff Springs, the intermediate station on the West Buchan Light Railway. The engine was diesel powered with a steam outline. A Dutch steam engine was also obtained. The line started at the site of Banff station and ran to Swordanes.

(Andrew Smith)

football club. It was subsequently replaced around 2006. Ladysbridge station site is largely under new housing. The Woodpark Asylum part of the hospital was demolished in the 1980s; Ladysbridge Hospital closed in 2003 and was converted into private residences. All traces of the three halts on the line have vanished. For a short period in the summers of 1984 and 1985 the privately owned West Buchan Light Railway operated a one-mile 15 inch gauge line from Banff Harbour to Swordanes near the Links Hotel using the former branch trackbed. There was an intermediate station at Banff Springs. Passenger numbers failed to meet expectations and the line closed in September 1985.

Inverboyndie Distillery, which had provided so much business to the railway at Boyndie Siding over the years, had a chequered history of fires, explosions and periods of closures. It pre-dated the Banff line and was bombed by the Luftwaffe on 16th August 1941 when warehouse No. 12 was destroyed. Local legend has it that neighbouring pigs reaped the benefit and became highly intoxicated! Rebuilt after the War the distillery was mothballed in 1983 and demolished in 1988. Banff station buildings were demolished in the late 1970s and the station site has recently been redeveloped for modern housing. The Railway Inn above the station continues to serve the locals.

Today the iron bridge over the River Isla to the north of the site of Grange North Junction Signal Box remains in use for the local post van and the platform at Knock survives along with the station nameboard posts and platform lamp-post frame. The old station buildings at Cornhill and Spey Bay survive as private residences. Glenbarry is all but completely lost. Portsoy is listed Category C(S) and is still used by the local scouts. Between 2011 and 2016 it was one of five buildings to be renovated by the Portsoy Conservation Area Regeneration Scheme funded by Historic Scotland. The station site is an attractive park and loch. The platform edges survive at both Glassaugh and Tochieneal. Cullen is a housing estate. Portknockie has been demolished and the whole station area levelled. Findochty

The steps at Strathlene, June 2024. (Keith Fenwick)

The railway is not quite forgotten in 2024 at the entrance to Portknockie. (Keith Fenwick)

station agent's house survives. At Portessie there are some remains of platforms along with the stone base of the water tower marking the junction of the two lines. Strathlene swimming pool closed in 1977 and the hotel was converted into four self-contained houses in the 1980s, but the golf course thrives. The Buckie station site has been landscaped and factory buildings have been erected, but steps from the High Street to the lower industrial area still pass under the former trackbed. The lifeboat station paid for by the Great North (but now unused) remains. Buckpool is a housing estate, but the western ends of the platforms remain. Portgordon was converted into a recreational park and bowling green in 1979. There has been agricultural land reclamation in the area of Lossie Junction but the field there is still referred to as *"the Junction field."*

Parts of the trackbed have disappeared due to agricultural reclamation and housing development, but there are several stretches which have been converted into attractive walkways. Some artefacts of interest to the railway historian remain, notably bridges, old fences and fenceposts. And what of the replacement bus services? It has to be conceded that the Buckie–Keith bus service over the B9016 offered a better line-of-route journey to Aberdeen than the rail service via Cullen and Portsoy but it was subsequently withdrawn, although in 2023 two rather unattractive early morning services had been reinstated. The Buckie–Aberdeen service via Macduff, Aberchirder and Rothienorman was axed many years ago. This is typical of what has happened following rail closures throughout the country. John Edser, the Beeching Report Implementation Officer, admitted later that *"in about 60-70% of the rail closures, very few of the replacement buses lasted more than three to four years"*. In fact, as Dr Beeching himself stated in his Report, both trains and buses served the same basic purpose [of carrying passengers] and that, not only were they competing with each other, they were both *"….fighting a losing battle against private transport"*.

The Spycatcher of Portgordon and....

Perhaps the most intriguing of several anecdotes of events and incidents on the Moray Firth Coast Line is the extraordinary tale of Portgordon Stationmaster John Donald in the Second World War.

Born in Fordyce in Banffshire in 1897, John Donald left school at the age of 14 to train as a junior railway clerk and subsequently worked at various stations throughout the north-east including Kintore and Banchory. In 1933 he gained promotion to Stationmaster at Portgordon and moved into the Agent's House with his wife and young daughter. As the War approached John, already proficient in First Aid, was trained in how to recognise and deal with enemy gas attacks. Accordingly, as hostilities commenced in 1939, he was appointed an Air Raid Warden and he started to train others in First Aid. British Intelligence officers in London could hardly have imagined that a sleepy railway station in the north-east of Scotland would be the scene of a John Le Carré espionage story. Indeed, they had probably never heard of Portgordon, but they were to become indebted to its vigilant Stationmaster.

Germany was increasing its spy network in Britain in the late 1930s and identified an Italian Countess in London who bore a grudge against the British. She had inherited a house in the Bavarian Alps but could not sell it due to Britain's increasing restrictions on currency exchange. The Germans quietly agreed to sell it on her behalf and pass the proceeds on to her. In return the Countess was to purchase a prestigious apartment in London from which she would build up useful contacts within London high society. And she was to spin a story that she had discovered a long-lost niece who was coming to stay with her. That was Vera Erikson, a 28 year-old professional ballet dancer of Russian extraction and a fully trained German spy, who went under the alias of Vera de Cottani de Chalbur – a suitably posh name.

John Donald, wearing his British Empire Medal.

On 29th September 1940, Vera and two other agents, Werner Walti and Karl Drucke, were flown from Norway on a seaplane which landed under cover of darkness onto the sea between Buckie and Portgordon. Their ultimate objective was to reach London and to infiltrate the RAF but matters went awry from the outset. They paddled ashore in a rubber dinghy but their three British-made bicycles, taken from the captured British Embassy in Norway and on which they were to cycle to London, were lost over the side in choppy waters. It was a cold and frosty night and all three were soaked through. They concealed the craft at the mouth of the Gollochy burn by covering it with stones.

Meanwhile, on the following morning, John Donald was early at work to oversee the departure of the 6.00am freight from Portgordon station. As he was about to nip home for his breakfast at about 7.30am a strange couple (Vera and Karl) appeared on the platform carrying a large suitcase and two smaller bags. They claimed to be refugees and enquired about trains to the south. John and duty porter Jocky Geddes were suspicious from the outset as Vera asked the name of the station. They both had wet feet and the lady had frost on her coat. Vera claimed they had been staying in a local hotel. John related the tale to his wife and daughter when he arrived home for his breakfast and, on their advice, he telephoned the local bobby Bob Grieve. He told John to delay them.

When the couple returned at 7.45am to purchase tickets the man pulled out a wallet stuffed with British notes – hardly likely for a newly arrived refugee. When Bob Grieve arrived he pretended to undertake routine personnel checks and did so on another passenger before approaching the couple. Their papers were clearly not in order as the printing was in continental-style lettering and numbers and there was no immigration stamp on their refugee cards. And so, it was off to the local police station for further checks.

Matters now took a turn worthy of a Brian Rix farce. Inspector

John Simpson arrived from Buckie and, on checking the couple's luggage, a Mauser pistol, wireless equipment, a list of RAF bases and a German torch were discovered. And so, it was off to Buckie. With such damning evidence it did not take long before Vera confessed about the whole operation and provided details about the third agent Werner Walti. He had separated from the other two and had, in fact, walked to Buckpool where the porter, George Smith, advised him that he had just missed an Aberdeen train. He walked on to Buckie carrying his two brown suitcases. Neither the Buckie nor Buckpool staff raised any suspicions, despite his odd appearance, and he successfully caught the train to Aberdeen. He was seen boarding a train for Edinburgh where he dropped his cases at left-luggage. Unbeknown to him he was now being tracked by diminutive police officer Willie Merrilees who, at only 5ft 5ins in height, had previously caught a criminal who was assaulting mothers pushing prams by squeezing his body into a pram to catch the offender. On this occasion Willie masqueraded as a railway porter at Waverley station to apprehend Walti when he returned to collect his luggage shortly before the departure of a night train to London. He was carrying a loaded pistol and flick knife. Willie Merrilees, perhaps not surprisingly, went on to become Chief Constable and was awarded an O.B.E. Back up north the dinghy in which the three had rowed ashore was found by the Buckie coastguard.

The three were transferred to London. John Donald found himself at the centre of great attention and congratulations. He had to write a brief note of the incident to his superiors. In

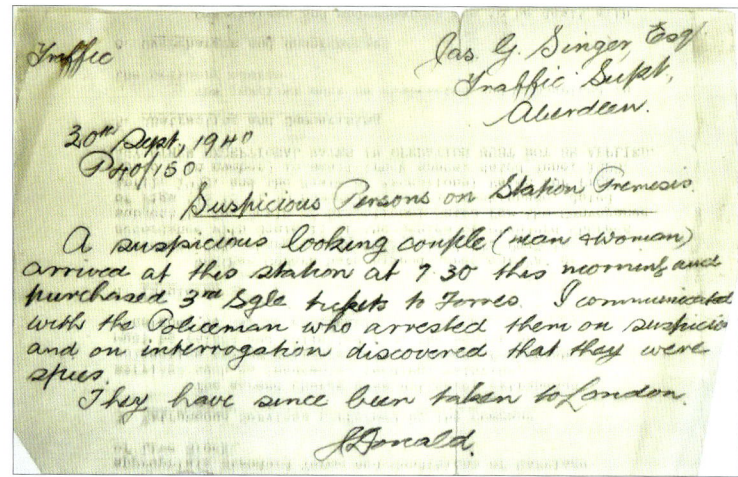
Report from John Donald to the Traffic Superintendent in Aberdeen.

January 1941 he received an invitation from Buckingham Palace to receive the British Empire Medal for his diligence. Due to the wartime dangers he travelled to London on his own to accept it. In June he was back in London to give evidence at the trial of the spies at the Old Bailey. Walti and Drucke were sentenced to death and hanged on 6th August 1941. Intriguingly, Vera was not called to trial and her future became a mystery. She may have traded important information in return for her life and was certainly sentenced to an indeterminate period in prison and shipped back to Germany at the end of the War. She disappeared although there were rumours that she quietly slipped back into Britain and saw out her days in the South of England, possibly in the Isle of Wight.

An eastbound train leaves Portgordon. The spies landed somewhere along the coast near here. (Mike Stephen)

....Other Coast Line Anecdotes

An unattributed newspaper cutting from the 1860s relates a couple of Coast Line stories which originated from the late Dr John Kerr, Chief Inspector of Education for Morayshire, Banffshire and Aberdeenshire during that decade:

"At Ordens, on the Banff and Tillynaught branch line, Dr. Kerr was instructed to go to the siding, and as the train approached, to set fire to a newspaper or other materials that would make a good blaze, and the train would stop. The night was very dark and windy, and he failed to set fire to the newspaper, but a stentorian shout had the same effect, and he was taken on board.

"One night the guard of the last train leaving Banff was reminded by one of the passengers that it was some minutes past the starting time, and replied: "Oh, ay, but Mr. F-----------has a denner pairty the nicht, an' I'm jist gi'ein' him twa or three meenits' preevilege.'"

One unusual load was carried in January 1871 when the railways delivered a new self-righting, 33-feet, 10-oar lifeboat, along with launching carriage, to Buckie for the RNLI. The three railway companies involved in the transport from London, the LNWR, Caledonian and Great North, made no charge which was normal practice. The "ensemble" arrived in Portsoy on 25th January 1871 and a team of horses hauled the load on to Buckie.

In January 1878 the *Banffshire Journal* reported that a parcel from London arrived at Banff Harbour instead of Banff Bridge. Rather than entrusting a porter to deliver the parcel on foot over the Deveron Bridge, a 20 minute walk, it was sent by rail on a 74-mile five hour journey via Grange and Inveramsay to Banff Bridge. A case of 19th century red tape?

In January 1897 the Great North announced a concession on Golfers' Fares: *"this month a new regulation giving cheap fares to golfers to both Highland and Great North stations is announced by the Great North of Scotland Railway. Members of golf clubs travelling for the purpose of playing golf may, on delivery of a voucher from the secretary of the club, be supplied with a first or third class return ticket at single fare and a quarter with a minimum as for five miles and not less charge than 9d.....Buckie golfers will shortly be able to obtain printed vouchers from Mr. Johnston, secretary of the Buckie club"*. As the concessionary tickets were limited to places not more than 50 miles from the "golf station", this initiative was targeting individuals wishing to visit neighbouring clubs. Previously concessions were only offered to parties of ten or more.

On trains from Aberdeen which carried portions for both Glen and Coast lines great care was taken to ensure that passengers were in the correct coaches. One porter rattled off the complete list of stations served in the local Doric, but with the advent of corridor carriages the ticket collector or guard undertook the checks in the Coast portion by asking *"A' Coast Wye?"* In the Glen portion it was *"Ony ane here for the Coast?"* which, according to A. G. Dunbar, reflected an unshakeable fondness for the Coast Line. Of course, they did not always get it right and one Englishman is known to have travelled from Aberdeen to Auchindachy (on the Glen Line) via the Coast!! Mr Dunbar also recorded a variation on *"Tillynaught, change for Banff"* as *"Ony ane here for Banff – get oot!"*.

On Saturday 23rd April 1898 the annual Buckie Fishermen's Excursion took place under the auspices of the Rolling Wave Lodge of Good Templars prior to the start of the herring season. The *Banffshire Advertiser* reported that a group of around 150 assembled in the Fishermen's Hall at 9.00am and marched with banners, along with the Portessie flute band and a piper, to the Great North Station. On a day of rain they caught the 10.25am train to Forres where dinner, tea and singing were organised. The group left for home at 6.05pm and arrived in Buckie at 7.51pm.

The annual Banff, Macduff and district holiday in July 1898 saw a busy Banff station as many left the town for a day in the country. The weather was glorious and the *Banffshire Journal* reported: *"The usual trains were well filled, but the two that were particularly patronised were a special train to Aberdeen and another special to Inverness, the latter run under the auspices of the Glenhauchie Lodge of Shepherds, Macduff. The low fare of 3/6d for the return journey to the Highland Capital attracted no fewer than 700 excursionists, the train being one of the largest that has left Banff for some time."*

The *Banffshire Advertiser* of 15th April 1900 commented on the local football: *"There was only a fair gate at the cup tie match between Buckie Thistle and Elgin City at Elgin on Saturday [7th April], but that was no fault of Buckie. By the train leaving at 3.13pm some 87 bookings were made for Elgin, and the carriages were taxed to their utmost. That number might have commanded a holiday fare, but the Railway company were inexorable, and all had to pay the regulation weekend fare of 1/8d. Such a crowd for a cup tie should give the Railway company an idea of how it would pay to run a special train from Buckie to Elgin on the occasion of the Glasgow Rangers visit to Elgin next month. The Elginshire Association might take note of this. Round the enclosure at Milnefield Park there would have been fully 100 Buckie folks, as about a score of cyclists were present at the match. Thistle's share of the gate was 16/3d [50%], while Buckie contributed 25/-. This speaks for itself."*

On Monday 25th June 1900 two Buckie Sunday School parties left both the Highland and Great North stations for their annual picnics. Some 200 children departed the former for Rathven and Ranas while 120 Episcopal children and teachers boarded the 1.40pm train at the Great North station for Tochieneal. Another contingent joined at Cullen and they all headed for a field on a farm near Tochieneal "....kindly granted by Mr. Bruce". Tea was served after games at 4.00pm and again after races at 7.00pm. The party returned by the last train and were assembled at the church to sing God Save The Queen before heading home.

The *Banffshire Advertiser* of 11th October 1900 touched upon the "Yarmouth Fishing": "*A special train arrived on Friday [5th October] at Yarmouth bringing 300 fisher girls from Aberdeen, Buckie and other towns in the North of Scotland. These will soon find employment in the famous bloater town during the herring season which lasts until Christmas. The girls travelled by train, which was composed of corridor carriages, and accomplished the journey of between five and six hundred miles, in about twelve hours. The special train travelled by the East Coast company's route, and was brought on from York over the Great Eastern Railway, the only stoppages being to change engines. A similar train arrived at Yarmouth on Saturday [6th October] from Fraserburgh. A special train also left Aberdeen on Monday night [8th October] for England, conveying between 200 and 300 fishworkers from Aberdeen, Peterhead, Fraserburgh and the Moray Firth.*"

On the same theme, GNSRA member Gordon Casely recalls being a young reporter for the long-dead *People's Journal* back in the mid-1960s: "*....on the stump one day in Buckie, I met an old worthy who related the days when herring quines from Buckie would travel in a reserved portion of a train to Yarmouth to work as fish gutters and packers....he pointed out: 'They'd ging there fae here in a presairved carriage!'*".

And the *Banffshire Journal* of 13th May 1902 noted: "*Today there will be landed the first fruits of the great herring fishing on the west coast. All along the shores of the Moray Firth, the harbours are almost depleted of fishing boats. A special train left Peterhead for Kyle of Lochalsh with over 100 coopers and herring workers. A special train left Buckie for the Kyle on Friday morning [9th May].*"

In April 1902 the *Banffshire Journal* commented: "*The Highland Railway Company are, we understand, to grant cheap fares between Keith and Fochabers (Spey Bay) on Wednesdays and Saturdays, commencing from 1st May. At present the Wednesday and Saturday cheap trips to Speyside by the Great North Railway and to Buckie by the Highland are much appreciated and taken advantage of. It has often been thought that the Great North might institute similar cheap trips to Cullen, seeing that the town is becoming such a favourite summer resort.*"

During that same month, April 1902, the *Banffshire Advertiser* reported: "*Peter Fair [at Rathven] and the lately established trades holiday week in Buckie have proved too much for the Great North. Their second application to the Town Council to change the date of the Buckie July holiday has proved abortive. Buckie really cannot disturb its equilibrium on account of the Highland Show at Aberdeen. I hope this action on the part of the Town Council does not mean that the local public are to be badly treated on 28th July by the Great North Railway Company, in the matter of travelling facilities in revenge for the stiff-necked attitude of their municipal representatives. I can recollect that on former holidays the Great North accommodation was not always up to the mark.*"

In July 1904 the *Banffshire Advertiser* reported: "*A labourer from Portknockie travelled by train from Buckie to Findochty without paying his fare. When challenged he claimed that he was drunk and had simply forgotten to buy a ticket and would do so now, but this was not accepted. He was fined £2 plus £1.12.6d expenses with the option of 20*

The gloomy interior of the train shed at Banff taken from a train for Tillynaught waiting for its next run to the junction. No doubt it was little changed from the days recalled in this chapter. There is a rich array of railway furniture to see, from the lamp on it's ornate bracket, the drinking fountain, platform bench and enamel signs that adorn the left hand wall. The bill posters advertise such diverse subjects as The Cairngorms, Lytham St. Annes and Barnardo's. The clock at the far end of the building looks to say 5.10pm and, if that is the case, then the next departure should be 5.25pm. There does not seem to be much custom just yet. (John Emslie)

days in jail for attempting to defraud the railway authorities. He was given a fortnight to pay. It worked out at 30/- per mile for his journey."

In late August 1904 Buffalo Bill and his Wild West Show performed in Aberdeen, Peterhead, Fraserburgh, Huntly and Elgin. The circus moved on consecutive days to each new location by three special trains, all double-headed and containing special American style vehicles (flat cars, stock cars, trunk cars and sleeping cars). The overnight journey on from Huntly to Elgin on Wednesday 31st August/Thursday 1st September was via the Coast Line and involved some tricky working at the Cairnie Junction/Grange triangle. The block telegraph at Cairnie was switched out for this special working. The two longest trains at 395 and 375 yards contained flat cars which were too long for the tight Cairnie–Grange North curve. Therefore, they both stopped short of the Grange cross-over points to allow the locomotives to use the triangle via Grange North to attach to the other end of the train at Cairnie. The train then reversed over the Grange cross-over and ran forward on to the Coast Line via the Grange–Grange North spur. The third train, with no flat cars, ran directly onto the Coast Line at Cairnie Junction. The trains ran at half-hour intervals and special arrangements were also required at sidings and crossing loops. In the early hours of Friday 2nd September all three trains were handed on to the Highland Railway at Elgin for onward movement to Inverness. The six Great North locomotives returned light to Aberdeen via the Glen Line.

Also in 1904, the working timetable shows a passenger train leaving Aberdeen at 10.05am for Buckie. It arrived at 12.53pm and set off back to Aberdeen at 1.15pm. It called at Cullen at 1.32pm and a former school pupil recalled that this train was known in Cullen as the "*Backlins Trainie*" or the "*Back to Fore Trainie*" because the locomotive ran tender-first back from Buckie as there was no turntable there. For the school children who lived underneath the viaduct in the Seatown of Cullen this train was the signal to return to the school (a fair way up the hill) after the lunch break. This train was still operating in 1914 but terminated at Tillynaught with a daily connection to Banff and a Wednesday and Saturday connection to Keith. By 1922 the train was working between Keith and Elgin.

The *Banffshire Advertiser* of January 1905 reported on golf fares: "*A meeting of the committee was held at Fochabers-on-Spey, Mr. J. Smith presiding. The Secretary submitted a reply from passenger superintendent of the GNS relative to cheap fares for golfers between Buckie and Fochabers. The Railway Company offered to give return tickets third class 6d instead of 10d and first class 10d instead of 1/8d.*"

Mr A. Hoggan of Bexleyheath recorded his memories of the Great North's Sorting Carriage in 1965: "*I worked on the Aberdeen-Elgin S.C. for around three years prior to being called up for military service on 4th August 1914. There were two of us – one for the sorting of ordinary and registered mail, the other struggled with surface mail (newspapers and large letter packets and circulars) despatched and received by apparatus. There was no double working of apparatus, the outward journey only dispatching, the home trips receiving…. There was not a spring in the whole [carriage] set-up and equilibrium could only be maintained by gripping tightly with the knee the irons supporting the wooden sorting frames…. The landmarks for most of the places for dropping off and receiving were their respective stations at the end of which the receiving net was set. It was a case of running thro' the station and then lowering. As a further precaution certain landmarks were to be noted, or if travelling at night, the guide would be the number of over and under bridges crossed before reaching the objective…. Cornhill was the one and only place where I ever overslipped the mark and missed the receipt, and as this had never been accomplished in the long history of the Sub-Postmaster's reign he did everything I should think except get in personal touch with the Postmaster General. Poor chap it did impact his applecart, and I had a few anxious moments wondering if next year's increment had gone for a Burton…. [At] Cairnie Junction…. we dispatched mail for Speyside – Aberlour, Dufftown, Craigellachie, etc. From the junction we got cracking for Elgin via the Coast, stopping at every town to handover the mail to the waiting postman. The return journey was the same in reverse until Cairnie Junction was reached where we had a heavy intake of mail from Speyside……*"

In November 1916 passengers on the Banff branch complained that station names were not being called out as trains arrived, a situation exacerbated by wartime lighting restrictions and drawn blinds. The Great North responded by ordering all trains to stop at all stations and halts whereas previously they had only called at halts during daylight hours. Footwarmers at this time were in short supply and were withdrawn, so winter journeys were cold ones!

Tanks first appeared as weapons of war in September 1916 and were so successful that the UK Government ordered 1,000 to be built. That required money and the National War Savings Committee capitalised on their popularity by dispatching six "travelling tanks" around the country to sell War Bonds and War Savings Certificates. A tank named *Julian 113* was sent to Aberdeen. "Tank Week" ran from 28th January to 2nd February 1918 and the good citizens of the Granite City contributed £2 million. Huge crowds turned out to greet *Julian* and to hear the patriotic speeches by both national and local dignitaries. After a spell back south *Julian* reappeared in the north-east in September 1918 for further fund-raising and was conveyed by goods train from Kittybrewster to Macduff where £12,000 was raised on Thursday 26th September. It was then transported by train along the Coast Line for fund-raising at Banff (£15,130), Portsoy (£10,786), Cullen (£5,000), Portknockie by road (£5,000), Findochty by road (£4,500) and Buckie by road. From Buckie the tank was conveyed on Wednesday 2nd October by the 5.10am goods train to Elgin. Unfortunately, while manoeuvring onto the rail wagon at Buckie station, *Julian* knocked over the hydrant handle which supplied the water from a line-side tank to the water crane and the support crew and members of the public were soaked by the escaping water. £175,132 was raised at Elgin. The whole operation was a credit to the Great North and its employees who had to manage the movement of a 28-ton tank and its support vehicles. Interestingly, the only hiccup was when *Julian* broke down on the road between Findochty and Buckie and required a night of repairs!

In 1993 GNSRA member Major E. K. Morrison recalled a childhood holiday to Banff in 1922: *"We went the long way round – not to Banff Bridge but via Tillynaught to Banff Harbour, possibly because it was through the Stationmaster there that my father had arranged our accommodation. I recall my mother being greatly agitated when our carriage appeared to stop short of the platform at the terminus. With all the assurance of an 8-year old I was able to tell her that this was only Golf Club House Halt! Banff Harbour station, of course, had no release road and an incoming train engine had to back its carriages along the line and then retreat on the engine shed siding while gravity saw the coaches back into the station. Once, to my great delight, I was allowed, under strict supervision, to operate the hand brake in the guard's van while this operation was carried out. Very much against the rule, but what an experience for a small boy!"*

On Thursday 5th May 1927 there were remarkable scenes on the line between Buckpool and Findochty. A bull escaped while cattle were being unloaded at Buckpool. He set off along the line towards Buckie with the 2.20pm Up express from Elgin to Aberdeen *"hard on his heels"*. Local butchers and other onlookers joined the chase and, on arrival in Buckie, the Stationmaster and staff joined the melée. Attempts were made to intercept or decoy the bull but he turned and charged them. Some of the pursuers practiced their bull-fighting skills as the bull continued ahead of the train which by now had several hanging onto the outside of the carriages. At one point the infuriated bull turned and charged and sent everyone running with some forced to jump for their lives over the lineside fence. After a 20 minute delay to the train at Findochty the bull turned off the line, but when the train passed he returned and pursued it to Portknockie. Here he retreated a few hundred yards to the shelter of an arched overbridge and waited patiently for an hour for the 4.00pm passenger train the engine of which he proceeded to attack with gusto. By this time the railway staff had reached the end of their tether and a car was sent to collect Sergeant James Reid from Buckie. He was a noted crack shot although it took him four attempts from 100 yards distance to kill the miscreant. All in the daily life of the railwaymen!

Bus services were becoming a threat to the railways by the late 1920s but the following letter, published in the *Aberdeen Evening Express* on 13th October 1928, demonstrates that trains were still very much part of everyday life. The letter does, however, highlight the potential for the buses:

"Sir – The 6.45pm train leaving Aberdeen for the Coast on Saturday night was very heavily laden, late comers having great difficulty in getting squeezed in. I myself was jammed in a corner so that I could hardly move.

"The next compartment was standing empty with the door locked and a card on the window marked "reserved". About five minutes before the train was due to leave along came three gentlemen. One took a key from his pocket, and the three entered and again had the door locked and this laden train left the station with these three gentlemen comfortably seated in this compartment.

"I would be pleased if some of the railway officials who were buzzing around this train before it left would explain why these gentlemen had a whole compartment to themselves. CURIOUS"

It is not known whether CURIOUS ever solved the mystery.

There was a New Year mishap during the night of Thursday 2nd January 1930 when two colts found their way from a lineside farm (Midton) on to the line between Cornhill and Tillynaught. Unfortunately, one was struck by a passing train and was found dead at the foot of an embankment. The other wandered along the line in darkness until the 5.20am Down goods from Cairnie appeared whereupon it tore down the line at full speed. The early duty shunter at Tillynaught watched in amazement as the horse appeared around a bend in the grey light of morning and sped through the station and headed for Portsoy. The news of the pending arrival was signalled to Portsoy from where a rather brave official, equipped with a hand lamp, set out to intercept the animal. The horse spotted officialdom at Huntly bridge (one mile from the station) and turned on its heels and made off at full speed back to Tillynaught. It arrived just ahead of the 6.10am Up passenger service. A group of railway men soon had it *"cornered on a flat piece of land east of the station"* but, after a failed attempt to break through a fence, it simply charged through the human cordon and made off back towards Portsoy. After a mile it reached the Baley level crossing where it took advantage of the left-hand gate being open and headed for Auchanachie. It was caught and taken to a steading to await its owner who arrived to claim it in a "motor car".

Glenbarry station was witness to a rather unusual, and possibly unique, occurrence on the dark winter's morning of Thursday 14th January 1932. As the 6.10am train pulled in there was apparent uproar in one of the corridor coaches and, as the train came to a halt, the doors were flung open and passengers *"….tumbled over each other to get out of their compartments"*. Many were screaming and a cry went up: *"the train is fu' o' futtrats"*. The bemused station and train staff searched and found that there were no weasels on board but that the culprit for the mayhem was a single working ferret! It transpired that it had escaped from the bag of a gentleman on his way to a day's shooting but who had alighted at an earlier stop. He had not noticed his companion's escape and the ferret was taking full advantage of its new freedom to explore the carriages. Having been glimpsed throughout the train at various times as it proceeded from compartment to compartment, the passengers became convinced that the entire train was infested. Hence the noise and panic. The errant ferret was eventually captured by a railway inspector and was reunited with its owner later in the day. And the passengers all had a grand tale to tell at the dinner table that evening!

In December 1934 the *Banffshire Herald* reported that the Buckie Traders Association had complained to the LNER that their special Christmas shopping excursions to Elgin were

Ex-Caledonian Railway 0-6-0 No. 57634 storms through the isolated station at Glenbarry on 12th August 1960. No ferrets on this train, as there was on a dark winter's morning in 1932.
(Sandy Edward)

adversely affecting their trade and requested that it withdraw them. The LNER refused on the basis that passengers would travel anyway!

In the April 1941 issue of the LNER magazine the following is recounted as to the origin of the name of "Lady's Bridge" station on the branch to Banff: *"In the course of Lady Banff's frequent visits from the Castle of Inchdrewer (her country residence) to Buchragie House, the Dower house of the Ogilvies of the Boyne, she had to cross the Burn of Boyndie which runs past the station. A bridge was erected about that time and became known as 'My Lady's Bridge'; hence the name of the station"*.

Jimmy Brown, the well-known former Supplies Officer at Inverurie Locomotive Works, recounted this ghostly tale based on a true story from the Second World War. The Coast Line carried heavy loads during the War, but one dark and stormy night an engine running light set down guard Joe Wood at Portsoy at the end of a long shift. The station was in complete darkness apart from the yellow light of the signal box. Joe climbed the stairs in the hope of a hot cup of tea and found Signalman Sandy Grant and Stationmaster Jimmy Grigor brewing up. Mr Grigor had been called out to attend to a signal lamp which had been blown out by the storm. Grant disliked Wood but he offered him a cup of tea at the side of his roaring fire. As the three men drank their tea they discussed the storm until a flash of lightning lit up the swaying trees and illuminated the outlines of ruined Portsoy House in the distance. *"Dae ye think she'll walk the nicht?"* asked Grant nodding towards the ruin. *"Fa?"* asked Wood, but he knew Sandy was referring to Kirsty Forbes a domestic who had died in the fire which destroyed the house several years before. *"This is just the nicht for her"* Grant said, to which Wood scornfully replied *"A lot o' auld wives blethers. There's nae sic' thing as ghosts"*. Mr Grigor, the Stationmaster, said nothing as he did not think it was appropriate to get involved in a discussion involving his inferiors. He listened as Wood and Grant discussed the subject of ghosts, then rose and with his back to Wood, he winked at Grant as he said: *"I think I'll check the lamp once more before I turn in, Sandy"*. He departed and Wood followed shortly to struggle down the dark road towards home to the sound of the wind and the distant roar of the sea. Suddenly a ghostly figure sprang out from behind a bush and danced on the path uttering eldritch screeches. Wood dropped his guard's kit and ran hell for leather back to the signal box where he crashed through the door. *"Ah've seen it....Ah've seen it....It's oot there.... Shut the door....Quick."* he gasped to Grant. *"Kirsty....she's oot there. Help me"* he implored Grant. Grant opened the window and, yes, he could discern a figure in white disappearing into the Stationmaster's house. He suddenly understood the meaning of the Stationmaster's wink as he helped Wood onto a seat by the fire. *"But you said yoursel'"* he said to Wood *"There's nae sic' thing as ghosts"*. *"Ah ken....Ah ken"* replied Wood *"but I've changed ma mind. Ah tak' it a' back noo that ah've seen 'er"*. To which Grant replied: *"Well, you can believe it if you like, but ah've been thinkin' ower whit ye said afore ye went oot an' ah'm fair convinced....There's nae sic' thing as ghosts"*!!! Mr Brown's tale was no doubt embellished in the telling, but be warned: old Portsoy station is not a place for the faint-hearted on dark and stormy nights!

In March 1945 passengers on the morning Coast Line mail train from Inverness to Aberdeen were unable to alight at Cornhill because the windows had frozen solid and could not be lowered to reach the outside door handles. Later during that same week drifting snow blocked the line from Banff to Tillynaught for the first time since 1942.

Prior to moving to its permanent base at Ingliston near Edinburgh, the Royal Highland Show was held in turn at various locations around Scotland. The first Show after the Second

World War was held in Inverness in 1948 and many special trains conveyed the farming communities and general public to the Highland capital. An interesting working on Thursday 24th June was the 6.4am departure from Grange to Elgin via the Coast Line. It was composed of six coaches, called at all stops, and arrived in Elgin at 7.43am. There it joined the 6.22am working from Keith Town which had run via the Glen Line to arrive in Elgin at 7.38am. The combined train of 12 coaches departed Elgin at 7.50am and arrived in Inverness at 9.12am. After a full and no doubt tiring day the return departed Inverness at 8.45pm and arrived in Elgin at 9.50pm. The Coast train departed Elgin at 10.5pm and arrived in Grange at 11.43pm. A grand day out no doubt tied in with a measure of Highland hospitality!

An anonymous contributor "The Great North Wanderer" commenced work as a 14 year-old Junior Porter at Tillynaught on 2nd August 1948. His starting wage was 23/- for a 48 hour week, but this increased to 25/- from his 15th birthday. He described some of the visitors to the station: *"Visiting workers included a man who opened a locked cupboard which was full of square jars linked by wires. These provided the electricity for the telegraph instrument and the phone to the signalbox. These jars were filled with electrodes and fluid and known as the Leyden electric system. The weighing machines were serviced regularly. A Pooley's wagon would arrive with weights, etc., and then a man came to service the machines. The wagon and man then moved on to the next station. Another man came to the station to dismantle, clean and maybe repair the station clock. The District Auditor would unexpectedly call and would firstly count all the cash in the till. Then he checked all the books with green pencil marks. A railway policeman, known locally as 'Dick Barton', kept an eye on the working of farm level crossings. The District Inspector was also seen at the station. He spent most of his time at the signal box overseeing the signalman and the shunters attaching vans of fish to the main line train. He also checked tickets on trains he travelled on."*

On Wednesday 13th August 1952 a special evening excursion departed Buckie at 3.37pm for Aberdeen. It arrived at 5.50pm and the "attractions" were the Aberdeen v. Hearts football match at Pittodrie (kick-off 6.45pm) or one of the evening shows including Harry Gordon in *"Half-past Eight"*. This performance could be booked in advance at Buckie station booking office. The return fare was 6/9d. (The attendance that evening at Pittodrie was 33,000 and, with the *"Terrible Trio"* of Conn, Bauld and Wardhaugh in the Hearts line-up, it is not surprising that the Edinburgh club won 4-2).

On 19th August 1952 the *Banffshire Journal* reported: *"The amount of drunkenness and hooliganism which occurred on trains between Aberdeen and Buckie was a public scandal, declared Sheriff Walker at Banff Sheriff Court, when he sentenced a Cullen trawl fisherman to thirty days for assaulting a Buckie engineer on a train on this line. Things had reached such a pass, declared the Sheriff, that decent people were unwilling to travel by that train [in all probability the 'Trawler Train'], and he was very glad that the railway authorities were at last taking steps to deal with the matter. The assault had taken place in a corridor on the train between Tillynaught and Cairnie Junction. A window was also broken."*

The same edition of the *Banffshire Journal* (19th August 1952) also had a few words for British Railways: *"British Railways have been coming in for much unofficial criticism in the North-East recently. The comments of amazed [Glasgow] Fair visitors who were stranded at Tillynaught a few weeks ago (when the train wasn't accommodating enough to take more than two thirds of the visitors to Aberdeen) have been followed up by more criticism of the excursion trains to Keith Show last week. An old lady making her first rail journey for several years was feeling a trifle unhappy after the special train completed the twenty mile run (with two changes) in 80 minutes. The train left Banff only five minutes behind schedule and passengers enjoyed a reasonably comfortable six mile run to Tillynaught Junction. After a wait of ten minutes, and a little confusion when some passengers for Keith tried to re-board the train they had just vacated, the connection arrived. Luckily this train was equipped with a corridor and the lady and her companion were able to stand wedged together outside the compartments already overflowing with 'through' passengers. Change again at Cairnie Junction, and the old lady had to be steadied as she jumped down onto a low platform. On the Keith train, they were able to find a seat, arriving at the upper town station."*

There are many tales of the "Great Gale" of 31st January 1953 and James MacLennan, a fireman based at Elgin Shed, recounted that, after abandoning B1 61242 *Alexander Reith Gray* at Drummuir when the locomotive was trapped by falling trees: *"I walked to Fife-Keith and managed to hitch a lift back to Elgin, and arrived just in time to see the spire of the church at the top of Moss Street fall. Elsewhere on the local rail network things were bad, the goods going to Cullen had problems, when the wind blew the telegraph wires into the engine, which wrapped themselves around the chimney with the result that the wires and poles were pulled over all the way into Cullen station. It was said that the seaward side of the D40 and its goods wagons were pure white from the foam being blown from the sea."*

In 1995 the well-known railway writer George Robin recounted this tale of the Banff Harbour – Tillynaught line from 1948: *"My wife has an aunt who stays just above the cramped terminus at Banff Harbour station, so one day I was determined to 'do' the branch instead of watching it. I got the slowest ever train going (it was worse than St. Combs), but coming back we fairly tore along. The line hugs the coast line to begin with, winding in and out with the contour of the cliffs, at the foot of which it runs, and passes two halts. These halts are open only in hours of daylight. We had a long stop on the level crossing at Ladysbridge, where the water was landed for the community. (In 1948, I believe, this practice is now stopped as the stop on the level crossing was 'just a bit over the score' for motorists). There was now nothing to report until climbing up into the branch platform at Tillynaught. This station, too, was a 'V' junction like Inveramsay, and I saw two main line trains cross. Our engine ran round and, after making the booked connections, set off again for Banff. This time we made good speed and stopped only at Ladysbridge, before threading our way into the 'goods shed' right up against the gasworks at Banff Harbour. Our engine was an ex-NER 0-4-4T."*

GNSRA member Donald Galloway recounted an incident at Glenbarry one warm Saturday morning in the late 1940s. By this time the Stationmaster was located at Knock: *"I had accepted a pick-up goods from Grange North and when I received 'Train Entering Section' for it, I obtained a key-token for it and pulled off the signals as he had no traffic for us....I sat on the end of the platform [at the Down catcher], listening to the songs of the birds, the noises of insects and all the sounds of the quiet countryside....I listened to see if I could hear the noise of the goods engine climbing the gradient through Knock Station or shunting in the distillery sidings, but no, not a sound.... We waited and listened....but nothing could be heard. Then we heard a 2-2-2 bell signal in the box from Tillynaught. This was an answer the phone – urgently."* Tillynaught were by now looking for the goods as it was due to pass a passenger train which had just been signalled from Portsoy. Tillynaught and Glenbarry agreed to send on the passenger train to Glenbarry who contacted Grange North for any information. While in discussion the Grange North signalman spotted the goods fireman running towards him down the track with the goods token. *"It transpired that the engine, a rather elderly D41, had blown a boiler tube near 'The Shiel', a farm about half way between Grange North and Knock station. Fortunately there were no injuries, but there could have been – and serious ones too."* Keith breakdown was summoned while the passenger sat simmering away at Glenbarry until the errant goods was towed back to Grange North and on to Cairnie to clear the line.

The Great North network suffered from snow on a regular basis throughout its life. Around 1950 Dr P. McDiarmid, the Fochabers GP, found the road to Garmouth impassable. He managed to drive his car to Spey Bay station where, due to the extreme cold, he purchased a first class return ticket to Garmouth. That was reputedly the first-ever first class ticket purchased for that journey! The north-east was hit by blizzards from Monday 18th January 1960 and the Coast Line remained blocked at Buckie until Friday 22nd. Normal services did not resume until the following day. The Banff branch also had a difficult week. On the Monday the 6.50am from Banff derailed at Tillynaught which resulted in a temporary bus service to Portsoy. The branch was then buried in snow with services not reinstated until Monday 25th.

Rather surprisingly, the railways were still moving circuses from venue to venue in the early 1950s. On the evening of Saturday 15th August 1953, 37 circus vehicles were shunted, loaded and marshalled into three specials for Bertram Mills' Circus at Kittybrewster. The first train (No. 600) hauled 24 vehicles of 620 tons weight and the second (No. 601) 22 vehicles of 635 tons weight (including the "Big Top" canvas). These trains were double-headed by two B1s. A single B1 pulled the third and lightest train (No. 602) of 17 vehicles weighing only 250 tons (elephants and horses). The initial destinations were Fraserburgh and Huntly. A B12 4-6-0 and a K2 2-6-0 substituted a couple of the B1s on the Huntly leg as Kittybrewster struggled to find suitable power. On arrival at Huntly there was a problem. With the goods yard trailing into the Up line and limited crossover space, only the lightest of the three trains (No. 602) could be accommodated in the runround and shunting facilities. Consequently, the two heavier trains ran on to the Grange Triangle. Each train in turn ran past Grange Junction and stopped. A B1 from Keith then attached at the rear of the train and pulled it up the Coast Line spur and clear of Grange North Junction towards Banff and detached. The train then headed back to Huntly via Cairnie Junction. The train locomotive carried the Grange–Grange North single line token while the Keith pilot was given that for the Grange–Glenbarry section. The pilot returned light to the Grange North Junction and surrendered the Glenbarry token and proceeded to Grange to repeat the exercise with the second train. All in a day's work for the BR staff with 67 years of using the Grange Triangle behind them and with minimum disruption to ordinary traffic.

On Wednesday 30th March 1955 a special train departed Buckie at 11.30am to Glasgow for the evangelist Billy Graham's evening meeting in the Kelvin Hall. The return fare was 28/4d but that included ticket entry to the event. The train arrived at Partick station at 6.15pm, departed for the return journey at 10pm, and arrived back in Buckie at 4.33am.

In July 1957 a nine-day bus strike resulted in a short boom in business at Elgin. Stationmaster Mr M. F. Beddow stated: *"This increase was especially noticeable on the Lossiemouth route. Instead of the normally sparsely filled three coach trains, we were running five coaches, which were full up."* A heavy increase in traffic was also reported on the Coast Line and from Forres to Speyside.

Fighting the snow in 1947 at Newmachar, an example of what railwaymen had to contend with. (Douglas Flett)

In January 1958 the 6.50pm train from Elgin hit an 8-foot snow drift two hours later a few miles from Cornhill. Nine passengers were on board. Although other engines pulled it free, it became stuck again near Inchford. A group of 20 men failed to dig it out and the passengers were forced to spend the night on the train. The driver kept up steam to maintain heating and local farmer John Gordon and his wife walked through the deep snow to provide hot tea. Two locomotives and a snow plough finally pulled the train clear about mid-day and it continued to Keith. Half the passengers alighted there with the rest continuing on to Aberdeen.

The Coast Line saw many Football Specials over the years. On Saturday 25th January 1964 Scottish First Division Club Ayr United travelled north by train to play Buckie Thistle at Victoria Park in a Scottish Cup tie. The DMU broke down near Cairnie Junction and the players and officials, who had stayed overnight in Aberdeen, had to scramble out of the train with their kit and hail taxis to get to Buckie in time for the 2.15pm kick-off. It was worth it, as Ayr won 3-1.

This is the story of the "other" Great Train Robbery in 1963 as recounted by Bill Falconer of the Keith & Dufftown Railway Association: *"When I was home on leave from the Army [in late 1963] I met up with friend Ewan Hay, and we decided to fish the Boyne Burn which runs beside the Coast Line between Glenbarry and Tillynaught Junction. Ewan's father's van was borrowed for transport and we set off discreetly parking the van a few hundred yards from Tillynaught while we went worm-drowning. I can't remember how successful we were, but no matter, after several hours we retrieved the van and headed home to Fordyce. Over the next few days we heard disconcerting stories about how a train carrying a valuable, but unspecified, consignment was due up the Coast Line when the sole member of staff at Tillynaught noticed the mystery van parked nearby; with memories of the Great Train Robbery [on 8th August 1963] fresh in his mind he alerted the police plus the stations up and down the line. Meanwhile, Ewan and I were peacefully fishing out of sight and earshot of all this fuss, and by the time we returned to the van the train had passed unmolested and the forces of law and order had gone home. This is the first time I have told this story as we had neglected to buy fishing permits and presumably a statute of limitation now applies!"*

Graham Maxtone recalls a tale of railway opportunism as recounted to him by signalman "wee" Johnny Murray. In the mid-1960s Johnny was signalman at Glenbarry supplementing his income as a local crofter near Yonderton of Knock. He was happy with his work as the early shift start and late shift finish at 6.50am and 8.40pm respectively was not too onerous and fitted well with his croft work. However, rumours started to circulate that the axe was to fall on Glenbarry box as part of wider economy measures and Johnny's mate on the opposite shift decided not to hang about and moved on. That resulted in a shortage of staff and every Thursday the roster clerk was on the internal railway phone circuit asking Johnny if he would work the double shift the following week. *"Nae buther at a' ma loon"* was Johnny's invariable reply as he contemplated the prospect of increased "siller". And so it started…6.50am to 8.40pm (13 hours 50 minutes) day after day, week after week, month after month. But the inevitable happened on 25th June 1966 when S&T arrived to disconnect the signals and points, remove the tablet instruments and lever frame, and switch out Glenbarry permanently. However, no one appeared to have updated the roster clerk who continued to phone what was left of Glenbarry box every Thursday afternoon to ask Johnny if he was willing to work the double shift. Johnny was only too happy to oblige and he placed some planks and a heavy carpet over the hole where the lever frame had been to keep out the draughts, kept the fire well stoked, and sat back in his comfortable chair. Life had suddenly become a lot easier as all Johnny had to do was sell the occasional ticket and tell folk heading west *"dinna gang ower the briggie, there's nae track there noo"*. As time went by Johnny called the "heid yins" at Buckie and asked if a meal could be provided due to his long hours and he was directed to Glenbarry Hotel with the railway picking up the tab. Of course, Johnny's utopian life couldn't last and, when Ronnie Munro (who started at Tillynaught) was appointed to the new post of Area Manager based in Buckie in 1967, the writing was on the wall. During his first week, on pay run day, Ronnie presented himself with a very fat pay packet at Glenbarry to find Johnny sitting in front of a roaring fire, a stone heavier, "sooking" on a King Edward cigar, with only a circuit phone to keep him company! Johnny was very quickly awarded a transfer to fill a desperately needed vacancy at Cairnie Junction which was still an extremely busy signal box. He was, in fact, the last signalman on duty at Cairnie for the last passenger trains to the Coast on Saturday 4th May 1968. He moved on to Tomatin in the 1970s and later to Ardlui. As with all such tales it is not unusual to suspect that it has been exaggerated and embellished down the years, but there is a sting in the tail. Ronnie Munro retired from Scotrail as Manager at Inverness many years later and he subsequently accorded the Association the privilege of recording details of his rich and varied career. He told almost exactly the same story with no name mentioned. It could only have been Johnny Murray!

The last Stationmaster at Portsoy when the Coast Line closed in 1968 was Harry Grant who, until then, had spent his entire LNER/BR career on the Moray Firth Coast Line including many years at Banff. In the final days at Portsoy he ran the station on his own undertaking porter work, trimming lamps, operating signals and issuing tickets. He had a sideline in vegetables and his prize carrots grew beside the track. He maintained that carrot-fly was unheard of in the days of steam and only appeared when diesels arrived! Although on his own, he did not lack company as he used the signal bell to communicate in code with his friend Bert Esslemont who was Stationmaster at Cullen. Usually, the messages related to private items to be conveyed for them by drivers including instructions from Bert for Harry to collect shopping items in Portsoy for his wife Jean. The last of an age going by!

Accidents and Incidents

There were relatively few serious accidents on the Great North system but, of those other incidents (including suicides) which did occur, the Coast Line had its share. Mention has already been made of the accident involving the Banff, Portsoy & Strathisla's celebratory train between Knock and Glenbarry on 30th July 1859 and the following is a selection of some others in subsequent years.

Probably the most spectacular and potentially serious accident occurred on Monday 16th May 1887 when the 10.10am mail from Aberdeen to Elgin, hauled by Manson Class G 4-4-0 No. 71, derailed between Buckpool and Portgordon because of track distortion due to excessive heat. The train, consisting of brake van, Composite, Post Office van and brake Third in that order was carrying seven passengers and was travelling at 35-40 mph. The locomotive and some carriages toppled down the embankment into a field of corn after ripping up 90 yards of track. Fortunately, there were no major injuries, although the guard suffered face cuts and leg injuries after being thrown across his van. Driver Andrew Black from Aberdeen and his Fireman William Laurie escaped with bruising. All but two passengers were able to walk to Portgordon station and a special train ran from Aberdeen with a squad of workmen and company officials, including Locomotive Superintendent James Manson, to make good the damage. The line re-opened to normal traffic the following day. The Board of Trade Inspector, Colonel Rich, criticised inadequate ballasting of track (an issue not unknown elsewhere to the Great North) and the Ibbotson's Patent fish bolts which gripped the rails too tightly and consequently prevented expansion. The local farmer was none too pleased at the damage to his crop!

Driver William Philip of Elgin shed recounted this report by fellow Driver Alex Boyle of an incident on 28th December 1894: *"When running the 1.5pm ex Portsoy and about halfway between Portgordon and Fochabers [Spey Bay] I observed something lying on the line. I thought when looking at it from a distance it was a piece of canvas or something blown with hurricane but when about 100 yards from it I saw it was a man lying with his back to us and sounding the whistle sharply he leaned up on his elbow and looked at us and he lay down again. When seeing this I used every endeavour to stop but was unable to do so until guard rail or bogie wheel struck him on the head and guides of axlebox struck him on the shoulder turning him on his face on sideway. I was an engine and two carriage lengths past him before I got stopped. We put him in van and took him to Elgin for medical assistance. He was able with assistance to walk. I understand the man's name is Morrison and lives at a place called Dallochy (12 miles from Elgin). 6 minutes lost thereby."*

On 29th July 1896 a late evening ballast train hauled by locomotive No. 52 and consisting of 12 loaded wagons, two carriages with 36 men, and a brake van was on its way from Portknockie to Grange when it was diverted without warning into a short siding at Knock station at 12.50am. It hit the buffers, derailing the engine and several wagons. The driver, fireman and

Builder's photograph of No. 52, Class L, which was involved in the accident in 1896. The locomotive was constructed by Neilson & Co. in 1876 and originally numbered 57 as shown here. It was extensively rebuilt in 1897. (GNSRA collection)

Buckpool station from the east from an early postcard. The headland in the distance was the location of the landslip in 1931. Midway Cottage is to the right of the line.

(Graham Maxtone collection)

district permanent way inspector Peter Sleigh, who was riding on the footplate, were all seriously injured. Peter Sleigh died the next day. The Stationmaster had misread the staff circular and thought the train was routed via the Rothes line (the train had originated at Glen of Rothes) and had therefore not set the road for the train to run through the station. He was exonerated before a jury at a Sherriff's enquiry in Banff which accepted the circular was open to misinterpretation, especially as he had been on duty for 18 hours to cover the annual Banff holiday. The train had also passed a danger signal although the driver claimed that ballast trains did not take account of signals!!

In June 1900 a nine year-old Portsoy lad, Joseph Smith, travelled from Buckie to Cullen to visit friends. He entered a compartment on his own at Buckie but on arrival at Cullen he found the carriage doors on the single platform side locked. It is believed that he panicked as he journeyed on in the train and attempted to get out near Glassaugh. His body was discovered by a surfaceman on the north side of the line just beyond Glassaugh station and was subsequently taken on to Portsoy before being returned to Portessie. It appears that, due to increased holiday traffic, several additional coaches were in service and that a number of other passengers were inconvenienced at Cullen due to locked doors. Such a practice led to several such deaths on UK railways and was strongly criticised by the Board of Trade.

In February 1901 at Banff Harbour a horse belonging to the Fife Arms Hotel which had pulled the mail truck to the station, was spooked by a shunting locomotive coming into contact with some wagons and started forward throwing the driver, Mr. William Hadden, to the ground. One of the lorry's wheels ran over his thigh. Fortunately, his injuries were limited to severe bruising and he was able, with assistance, to walk home.

In June 1902 two carriages and three wagons, were derailed while the 8.16am train was reversing into a siding at Buckie to collect a truck containing camels belonging to the circus of Lord George Sangor. This was due to defective points. There was no reported damage to track, trucks or camels. The popular circus had given two performances in the town the previous day attracting a large influx of visitors. The circus had previously performed to several thousand spectators in Banff and a special train was run from and to Fyvie.

On 23rd April 1913 a Tillynaught porter, William McWilliam, fell while attempting to board a train arriving at the main line platform in order to transfer luggage and parcels on to the Banff branch train. His right leg was subsequently amputated. The Company refused compensation as his actions were strictly prohibited by the Company Rules, but in an Appeal to the Court of Session the judge ruled that he was due compensation because: *"He was performing his duty in an indiscreet and wrong manner, but still performing it."* Mr. McWilliam claimed to be ignorant of the rule.

At around 5.30pm on Tuesday 24th March 1931 an estimated 100 tons of the southern cutting at Midway Cottage, between Buckie and Portgordon, collapsed and blocked the Coast Line to a depth of several feet. It was triggered by a thaw following a severe frost. Fortunately, the landslip was witnessed by five young lads aged nine to eleven who were fishing for tadpoles in a nearby burn. They ran half a mile to Buckpool station to raise the alarm with the station porter. The next two trains from Aberdeen and Elgin were not due for over an hour and were halted at Buckie and Portgordon respectively. Buses came to the rescue but the debris was dug out and removed in time to allow the 9.00pm train from Buckie to Elgin to pass, albeit one hour late. The five boys each received a watch and a letter of thanks from the LNER.

On Wednesday 10th June 1931 ten cattle owned by Mr Adam Michie of Claymyers strayed on to the line between Glenbarry and Cornhill. The 1.20pm Keith to Elgin was due, and they were spotted by local man Mr W. Gray and his son Bennet who ran across fields and on to the line to warn the driver. However, they were just too late as the train appeared around a bend and the cattle stampeded, one knocking the boy Bennet to the ground. He suffered a bad cut to his forehead. The train hit and killed one stirk and pulled up. The rest of the cattle were unharmed.

On Saturday 30th July 1932 tremendous rainstorms hit the north-east. Rettie's Burn at Ordens flooded and passengers alighting at Banff just after 9.00pm described how water had rushed in to the carriages as their train negotiated the flooded section of line. On Sunday morning a farm worker noticed that part of a railway bridge's masonry had been washed away and notified Banff station. The entire branch was closed for two days while repairs were undertaken. Passengers were diverted to Macduff and Portsoy with an hourly bus service from Banff serving the latter. A locomotive running slowly through flood water on the main line derailed ¾ mile from Grange and 20 passengers were rescued by a relief train dispatched from Keith. Fortunately, the incident occurred on the double track and the rescue engine was able to draw alongside the stricken train to allow passengers to cross directly from train to train. There were no injuries to passengers and staff, but there were significant losses of farm animals and damage to properties and fields throughout the area.

Perhaps the most sobering of accidents on the Coast Line is that which occurred in Knock station goods yard on 2nd December 1943. Karam Dad was the 22 year-old son of Rahmat Khan of Chak Pinana, Gujrat, Pakistan and he was serving in the Royal Indian Army Service Corps. He was a mule driver who, with his transport company, worked alongside the British Army and was evacuated from Dunkirk. His company was sent to north-east Scotland to train in Arctic warfare for a possible invasion of occupied Norway. The exact circumstances of how he ended up walking on the railway and the accident in which he was involved is shrouded in mystery. It is known, however, that he died at the scene *"from internal injuries and accidental shock"*. The adjacent Knockdhu distillery was closed at the time. Karam Dad is buried in a corner of Grange Church cemetery.

In the early hours of Tuesday 10th December 1957 the waiting room on the Down platform of Buckie station was damaged by tons of earth and masonry crashing 30 feet down the hillside onto the station. This was the most serious landslide at Buckie but fortunately, as it occurred during the night, the station was deserted and no one was injured.

On Thursday 20th February 1958 a potentially serious accident was averted. Over 500 tons of earth and mud slid onto and blocked the Coast Line between Tochieneal and Cullen in a narrow cutting about ¾ mile to the east of Cullen station. James Moir, a 58 year-old railway ganger from Cullen, averted a disaster by running ¾ mile to Tochieneal to raise the alarm. He approached the signal box waving his arms and blowing his whistle and was just in time to have the signals set against the 8.50am Aberdeen–Elgin train. A telephone call to Portknockie box halted the eastbound passenger train on the other side of the landslide.

Two incidents with potentially fatal consequences occurred at level crossings on the Banff branch in quick succession. On 21st January 1959 the hired car of local County Councillor and farmer John Milne of Paddocklaw Farm, Banff smashed through the gates of Ladysbridge level crossing and became stuck on the railway line. An effort by a passing motorist Norman Rothnie to rescue the driver failed as, shortly after 1.30pm, a train from Tillynaught to Banff approached. The signals had been set in favour of the train by Ladysbridge porter Alistair McHardy and he immediately set them against it when he witnessed the accident. It was, however, too late for the train to pull up and the locomotive, hauled by a Caledonian 0-4-4 tank engine running bunker first, hit the vehicle at about 25mph which caused the main Westinghouse air pipe to the brakes to fracture. Relief driver

Rather forlornly in a far-flung corner of Grange Church cemetery lies the lone grave of Karam Dad. (David Fasken)

The level crossing gates at Ladysbridge. These were typical wooden gates which would not stand up to any runaway vehicles.
(John Emslie)

James Fraser threw the engine into forward gear but the train pushed the car about 200 yards along the track before it came to a halt. Fireman Alexander Taylor ran back to Ladysbridge station to summon help to extricate the driver. Mr Milne was seriously injured and was taken to Chalmers Hospital in Banff with arm injuries and suffering from shock. He survived.

On Christmas Day 1961 Bob Smith, the gatekeeper at Boyndie level crossing, received a telephone message from Tillynaught at 8.56am that the train for Banff was on its way. As he proceeded to open the gates a bus of 40 Buckie fishermen on their way to Aberdeen skidded off the road, smashed into a fence, snapped a telegraph pole and rammed into the gates. With the wires down there was no way of stopping the train and Mr Smith jumped on his bike and rode furiously to Ladysbridge station over ice-bound roads. He had four minutes in which to meet the train and he was just in time to warn driver Tom Ross, fireman James Fraser and guard Harry McDonald. A disaster averted.

Boyndie Crossing, where the Banff line crossed the Banff to Portsoy road. This faded postcard was sent on 9th July 1909. Ice on the sharp bend in the road was the cause of the accident here in 1961.
(GNSRA collection)

Appendix 1: Coast Line Stations and Sidings

	Miles	Height (Feet ASL)	Date Opened Passengers	Goods	Date Closed Passengers	Goods
Grange South Junction (1)	0	314	Signal Box only			
Cairnie Junction (2)	0	314	1st Jun 1898		6th May 1968	
Grange North Junction (3)	0½	308	Signal Box only			
Millegan	1½	N/A	1st Oct 1859	1st Oct 1859	1st July 1875	Not known
Shiel Wood Timber Siding (4)	2½	N/A		15th May 1916		28th Apr 1921
Knock (5)	3¼	400	30th Jul 1859	30th Jul 1859	6th May 1968	6th May 1968
Glenbarry (6)	4½	476	1st Oct 1859	1st Oct 1859	6th May 1968	2nd Nov 1964
Cornhill	7½	258	30th Jul 1859	30th Jul 1859	6th May 1968	6th May 1968
Tillynaught Junction	10	180	1st Sep 1859	Not known	6th May 1968	10th Aug 1964
Tillynaught Ballast Pit (7)	N/A	N/A		14th Jan 1888		Not known
Smiddyboyne LC	10½	N/A	Level Crossing			
Portsoy (first station)	12¾	60	30th Jul 1859		1st Apr 1884	6th May 1968
Portsoy Harbour Branch	N/A	N/A		c. 1860		c. 1885
Portsoy (second station)	12¾	60	1st Apr 1884		6th May 1968	
Glassaugh	14¾	103	1st Apr 1884		21st Sep 1953	20th Apr 1964
Tochieneal	17	125	1st Apr 1884		1st Oct 1951	20th Apr 1964
Gillyfurry Cutting Siding	18	N/A		14th Jan 1888		Not known
Cullen	18¼	123	1st May 1886	5th Apr 1886	6th May 1968	6th May 1968
Portknockie	20¼	146	1st May 1886	5th Apr 1886	6th May 1968	18th Jul 1966
Findochty	21½	136	1st May 1886	5th Apr 1886	6th May 1968	20th Apr 1964
Portessie	23	88	1st May 1886	5th Apr 1886	6th May 1968	20th Apr 1964
Buckie	24¼	28	1st May 1886	5th Apr 1886	6th May 1968	6th May 1968
Buckpool (8)	25¼	35	1st May 1886	5th Apr 1886	7th Mar 1960	7th Mar 1960
Portgordon	26¾	46	1st May 1886	5th Apr 1886	6th May 1968	20th Apr 1964
Spey Bay (9)	29	18	1st May 1886	5th Apr 1886	6th May 1968	20th Apr 1964
Garmouth	30¼	57	12th Aug 1884	12th Aug 1884	6th May 1968	20th Apr 1964
Garmouth Timber Siding (10)	31½	N/A		23rd Mar 1917		21st Jun 1921
Urquhart	33½	77	12th Aug 1884	12th Aug 1884	6th May 1968	20th Apr 1964
Meft Siding	34¼	N/A		14th Jan 1888		19th Jan 1888
Calcots	36	14	12th Aug 1884	12th Aug 1884	6th May 1968	20th Apr 1964
Lossie Junction (11)	38	63	Signal Box only			
Elgin (Great North)	39	36	11th Aug 1852	11th Aug 1852	6th May 1968	
Grange	0	320	11th Oct 1856	11th Oct 1856	6th May 1968	4th Dec 1961
Grange North Junction (3)	0¾	308	Signal Box only			
Tillynaught Junction	10¼	180	See above			
Ordens Halt (12)	11¾	N/A	1st Oct 1859		6th Jul 1964	
Blairshinnock LC	13¼	N/A	Level Crossing			
Ladysbridge (13)	13¾	80	1st Oct 1859	1st Oct 1959	6th Jul 1964	6th May 1968
Boyndie Siding (14)	14½	N/A		By 1867		Early 1960s
Bridgefoot Halt	15	N/A	1st Oct 1913		6th Jul 1964	
Golf Club House Halt (15)	15½	N/A	1st Oct 1913		6th Jul 1964	
Banff (Temporary) (16)	15½	N/A	30th Jul 1859	30th Jul 1859	1st May 1860	31st Mar 1860
Banff Links (17)	15¾	N/A	2nd Jun 1886		7th Jun 1886	
Banff Harbour (18)	16¼	22	1st May 1860	31st Mar 1860	6th Jul 1964	6th May 1968

1. Grange South Junction opened as a signal box only on 5th April 1886.
2. Cairnie Platform from 1st June 1898 until 1919 when renamed Cairnie Junction. It was an exchange platform only, no public access. Gained public status from 14th January 1965.
3. Grange North Junction Signal box opened 5th April 1886; closed 29th September 1968. Grange to Grange North closed 7th March 1960.

4. Points faced Down trains. Worked by tablet locking frame.
5. The original Knock station was situated 110 yards to the south of the road bridge. The new station opened on 20th December 1893.
6. Originally opened as Barry on 1st October 1859 and was closed in October 1863. Re-opened in 1870 on a slightly different site and was renamed Glenbarry on 19th February 1872.
7. 200 yards north of Tillynaught station house.
8. Originally called Nether Buckie. Buckpool from 1st January 1887.
9. Fochabers-On-Spey from 5th April 1886 to November 1893. Fochabers until 1st January 1916. Fochabers and Spey Bay until 1st January 1918. Spey Bay from 1st January 1918.
10. Points faced Down trains. Worked by tablet locking frame.
11. Lossie Junction signal box opened 12th Aug 1884; closed 29th Sep 1968.
12. Indication of early siding at Ordens, but no details known. Not advertised as a public station between October 1863 and 14th July 1924.
13. Lady's Bridge 1859 to 1886, Ladysbridge thereafter.
14. Served Inverboyndie Distillery. Tablet controlled ground frame. Signals introduced 22nd October 1888, altered 28th June 1933.
15. Golf Club House Halt was originally operated all year. By 1920 closed December to April inclusive. By 1960 closed October to April inclusive.
16. The temporary Banff terminus (when the line opened) is thought to have been situated near to where Golf Club House Halt was later built.
17. Temporary platform erected at Banff Links for Banff Artillery Volunteers (at their expense) to serve encampment from 2nd to 7th June 1886. The trackbed from Banff to Banff Links was used for the West Buchan Light Railway in the summers of 1984 and 1985.
18. "Harbour" was dropped from June 1928 and the station name became Banff.

The Manson auto tablet exchanger. The arm in the foreground is attached to the trackside equipment while the upper one is fixed to the locomotive. The tablets were held in the leather pouches.
(GNSRA collection)

Key token, as introduced by the LNER, for the section from Portknockie to Portessie. It is sitting on top of the leather pouch used for the exchange. (Graham Maxtone)

Tyer's No. 6 Tablet instrument as used by the GNS. Tablets are withdrawn and inserted via the slide at the bottom and held in a tube above the slide. (Graham Maxtone)

Appendix 2: Coast Line Signalling

The Great North was one of the earliest to apply block signalling to the control of trains. The Banffshire Railway used Telegraph Speaking Instruments and this was subsequently adopted for the Coast Line from 5th April 1886.

When the section from Portsoy to Tochieneal was opened on 1st April 1884 it was worked on the "one engine in steam" rule. From opening on 12th August 1884 the section from Elgin to Garmouth was signalled "....*by Tyer's Train Signalling Instruments between the following stations, in accordance with the Company's Regulations and Special Instructions: Elgin and Lossie Junction; Lossie Junction and Calcots; Calcots and Urquhart; Urquhart and Garmouth. Telegraph Single Needle Speaking Instruments will be put in....*" The Lossiemouth branch was also covered by the same procedures from this date.

On 20th July 1885 the Great North, anticipating completion of the new Coast Line, wrote to the Board of Trade: "*I may mention that the system under which the Company's single lines are worked is to have only one Engine in Steam or two or more engines coupled together upon the Single Line or portion thereof at one and the same time, and in addition to that the sections are worked by Tyer's Block Train Signal Instruments – the whole service being controlled from the Train Superintendent's office here [Aberdeen].*" After opening to freight on 5th April 1886 tablet stations were established at Portsoy, Tochieneal, Portknockie, Portessie, Buckie, Fochabers-on-Spey, Garmouth, Calcots and Lossie Junction. The Coast Line telegraph had, in addition to any block telegraph circuits, two circuits. One was for train messages and the other for all other messages.

Tablet working was introduced as follows:

	Introduction	Renewed
Grange to Grange North	27th Jan 1896	
Grange North to Tillynaught	Not known	31st Dec 1894
Tillynaught to Banff	14th Jan 1895	
Tillynaught to Portsoy	12th Jan 1894	
Portsoy to Tochieneal	1st Apr 1884	2nd Jan 1893
Tochieneal to Garmouth	5th Apr 1886	2nd Jan 1893
Garmouth to Lossie Junction	12th Aug 1884	2nd Jan 1893
Lossie Junction to Elgin East	2nd May 1904	

Due to the risk of injury to staff while manually exchanging tablets at stations, the Great North designed and developed the automatic tablet exchange apparatus which allowed the tablets to be exchanged while trains were moving. Following successful trials at Kittybrewster and then on the Buchan Line they were introduced on the Coast Line from 1889. By January 1893 five stations had the new apparatus and all were on the Coast Line: Tochieneal, Portknockie, Portessie, Calcots and Lossie Junction. Portessie and Lossie Junction were both restricted to receipt only from Down trains and delivery only to Up trains. By 1895 they were installed at all passing places on the line between Grange North Signal Box and Portessie with the exception of Portsoy. Initially the apparatus was not wholly reliable, but this was often due to improper use or to inadequate maintenance. As staff became more conversant with its use and confidence grew, tablet exchange at speeds of up to 50mph was regularly achieved. This allowed the acceleration of passenger services on the Great North system, including the Coast Line, and the system was adopted by other railway companies including the Highland Railway and the Glasgow & South Western Railway. The design and development of the apparatus is attributed to three Great North employees: James Manson (Locomotive Superintendent); Robert G. Sharp (Draughtsman); John Duncan (Blacksmith).

Shortly after Grouping the LNER moved from the original "tablet" system to the simpler "Key Token" system, as follows:

2nd October 1927: Grange to Grange North; Grange North to Knock; Knock to Glenbarry; Glenbarry to Tillynaught.

9th October 1927: Tillynaught to Portsoy; Portsoy to Tochieneal; Tochieneal to Portknockie; Portknockie to Portessie.

8th January 1928: Buckie to Spey Bay; Spey Bay to Calcots; Calcots to Lossie Junction; Lossie Junction to Elgin East.

Key Tokens were also introduced on 2nd October 1927 to access the sidings at Glenbarry and Cornhill; on 9th October 1927 at Glassaugh, Cullen, and Findochty; and on 8th January 1928 at Buckpool, Portgordon, Garmouth, and Urquhart.

A Long Section Token was introduced between Tillynaught and Tochieneal on 9th March 1936. The token for this section allowed access to the sidings at Portsoy via a ground frame until 24th January 1953 when the ground frame was removed and the points were operated from the signal box.

Signal Boxes

Signal Box	Opened	Closed	Levers
Grange South	5th Apr 1886	31st May 1898	
Cairnie Junction (1)	1st Jun 1898	29th Sep 1968	
Grange North (2)	5th Apr 1886	29th Sep 1968	
Grange (3)	17th Jan 1898	18th Mar 1963	
Knock (4)	20th Dec 1893	16th Sep 1928	
Glenbarry (5)	13th Jun 1887	25th Jun 1966	
Tillynaught S. (6)	4th Aug 1890	29th Sep 1968	35
Tillynaught North	18th Jul 1890	27th Aug 1933	(worked from South)
Banff (7)	3rd Dec 1900	29th May 1960	14 (+ 2 spaces)
Portsoy South (8)	1st Apr 1884	28th Aug 1959	11
Portsoy North	1st Apr 1884	9th Feb 1936	7 (worked from South)
Glassaugh (9)	1st Apr 1884	27th Oct 1896	9
Glassaugh (re-opened)	1st Jun 1898	14th Nov 1921	
Tochieneal South (10)	1st Apr 1884	24th Jul 1966	10
Tochieneal North	5th Apr 1886	27th Oct 1917	6 (worked from South)
Cullen (11)	5th Apr 1886	15th Jun 1896	9
Portknockie East (12)	5th Apr 1886	24th Jul 1966	10
Portknockie West	5th Apr 1886	29th May 1927	6 (worked from East)
Findochty (13)	5th Apr 1886	26th Oct 1896	9
Portessie	5th Apr 1886	29th Sep 1968	25
Buckie East	5th Apr 1886	30th Mar 1903	11
Buckie West	5th Apr 1886	30th Mar 1903	6
Buckie Station (14)	30th Mar 1903	29th Sep 1968	
Buckpool (15)	5th Apr 1886	14th Oct 1896	14
Portgordon (16)	5th Apr 1886	13th Oct 1896	9
Fochabers East (17)	5th Apr 1886	2nd Jan 1912	10
Fochabers West	5th Apr 1886	2nd Jan 1912	6 (worked from East)
Fochabers (Spey Bay)	19th Feb 1912	18th Jun 1966	
Garmouth East (18)	12th Aug 1884	14th Mar 1922	6
Garmouth West	12th Aug 1884	8th Jul 1917	11 (worked from East)
Urquhart (19)	12th Aug 1884	12th Oct 1896	10
Calcots East (20)	12th Aug 1884	29th Sep 1968	6
Calcots West	12th Aug 1884	27th Aug 1930	11 (worked from East)
Lossie Junction	12th Aug 1884	11th Jun 1966	9
Elgin East (21)	30th Apr 1888	15th Dec 1968	
Elgin West (22)	1st May 1888	11th Nov 1973	
Lossiemouth (23)	21st Sep 1896	26th Mar 1966	13

Notes

1. Cairnie Junction replaced Grange South Junction on 1st June 1898.
2. Grange North controlled the junction and the two adjacent wheel-operated level crossing gates. Signals altered on doubling of line from Cairnie Junction on 17th January 1898.
3. Grange station box opened for line doubling to Newmill (Keith) and included Coast arrangements. The spur to Grange North closed in 1960.
4. Replacement of older (original) Knock box on 20th December 1893 (date of opening unknown), with new station and sidings adjacent to new Knockdhu distillery. Crossing loop from 20th December 1893 to 16th September 1928 when loop removed, Down platform demolished and sidings accessed by tablet operated ground frame.
5. New crossing loop and signals were introduced along with the new box on 13th June 1887.
6. Tillynaught South (which carried a nameboard "Tillynaught South Cabin") was renamed Tillynaught Junction when Tillynaught North closed on 27th August 1933. Signalling alterations were made in June 1933 in preparation for this change. Long section token to Tochieneal introduced 9th March 1936.
7. Interlocking of signals and points from December 1900 brought Banff into line with the rest of the Coast Line in compliance with the Regulation of Railways Act 1889! "One Engine in Steam" and sidings accessed by tablet operated ground frame from May 1960.
8. Portsoy (and Calcots West) were the only two boxes on the Coast Line to have track-circuits outwith their respective Up home signals, as both had road bridges over the track which hid these areas from the signal boxes. From 9th March 1936 "switching out" was provided and the goods sidings could also be controlled by a ground frame operated by the long section token. Ground frame was removed on 24th January 1953 and the points became operational only from the signal box. The box was reduced to ground frame operation only on 29th June 1959 and was replaced by tablet operated ground frame on box closure on 28th August 1959. The Up loop became the single line.
9. Glassaugh loop removed and sidings accessed by tablet operated ground frame from 27th October 1896. New cabin with new crossing loop, interlocking signals and points from 1st June 1898. Unusually, the new box had a masonry base. From 14th November 1921 the Up loop line became the single line.
10. Tochieneal loop removed on 24th July 1966.
11. Sidings accessed by tablet operated ground frame on box closure on 15th June 1896.
12. Portknockie East was destroyed by fire in November 1892 and tablet working between Tochieneal and Portessie was suspended. Electric Block instruments brought into use between these stations. Portknockie loop and siding points (not interlocked with the signals) worked by hand until Locking Frame restored. A rebuilt box opened on 2nd January 1893 with new tablet instruments and interlocking points and signals.
13. Sidings accessed by tablet operated ground frame on box closure on 26th October 1896.

14. The new Buckie box was on the Up platform and had speaking instrument, block telegraph and tablet instruments. It cost £151 and replaced the East and West boxes as a cost cutting measure (reduction of staff). Electrically released ground frame controlled the west end of the station.

15. Sidings accessed by tablet operated ground frame on box closure on 14th October 1896.

16. Sidings accessed by tablet operated ground frame on box closure on 13th October 1896.

17. As a result of fire destroying Fochabers East box on 2nd January 1912 and the relaxation of the maximum distance manually operated points could be worked from a lever frame, a more central signal box midway along the Down platform replaced both East and West cabins on 19th February 1912. Fochabers West box remained in situ following closure (it is not known if it was put to alternative use) until the line closed in May 1968.

18. On box closure on 14th March 1922 the Garmouth Up loop became the single line and the sidings were accessed by a tablet operated ground frame. The box, footbridge, Down platform and Down track were removed.

19. Sidings accessed by tablet operated ground frame on box closure on 12th October 1896.

20. Calcots East was renamed Calcots on 27th August 1930. Destroyed by fire on 2nd March 1934. Rebuilt and operational from 22nd August 1934.

21. Elgin East's signalling was arranged to allow Coast Line and Glen Line trains to arrive and depart simultaneously.

22. Named Elgin West to 7th September 1934, thereafter Elgin Central. From box closure on 11th November 1973 the ground frames were released by the former Highland signal box. Box still standing in a dilapidated state in 2024; it is a listed structure.

23. Replacement of older Lossiemouth box on 21st September 1896, (date of opening unknown).

Additional Note: There were no passing loops at Cullen, Findochty, Portgordon and Urquhart. There were no passing loops or signal boxes at Cornhill and Ladysbridge where access to sidings was always by tablet operated ground frames. There is a map indication of an early siding at Ordens Halt on the Banff branch but for most of its life it was a single through line only. There were no sidings at Golf Club House Halt and Bridgefoot Halt. The various sidings between stations were accessed by tablet operated ground frames.

Classification of Coast Line Signal Boxes as at 20th September 1912

Second Class: Elgin East.
Fourth Class: Cairnie Junction; Grange; Tillynaught Junction.
Fifth Class: Lossie Junction; Banff; Portsoy; Portessie; Buckie.
Sixth Class: Knock; Glenbarry; Glassaugh; Tochieneal; Portknockie; Fochabers (Spey Bay); Garmouth; Calcots.

The hours of duty for First and Second Class boxes was 8 hours per day. Pay per week after 3 years' service: 29/- and 27/- respectively.

The hours of duty for Third and Fourth Class boxes was 10 hours per day, although Tillynaught Junction was an exception at 12 hours per day. Pay per week after 3 years' service: 25/- and 23/- respectively.

The hours of duty for Fifth and Sixth Class boxes was 12 hours per day. Pay per week after 3 years' service: 21/- and 20/- respectively.

All time worked between midnight on Saturday and midnight on Sunday was paid at time and a half. If an employee was called out for extra duty on a Sunday, half a days' wages were paid in addition to the hourly rate, irrespective of actual hours worked.

Ladysbridge ground frame was typical of those installed where a full signal box was not needed. Here there are two levers for the signals linked to the crossing gates.
(John Emslie)

Signal Box Types

Using the types defined by the Signalling Study Group with further distinctions: Type 1 was a hipped roof design with stone/brick to floor and vertical boarding above; Type 2a was to a much plainer design of all wooden construction with horizontal boarding and with gable roof; Type 2b was very similar apart from the roof which finished flush (rather than overhanging) the sides. Type 2 boxes were first constructed by the Great North on the Coast Line from 1884; Type 3a was a hipped roof, all wooden construction with horizontal boarding, not too dissimilar from Type 2a apart from the hipped roof and additional ornamentation. Fuller details can be found in the "Signalling" section of the GNSRA website.

Spey Bay West box in February 2003 before it moved to Dufftown. Standing next to it is Bob Robertson from the development company which bought the site.
(Northern Scot/Bob Robertson)

Type 1: Cairnie Junction, Portsoy South, Portsoy North, Glassaugh, Tochieneal South, Buckie East.

Type 2a: Grange (Station), Grange North, Glenbarry, Banff, Portknockie East, Cullen, Portessie (illustrated on page 48), Buckpool, Fochabers East, Garmouth East, Urquhart, Calcots East, Lossie Junction, Elgin East, Elgin West (Centre).

Type 2b: Knock, Tillynaught South (illustrated on page 44), Tillynaught North.

Type 3a: Buckie (station).

Unclassified: Tochieneal North, Findochty, Buckie West, Portgordon, Fochabers West, Garmouth West.

The Coast Line boasted four signal boxes of unusual design. These were at the west ends of Tochieneal, Portknockie, Buckie and Spey Bay stations. The boxes are square with hipped roof, horizontal weather boarding and nine-pane windows. There were three rows of weatherboarding below the windows and the structures sat on a stone base. The boxes date from the construction of the Coast Line in 1886. The Spey Bay box having survived since closure in 1912, was moved (allegedly by tipper lorry) in 1968 to a private house at Clochan near Portgordon where it was used as a garden summer house for about 35 years. On 13th February 2003 it was moved to the Keith & Dufftown Railway and restoration is imminent at the time of writing.

Type 1 signal box at Portsoy South on 19th July 1938. (J L Stevenson collection)

Appendix 2: Coast Line Signalling 117

Signal Box Diagrams

Drawn by Robert Dey based on files in The National Archives, Kew. The date is when the file was completed.

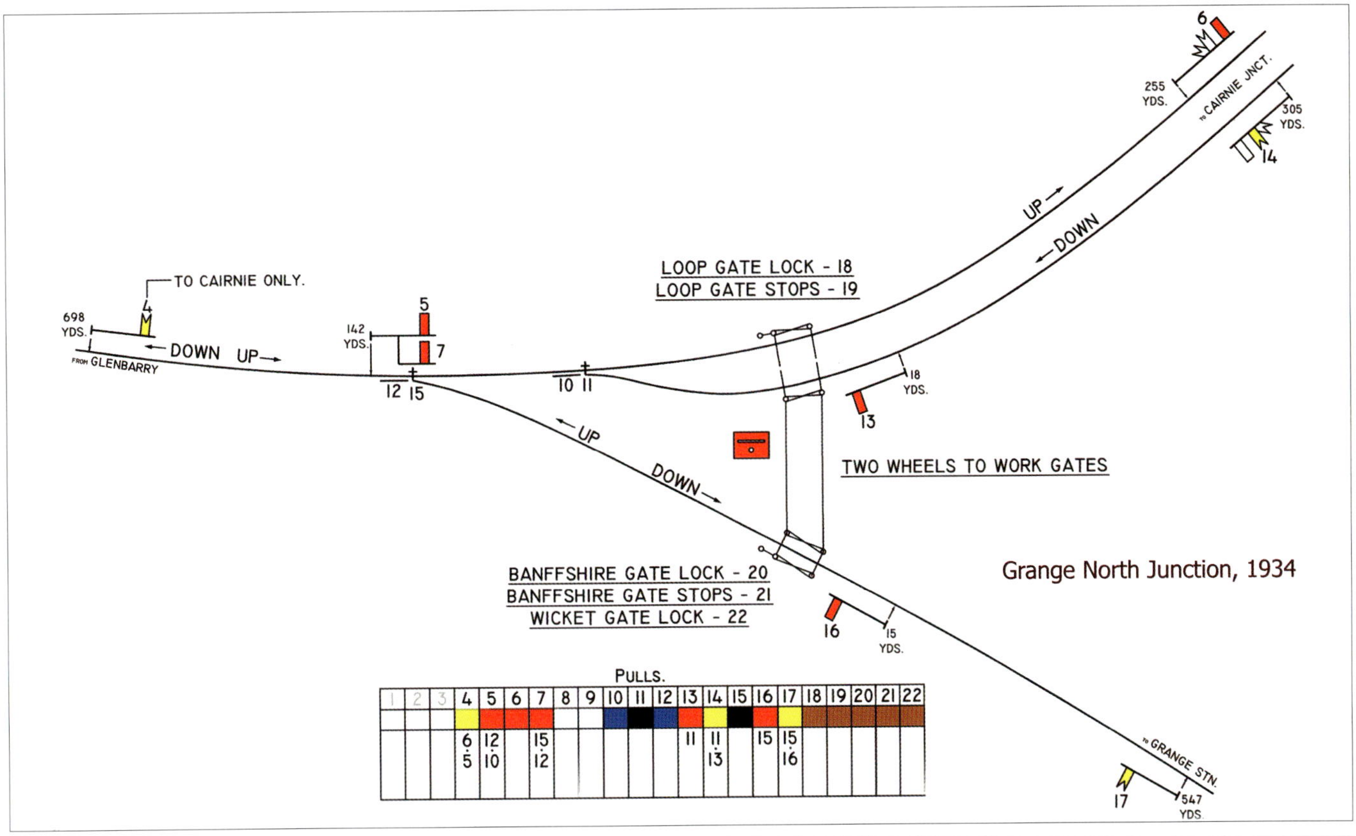

Grange North Junction, 1934

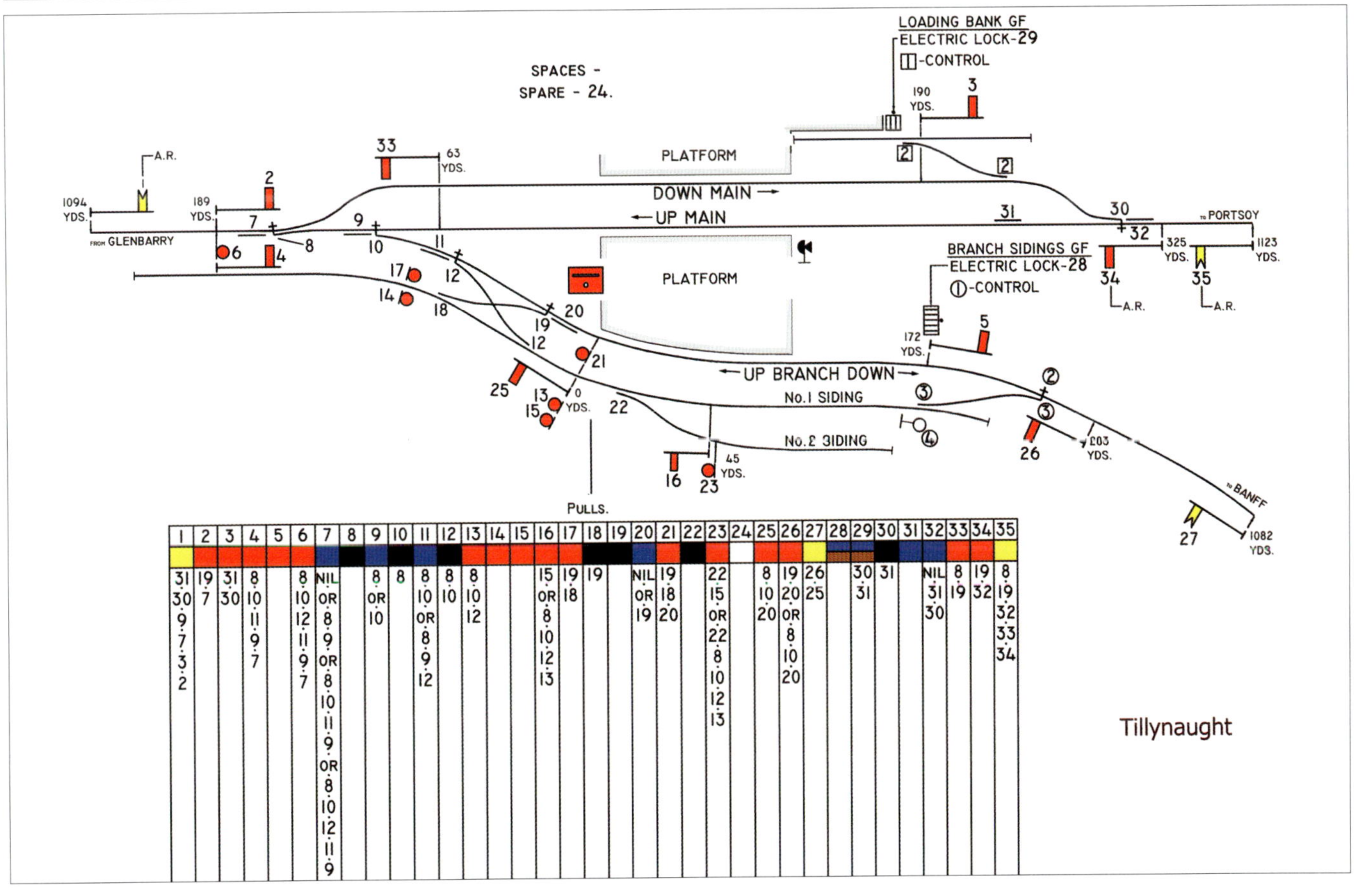

	1	2	3	4	5	6	7	8	9	10	11	12	13	14	15	16	17	18	19	20	21	22
Pulls																						
					6 5	12 10	15 12							11 13	11	15 16	15					

Tillynaught

1	2	3	4	5	6	7	8	9	10	11	12	13	14	15	16	17	18	19	20	21	22	23	24	25	26	27	28	29	30	31	32	33	34	35
31 30 9 7 3 2	19 7	31 30	8 10 11 9 7	8 10 12 11 9 7	NIL 10 OR 8 9 OR 8 10 11 9 OR 8 10 12 11 9	8 OR 10	8	8 10 OR 8 9 12	8 10	8 10 12			15 OR 8 10 12 13	19 18	19	NIL OR 19 20	19 18 20	22 15 OR 22 8 10 12 13		8 10 OR 20	19 20 OR 8 10 20	26 25		30 31	31	NIL 31 30	8 19	19 32	8 19 32 33 34

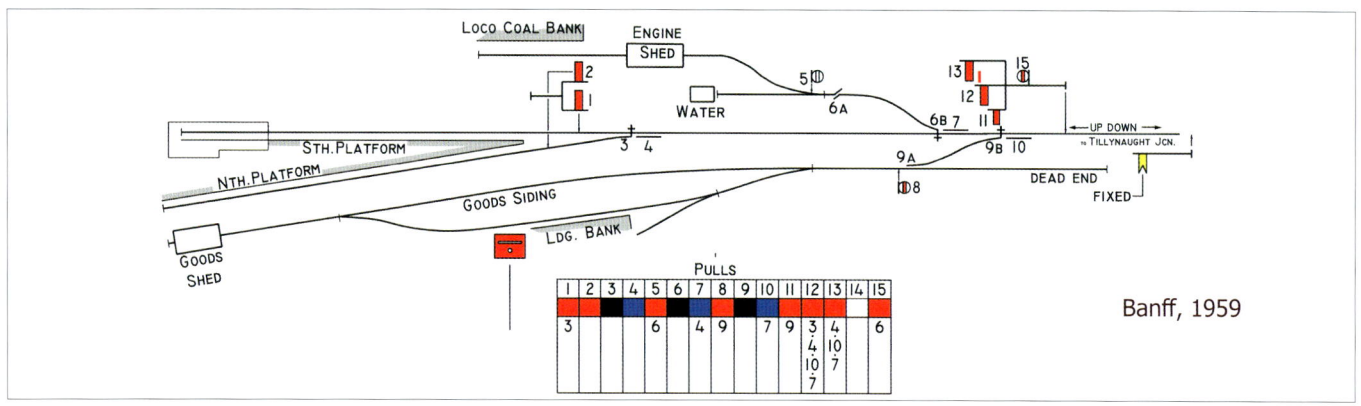

Banff, 1959

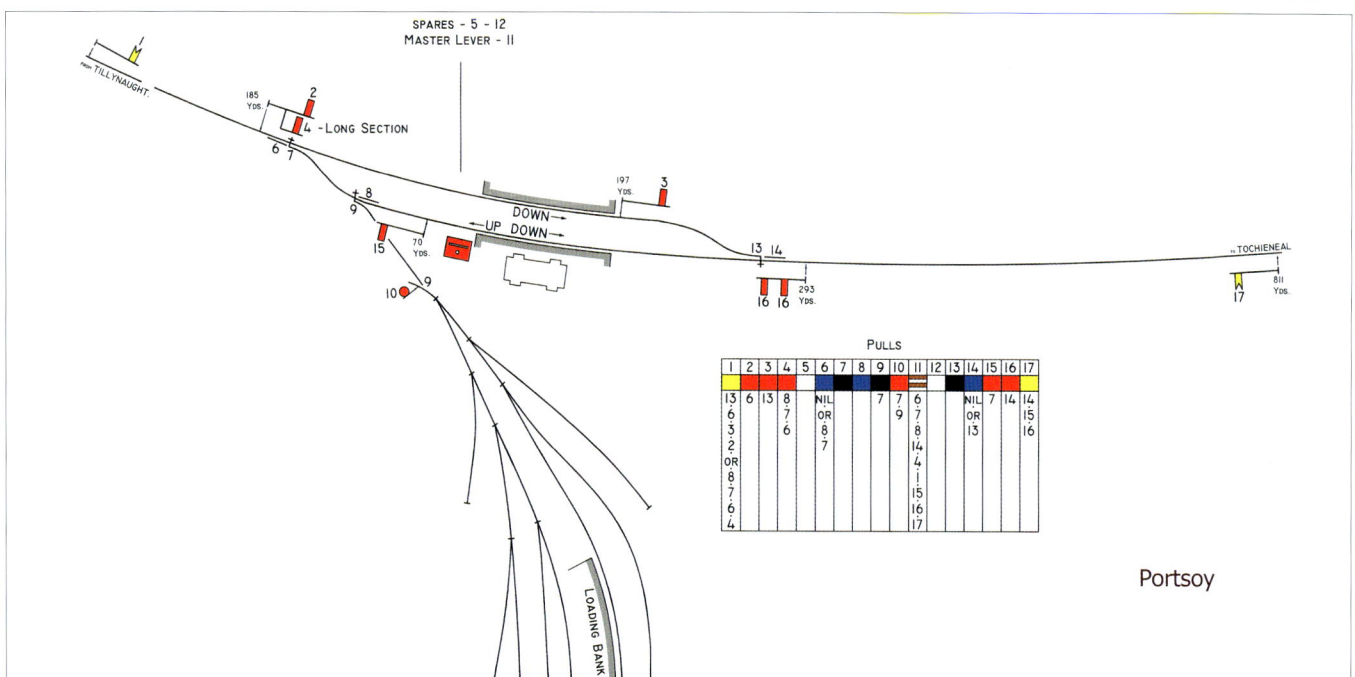

Portsoy

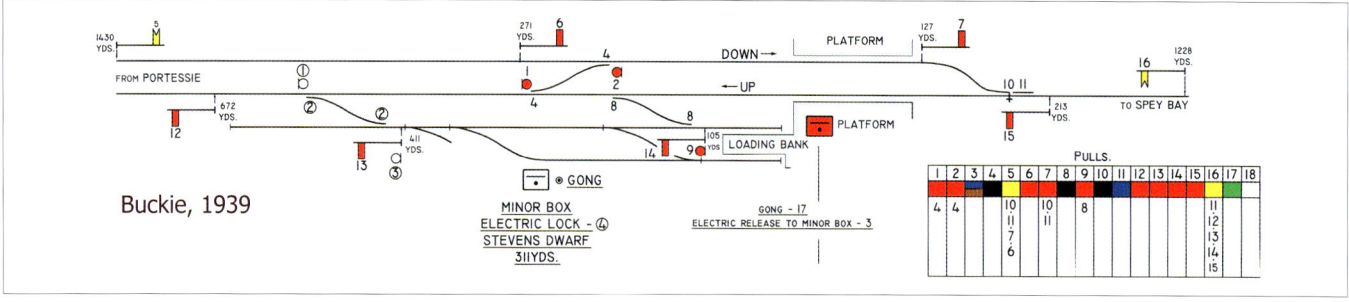

Buckie, 1939

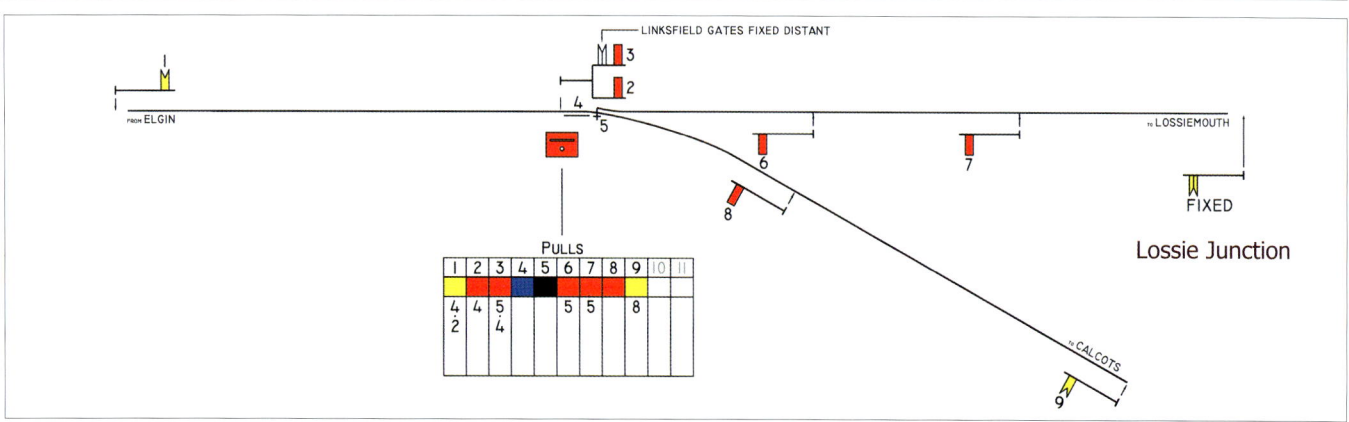

Lossie Junction

Appendix 3: Coast Line Operations

Locomotive Watering Facilities 1916
There were locomotive watering facilities at the following stations:
  Glenbarry: Tank west end of Down platform; column east end of Up platform.
  Banff: Tank north end of engine shed (engines can water from either side).
  Portsoy: Tank (small) west end of Down platform.
  Tochieneal: Tank (small) east end of Up platform.
  Buckie: Tank west end of Down platform; column east end of Up platform.
  Elgin: Tank between turntable and engine shed (engines can water from either side).

Turntables 1887 - 1928
There were engine turntables of various lengths at the following stations recorded on the dates shown:
  Banff: 1887 – 1902: 22 feet.
  Portsoy: 1894 – 1902: 22 feet.
  Elgin: 1887 – 1890: 44 feet 11 ins.; 1891 – 1922: 50 feet; 1928: 50 feet 10 ins.
  Portessie (Highland): 1908, 1916, 1922: 45 feet (Great North locomotives permitted to use).

Station Staff 1903
The Great North undertook an economic review of its branch lines in 1903 (based on the year to 31st July 1903). As the Coast Line was not a "branch" it was not included, but the line from Tillynaught to Banff was reviewed and the following staffing levels at Banff and Ladysbridge recorded. These give an indication of the staff at the Coast Line stations. Branch revenue was also included.

Station Staffs

Banff	Cost	Ladysbridge	Cost
1 station master	£73 15/1d	1 station master	£60 7/8d
1 goods clerk	£56 15/6d	1 clerk	£15 0/-
1 passenger clerk	£24 19/7d	1 porter	£44 5/-
1 platform porter	£49 2/8d	1 cleaner	£2 12/-
1 foreman goods porter	£47 19/5d	1 gate keeper (Blairshinnoch)	£26 0/-
2 porters	£86 15/-	1 gate keeper (Boyndie)	£18 14/-
1 office cleaner	£6 10/-	Total	£166 18/8d
1 signalman	£52 0/-		
1 guard	£66 6/-		
Total	£464 3/3d		

Revenue Banff to Tillynaught in 1903

Passengers	Single	Return	Total	Journeys	Value
Banff to Ladysbridge and Tillynaught	6,085	1,840	7,925	9,765	£162.12.5d
Ladysbridge to Banff and Tillynaught	3,640	1,836	5,476	7,312	£77.19.10d
Tillynaught to Ladysbridge and Banff	2,353	1,713	4,066	5,779	£127.14.4d
Banff to stations beyond Tillynaught	19,623	15,118	34,741	49,859	£1,044.17.8d
Ladysbridge to stations beyond Tillynaught	5,400	7,676	13,076	20,752	£257.7.8d
Total	37,101	28,183	65,284	93,467	£1,670.11.11d
Plus					
Season Tickets: Local 81 x 52 weeks				4,212	£16.4.9d
Beyond Tillynaught				2,000	£7.16.0d
Parcels (mails not included)					£93.0.0d
Freight					£1,351.6.0d

In comparison to the Great North's other branches (Alford, Cruden, Lossiemouth, Macduff, Oldmeldrum, Strathspey and St. Combs) in 1903, the Banff branch was second worst only to the Cruden Bay line with net receipts of 2.82d per train mile (Cruden 2.20d). At the other end of the scale the Alford branch returned 22.24d per train mile. This demonstrates just how much of a branch the Tillynaught to Banff section had become since the Coast Line was opened on 1st May 1886.

Station Facilities

From 1925 Railway Clearing House Handbook of Stations.

G: Goods; P: Passenger & Parcels; P*: Passengers Only (not parcels nor miscellaneous traffic); F: Furniture, Vans, Carriages, Portable Engines, Machines on Wheels; L: Livestock; H: Horse Boxes & Prize Cattle Vans; C: Carriages by Passenger Train.

	Crane Capacity		
	Tons	Cwt	
Cairnie Junction: P*	None		
Grange: GPLH	1	10	
Knock: GPLH	1	10	(removed by 1956)
Glenbarry: GPLH	None		
Cornhill: GPLH	1	5	(removed by 1956)
Tillynaught: GPLH	None		
Ordens Platform: P*	None		
Ladysbridge: GPLH	2	0	
Banff: GPFLHC	5	0	(originally 2 tons 10 cwt.)
Portsoy: GPFLHC	4	0	
Glassaugh: GPFLHC	1	5	(removed by 1956)
Tochieneal: GPFLHC	1	5	(removed by 1956)
Cullen: GPFLHC	1	5	(1 ton 10 cwt by 1956)
Portknockie: GPLH	2	0	(removed by 1956)
Findochty: GPLH	3	0	(removed by 1956)
Portessie: GPLHC	1	5	(removed by 1956)
Buckie: GPFLHC	4	0	
Buckie (HR): GPFLHC	4	0	
Buckpool: GPFLHC	3	0	(removed by 1956)
Portgordon: GPFLHC	1	5	
Spey Bay: GPFLHC	1	5	
Garmouth: GPFLHC	1	10	(originally 2 tons)
Urquhart: GPFLHC	1	5	
Calcots: GPFLHC	1	5	(removed by 1956)
Elgin East: GPFLHC	5	0	

Coast Mail Train Timetables

The Aberdeen – Elgin mail train (Monday – Saturday) via the Coast called at Inverurie, Inveramsay, Insch, Gartly (from 1897) and Huntly on the main line. The following timetable shows Coast stations only.

Station	Jun 1888	Mar 1891	Sep 1895	Apr 1897
Aberdeen	10.10	09.30	09.30	07.55
Grange South	11.35	10.55	10.55	09.20
Tillynaught	11.55	11.15	11.15	09.30
Portsoy	12.00	11.20	11.20	09.44
Cullen	12.10	11.30	11.30	09.54
Buckie (1)	12.25	11.45	11.45	10.04
Fochabers	12.33	11.53	11.53	
Garmouth	12.37	11.57	11.57	10.15
Elgin East (Arr) (1)	12.52	12.12	12.12	10.32

Station	Jun 1888	Mar 1891	Sep 1895	Apr 1897
Elgin East (1)	1.35	2.25	2.50	2.50
Garmouth	1.50	2.40	3.03	3.03
Fochabers	1.52	2.42	2.42	
Buckie (1)	2.00	2.52	3.13	3.13
Cullen	2.11	3.03	3.23	3.23
Portsoy	2.21	3.13	3.31	3.31
Tillynaught	2.29	3.20	3.37	3.37
Grange South	2.51	3.44	3.55	3.55
Aberdeen (Arr)	4.20	5.15	5.10	5.10

Note 1: From the 1888 timings the longer turnround at Buckie afforded the two postal sorters a break of 1 hour 35 minutes as opposed to the alternative of only 43 minutes at Elgin. When the sorters worked right through to Elgin from 1896 a seven hour working day was extended to ten hours.

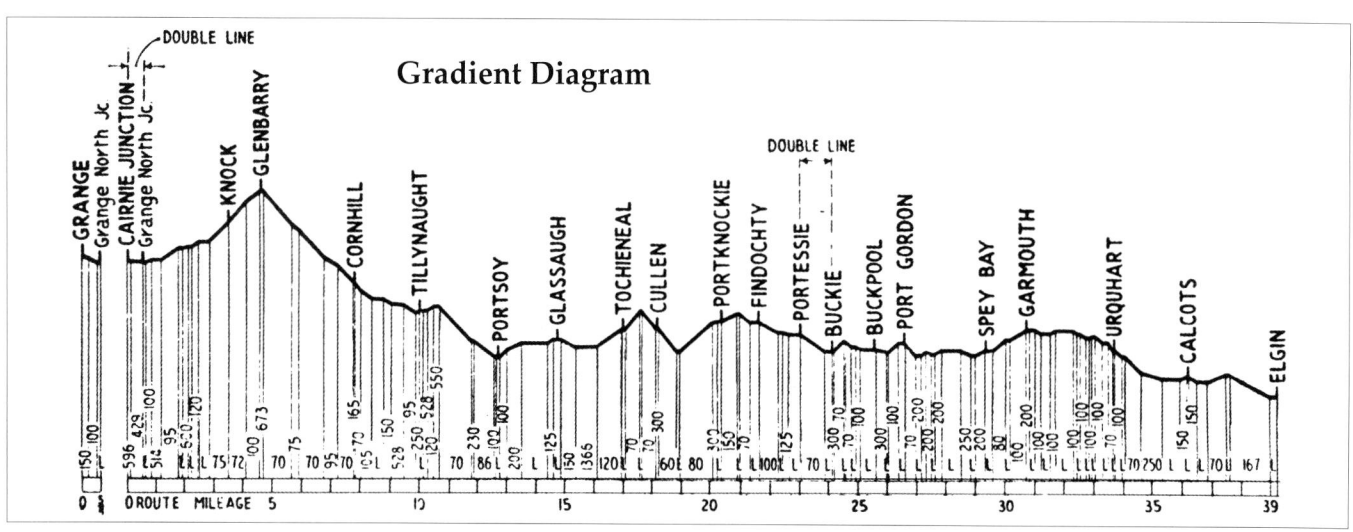

Gradient Diagram

Working Timetable, 1947

The last published by the LNER. See overleaf for the Coast Line.

WEEKDAYS — DOWN TRAINS—TILLYNAUGHT TO BANFF

M.C.	No.	2	3	4	5		6	7	8	9	10	11
	Description	OP	LE	OP	OP		OP	OP	OP	OP		OP
	Class	Mixd.		Mixd.			Mixd.				D	
	Departs from											
	Previous Times on Page											
					SO						Q	SO
		am	am	am	am		PM	PM	PM	PM	PM	PM
	Tillynaught ......⊕......	7 35	9 15	10 40	11 58	....	1 45	3 28	4 52	6 10	7 30	9 5
1 46	Ordens Halt	*		*	*		*	*	*	*	*	*
3 45	Ladysbridge	7 50	....	10N50	12 4	....	1 f51	3 43	4 58	6 16	7 50	9 11
4 56	*Boyndie Siding*											
4 70	Bridgefoot Halt	*		*	*		*	*	*	*	*	*
5 25	Golf Club House Halt	*		*	*		*	*	*	*	*	*
6 1	Banff ......⊕......	8 0	9 27	11 0	12 13	....	2 f0	3 53	5 7	6 25	8 5	9 20

No. 2—Goods portion not to exceed 10 vehicles.
No. 4—N Wagons for Ladysbridge to be worked via Banff for No. 6 Up. Goods portion not to exceed 10 vehicles.
No. 5—Will lift whisky traffic from Boyndie Siding when required and run as OP Mixed, Tillynaught to Banff, due at 12.20 p.m. (not advertised).
No. 6—f Calls at Boyndie Level Crossing when required to put off Water Barrels, and when such done will be due to leave Ladysbridge 1.52 p.m. and arrive Banff 2.3 p.m. Not advertised.
No. 7—Goods portion not to exceed 10 Vehicles.

WEEKDAYS — UP TRAINS—BANFF TO TILLYNAUGHT

M.C.	No.	2	3	4	5		6	7	8	9	10	11
	Description	OP		OP	OP		OP	OP	OP	OP	Fish	OP
	Class		D				Mixd.				No. 1 Exp.	
	Departs from											
	Previous Times on Page											
					SO						Q	SO
		am	am	am	am		PM	PM	PM	PM	PM	PM
	Banff ......⊕......	6 55	8 30	9 55	11 30	....	1 0	2 45	4 15	5 35	6 40	8 30
0 56	Golf Club House Halt	*		*	*		*	*	*	*		*
1 11	Bridgefoot Halt	*		*	*		*	*	*	*		*
1 25	*Boyndie Siding*											
2 36	Ladysbridge	7 2	8 50	10 2	11 37	....	1 16	2 52	4 22	5 42	7 0	8 37
4 35	Ordens Halt	*		*	*		*	*	*	*		*
6 1	Tillynaught ......⊕......	7 11	9 5	10 11	11 46	....	1 28	3 1	4 31	5 51	7 15	8 46

No. 3—Calls at Blairshinnoch Level Crossing when required to put off Water Barrels.
No. 6—Goods portion not to exceed 12 Vehicles.
Nos. 4, 7 and 8—Will be due Tillynaught 5 minutes later when fish traffic lifted at Ladysbridge. Not advertised.
No. 10—When not run Engine will be used to marshal No. 3 Up.

DOWN TRAINS—KEITH TO ELGIN, via Buckie — WEEKDAYS

No.	1	256	567	245	21	551	22	246	247	1a	27
Description		OP		OP	OP		OP	OP	Fish No. I Exp.	LE	OP
Class	D		D			D					
Departs from	Keith 4.10 a.m. EBV			Lossiemouth 8.45 a.m.	Keith Town 9.2 a.m.	Lossiemouth 10.30 a.m.	Aberdeen 8.5 a.m.	Lossiemouth 11.55 a.m.	Lossiemouth 12.20 p.m.		Aberdeen 9.30 a.m.
Previous Times on Page	14			32	16	32	6	32	32		7

Distance from Aberdeen M.C.	Station		am	am	am	am	am	am	PM	PM	PM	am
48 15	Keith	1		6 50	5 40							11 30
	Grange	2		6 58	5 50							11 31
	Grange	3		6 59	6 0							11 36
	Cairnie Junction	4	5 10		6 3		9 15		9 42			11 40
	Cairnie Junction	5			6 15				9 48			11 46
49 0	Grange North Junction	6	5 12	7 6	7 17				9 52			11 50
51 55	Knock	7			7**37				9 58			11 58
52 79	Glenbarry	8	5 26	7 10	7W44				10 2			12 3
56 7	Glenbarry	9		7 16		8T0						
58 26	Cornhill	10	5 38	7 20	8 17				10 4			12 7
	Tillynaught Junction	11										
61 0	Tillynaught Junction	12	5 50	7 24	8 27				10 8			12T16
	Portsoy	13		7 29	8**36				10 13			12 20
	Portsoy	14	6 5	7 29	8 42				10 17			12 23
63 9	Glassaugh	15		7 34	8 57				10 22			12 27
65 26	Tochieneal	16		7 40	9T1				10 26			
	Tochieneal	17		7 45	9 15				10 31			
66 44	Cullen	18	6 30	7 50	9 35				10 35			
68 52	Portknockie	19	6 38	7 55	9 58				10 39			12T16
	Portknockie	20	6 55						10 42			12 20
69 78	Findochty	21	7 10	7 59	10 10				10 44			12 24
71 34	Portessie	22			10 20				10 48			12 27
	Portessie	23		7 30	10 25				10 52			
72 50	Buckie	24		8T4					10 57			
73 56	Buckie	25	8 26	8 6		8 54		10 46	11 8			
75 8	Buckpool	26	8 40	8T10				10 50	11 14		12 40	12T29
77 41	Portgordon	27	8 58	8 14					11 18			12 33
	Spey Bay	28	9 4						11 21		12 47	12 39
	Spey Bay	29	9W30	8 19						4 12		12 43
78 60	Garmouth	30	9 38	8T27			10 57					12T47
82 20	Urquhart	31	9 56	8 30			11 8					12 54
84 32	Calcots	32	10 15	8B36			11 14			4 29		1 0
	Calcots	33	10 21	8B40			11 18				12 50	
86 20	Lossie Junction	34	10 21				11 21			4 12	12 50	1 7
87 36	Elgin	35	10 25	8845		8 57	11 25					

| Arrives at | | | | | | | | | | | |

Forward Times on Page

No. 1—▼SX Enginemen only with 6.50 a.m. OP, Keith to Elgin. SO—▼Enginemen only with 6.10 a.m. Goods, Elgin to Keith. ‡—When 9.20 a.m. LE Q, Elgin to Buckie, runs, will be retimed Spey Bay dep. 9.38 a.m. and run 8 minutes later to Elgin.
No. 1a—Engine off 5.40 a.m. ex Keith.
No. 27—▼Guard only with 11.55 a.m. Goods ex Buckie. P Buckie to Elgin. Engine off 5.40 a.m. ex Keith.
No. 256—▼SX At Buckie Enginemen only with 5.10 a.m. Goods, Cairnie Jct. to Elgin SO At Portessie, Enginemen only with 6.10 a.m. Goods, Elgin to Keith. ▼At Tochieneal with 6.10 a.m. Goods, Elgin to Keith. At Buckie SX with Trainmen
No. 567—** Van Goods only. ▼At Tochieneal with 6.10 a.m. Goods, Elgin to Keith. B—2 minutes recovery time. Passengers by 9.5 a.m. OP, Keith to Elgin.

DOWN TRAINS—KEITH TO ELGIN, via Buckie — WEEKDAYS

No.	248	2	568	257	258	258	552	48	249	3	4	259	80	252	214	214	5
Description	OP	LE	OP	EBV	OP	OP		EP	OP			OP	OP	OP	EP	EP	ECS
Class		Q		ThO Q	FX	FO	D			D	D						
Departs from	Lossiemouth 1.46 p.m.			Keith 12 noon	Keith Town 12.57 p.m.	Keith Town 12.57 p.m.	Lossiemouth 4.15 p.m.	Aberdeen 2.15 p.m.	Lossiemouth 5.33 p.m.	Keith 12 noon EBV		Keith Town 5.15 p.m.	Keith Town 8.12 p.m.	Lossiemouth 8.20 p.m.	Aberdeen 7.15 p.m.	Aberdeen 7.15 p.m.	
Previous Times on Page	32			17	19	19	32	9	32	17		22	25	32	SX	SO	

		PM	PM	PM	PM	PM	PM	PM	PM	PM	PM	PM	PM	PM	PM	PM	PM
1	Keith			10Q50	4 12	1 2	1 2		3 50			5 20					
2	Grange			10 58	4 17	1 7	1 7		3 51	1 20		5 28			8 37		
3	Grange			11 7	4/2d/5	1 10	1 10		3 57			5d37					
4	Cairnie Junction		12 2	11 2													
5	Cairnie Junction		12 12	12 22		1 17	1 17		4 6					8 25			
6	Grange North Junction		12 10	12 30		1 21	1 21		4 13	1 40		5 44			8 44	8 37	
7	Knock		12 21	12 36		1 28	1 28		4 18	1 48		5 49			8 46	8 49	
8	Glenbarry			12 36		12 36											
9	Glenbarry		12 36	12 47					4 22	1 52		5 56			8 54	8 57	
10	Cornhill											6 0					
11	Tillynaught Junction		12 55	1 18						2 10							
12	Tillynaught Junction		12 46	1 37	1s37	1 37			4	2 20		6 3			8 55	8 58	
13	Portsoy		12 52		1T2	1T2			4 12	2 30		6 9			9 0	9 3 9 25	
14	Portsoy		1 28		1 43	1 43			4 15	2 42		6 15					
15	Glassaugh				1 48	1 48				2 55							
16	Tochieneal		1 35		1 52	1 52			4 22	3 17		6 19				9 8	
17	Tochieneal				1 56	1 56			4 25	3 28		6 24				9T12	
18	Cullen		1 42		2 2	2 2			4 31	3 35		6 30			9 9	9 14 9 17	9 40
19	Portknockie				2 6	2 6			4 35	3 40		6 34			9 14 9 17	9 18 9 21	
20	Portknockie				2 10	2 10			4 35			6 37			9 18 9 21		
21	Findochty		1 52		2 11	2 11			4 39	4 0							
22	Portessie				2 14	2 14			4 42	4T2		6 39			9 23	9 26	
23	Portessie									4T20		6 42					
24	Buckie				2 16	2 16			4 44	5d 0 5 45		6 45			9 24	9 27 9 48	
25	Buckie				2s22	2 22			4 48	5 59		6 49			9 30	9 33	
26	Buckpool				2 26	2 26			4 52	5 20 6 14		6 54			9 35	9 38 9 58	
27	Portgordon				2 31	2 31			4 57	5 30 6 20		7 0			9 39	9 39 9 42	
28	Spey Bay				2 38	2 38			5 1	6 37		7 4					
29	Spey Bay				2T45	2T49			5 14	**		7 12					
30	Garmouth				2 51	2 55			5 15			7B18			9 52 9 55	9 55 9 56	
31	Urquhart		1 55		2 55	2 59			5 19	5 56 6 13	7 1		8 29		9 53		
32	Calcots		1 58		2 58	3 2			5 23	4T22	7 6						
33	Calcots																
34	Lossie Junction																
35	Elgin				2 58	3 2			5 23		7 11	7B27	8 32	10 15		0 0 11	3 0 10 15

No. 2—Engine and Guard off 10.32 a.m. Fish ex Buckie. No. 4—No. 3 retired, Buckie to Elgin.
No. 3—** LS at Buckpool, also when time permits will put off traffic at Buckpool, Portgordon, Garmouth and Urquhart. s LS Will work wagons, Cornhill to Tillynaught, for Up Trains. f Will detach at Findochty, but must arrive Portessie by 4.0 p.m. ▼ With 12.30 p.m. Goods, Elgin to Keith. g Th O on arrival makes trip to Buckpool with Live Stock when necessary. d May be detained at Buckie, if necessary, and run as No. 4 to convey Passenger rated Fish traffic for Glasgow, from Buckie to Elgin.
No. 257—d Engine tender first and coupled to No. 33 Up, Keith to Grange. Works LS, Cornhill to Tillynaught. If required will work Empty Cattle Trucks, Glenbarry to Cornhill.
No. 258—s LS, MO. Lifts not more than 4 fitted trucks (ex Banff), Tillynaught to Buckpool.
No. 259—d Advertised to leave at 5.28 p.m. B—2 minutes recovery time.
No. 568—d Engine tender first from Cairnie Jct. s LS—Will work wagons, Cornhill to Tillynaught for Up Trains. f Engine and Guard to work from Portsoy to Control orders.

Appendix 3: Coast Line Operations

UP TRAINS—ELGIN TO KEITH, via Buckie — WEEKDAYS

Distance from Elgin M.C.	No.	2	221	541	2	222	223‡	225	3	542	226‡	227	543‡
	Description						No. 1 Exp.				No. 1 Exp.		
	Class	LE	OP	D	LE	OP Mxd.	Fish	EP	LE	D	Fish	OP	D
	Departs from												
	Previous Times on Page												
		am	am	am	am	am	am	am	am	am	am	am	am
—	Elgin	5 40	5 55	6 10		7 30	8 45	9 10			10 32	11*28	11 25
1 16	Lossie Junction	5 5	5 57	6 14		7 32			9 22	9 30	10 36		
3 4	Calcots	5 6	6 1	6 22		7 36	8 49	9 16	9 24	9 34	10 39		12*2
5 36	Urquhart		6 8	6 29			8 57	9 23	9 28		10 47		12*9
8 56	Garmouth		6 14	6 35		7 0	9 2	9 27			10 52		12 25
9 75	Spey Bay	5 26	6 19	7 5		7 5	9 7	9 32	9 38				12 37
12 28	Porgordon		6 25	**		7 15	9 18 10	10 6	9 47				12 47
13 60	Buckpool		6 29	7 38	7 55	7 46	9 23	10 12			11 0		1 0
14 66	Buckie	6 5	6 32				9 30	10 20			11 13		2 5
	Buckie		6 35	7 56			9 35 10 26				11 25		2 30
16 2	Portessie		6 39	8 0			9 50 10 32				11 39		s
17 38	Portessie		6 44	8 12			9 53 10 40				11 41		3 10
18 64	Findochty		6 47	8 22			10 32				11 49		3s20
20 72	Porknockie		6 49	8 27			10 47				11 f51		
22 10	Cullen		6 54	8 38			10 49						
	Tochieneal		6 59	8 50			10 3						
24 27	Glassaugh		7 4	9 24			9 18 10 12						2 15
26 36	Portsoy		7 9	9 33			10 14						
29 10	Tillynaught Junction		7 11	9 40			10 18						3 28
	Tillynaught Junction		7 17	10 40			10 30						3 51
31 29	Cornhill		7 21	11 56			9 50						
34 37	Glenbarry		7W35	12 34			9 53						
35 61	Glenbarry		7 39	12 43			10 47						
38 41	Knock		7 43	12 55			10 49						
29 30	Grange North Junction		7 49 8 0										
39 21	Cairnie Junction		8 3	1 3									
32	Cairnie Junction		8 12	1 10									
39 30	Grange												3 28
43 53	Grange / Keith			1 20									4 0
	Arrives at		Keith Town 8.15 a.m.			Lossiemouth 7.55 a.m.	Aberdeen 11.22 a.m.	Aberdeen 12.21 p.m.	Lossiemouth 9.50 a.m.		Aberdeen 1.11 p.m.	Lossiemouth 11.37 a.m.	
	Forward Times on Page	15	5			32	16	17	32	32	18	32	

No. 1—Engine to shunt at Buckie and work 11.55 a.m. Goods, Buckie to Keith.
No. 2—Works No. 223 Up to Aberdeen.
No. 3—Engine to work 10.32 a.m. Fish Train.
No. 226—f Engine and Guard thence to Buckie at 12.2 p.m. No. 227—* To set down Stationmaster when required.
No. 541—d When working permits runs EBV to Cornhill with and for wagons as required. ** Urgent Traffic only. ᵞSX At Tochieneal with 5.40 a.m. Goods, Keith to Buckie. SO—At Buckie, Enginemen only with 5.10 a.m. Goods, Cairnie Jct. to Elgin. At Portessie, Enginemen only with 6.55 a.m. OP, Keith to Elgin. At Portknockie with 4.45 a.m. Q Goods or at Tochieneal with 5.40 a.m. Goods, Keith to Buckie.
No. 543 SO-SX—* Van Goods only. d—Calls Smiddyboyne Level Crossing when required to set down Portsoy Stationmaster. s—LS also Urgent and Perishable traffic. Stationmasters to advise Tillynaught.

UP TRAINS—ELGIN TO KEITH, via Buckie — WEEKDAYS

No.	543‡	228	544	247‡	229	4	231‡	232‡	233	545‡	234	235	238	240	241	242	243
Description				No. 1 Exp.			Inverness LMS 12.45 p.m.	Inverness LMS 12.45 p.m.		Huntly							
Class		OP	D	Fish	OP	LE	EP	EP	OP	Mixed B	OP	OP	OP	EP	EP	OP	OP
	SO am	SO PM	SX PM	PM	PM	SX PM	PM	FO PM	Th O PM	PM	PM	PM	SX PM	SO PM	SO PM	PM	
Elgin	11 55	12 18	12 30	12*48	1 16	1 45	2 16	2 16	2 30		3 20	5 8	6 5	7 48	7 48	8 10	7 55
Lossie Junction	12* 2	12 20	12 34	12*51	1 19		2 18	2 18	2*34		3 22	5 11	6 7	7 50	7 50	8 13	7 58
Calcots	12* 2	12 24	12 42	12*56			2 22	2 22			3 26		6 11	8 1	7 55	8 17	
Calcots	12 9	12 30	12 48	1d 2		1 52		2 26			3 32		6f19	8 3	8 1	8 23	
Urquhart	12 14	12 36	1 18	1d18			2 29	2 33			3 39		6 25		8 6	8 30	
Garmouth	12 25	12 41	1 23				2 33	2 37			3 42		6 29	8 4	8 11	8 35	
Spey Bay	12 37	12 43	1 28								3 48		6 34	8 9	8 13	8 40	
Spey Bay		12 48	1 38	1d28		2 10	2 40	2 44			3 52		6 38	8 13	8 15	8 45	
Porgordon	12 47	12 52	1 53								3 55		6f41				
Buckpool	1 10	12 55	1 58										6 45				
Buckie				2 55			2 47	2 49			3 58		6 49		8 17	8 46	
Buckie	1d55	12*57		2 59			2 50	2 52			4 7		6 53	8 23	8 23	8 52	
Portessie	1Y27	1 4 9	4Y 4														
Portessie	2 5	1 13	4 22	3 7			2 54	2 56			4 11		6 57	8 28	8 28	8 57	
Findochty		1 14	4 28				3 0	3 2			4 16		7 3	8 34	8 34	9 7	
Porknockie		1 18	5 0					3 6			4 20					9 9	
Cullen	12 37	1 25	5 13	3 15			3 4				4Y22		7 10	8 44	8 44	9 16	
Tochieneal		1 28	5 33	3 23							4 26			8 46	8 46		
Glassaugh		1 42	5 48	3 28			3 10	3 12			4 32		7 15	8 48	8 48		
Portsoy	2 15	1 36	6 2	3 35			3 16	3 18			4 38		7 21	8 52	8 52		
Tillynaught Junction	2 50	1W50	6 27	3 40			3 24	3 24		4Y 8	4 42		7 24	8 55	8 58		
Tillynaught Junction	3s 0	1 55	5 10							4S25	4 48		7 30				
Cornhill	3 8	1 58									4 58		7 39	9 5	9 8		
Glenbarry	3 18	2 6	6 44	3 58			3 36	3 36		4 40	5 2		7 44				
Glenbarry	3 28	2 13	6 54														
Knock																	
Grange North Junction				4Y 8			3 43	3 43		4 52			7 50	9 12	9 15		
Cairnie Junction																	
Cairnie Junction																	
Grange											5 8						
Grange / Keith											5 9		8 58				
											5 16						
Arrives at		Keith Town 2.16 p.m.		Lossiemouth 5.32 p.m.	Lossiemouth 1.28 p.m.		Aberdeen 5.5 p.m.	Aberdeen 5.5 p.m.	Lossiemouth 2.45 p.m.	Huntly 5.10 p.m.	Lossiemouth 5.20 p.m.		Aberdeen 9.16 p.m.	Aberdeen 10.29 p.m.	Aberdeen 10.35 p.m.	E.C.S. Elgin 10.15 p.m.	Lossiemouth 8.7 p.m.
Forward Times on Page		8	21	21	32		21	21	32	22	32		24	25	25	29	32

No. 4—Will not run when 9.22 a.m. LE runs.
No. 228—ᵞ At Portsoy Enginemen only with 11.55 a.m. Goods, Buckie to Keith. SO Works Urgent Van Goods to and from Portgordon and Buckpool.
No. 233—* To set down Stationmaster when required.
No. 240—B 2 minutes recovery time.
No. 247—d Runs SO Elgin to Buckie. ᵞ At Cairnie Jct., or as otherwise arranged.
No. 543—ᵞ SO Guard only at Portknockie with 11.30 a.m. OP, Cairnie Jct. to Elgin. ᵞ Enginemen only at Portsoy with 12.18 p.m. OP, Keith to Keith.
No. 544—ᵞ At Portessie with 1.20 p.m. Goods, Cairnie Junction to Elgin. SO Urgent Van Goods to and from Portgordon and Buckpool to be dealt with by No. 228 Up.
No. 545—ᵞ Propel EBV to Cornhill (arrive 4.14 p.m.). S—LS.

Appendix 4: Coast Line Excursions

In addition to normal day-to-day passenger traffic the Great North promoted its railway network through "Specials" and regular programmes of tours and excursions. Local groups such as the Boys Brigade, Sunday Schools and Operatic Societies used the trains for their outings. For example, on Monday 2nd January 1922, the Company laid on "Late Trains" for attendees of the Buckie Oratorio and Operatic Society's New Year concert to allow them to get home along the Coast. An eastbound train left Buckie at 10.30pm for Portessie (10.35pm), Findochty (10.39pm), Portknockie (10.43pm), Cullen (10.49pm) and Portsoy (11.00pm). A westbound one left Buckie at 11.30pm, presumably the same train after it had returned from Portsoy, for Portgordon (11.37pm), Spey Bay (11.42pm), Garmouth (11.46pm) and Elgin (12midnight). Special trains ran to the Royal Northern Agricultural Society's Summer Show in Aberdeen and to the annual Keith Show. Both the LNER and British Railways continued the policy of full and half-day excursions and, for those living along the Coast, two popular and regular trips were to Aberdeen and Elgin. "Springtime Cheap Tickets" and "Special Cheap Day Tickets" were offered.

Football Specials ran regularly along the Coast throughout the life of the line. On Saturday 10th February 1906 the Company ran a Special from Elgin for the Aberdeen – Rangers match at Pittodrie Park calling at Garmouth, Buckie, Findochty, Portknockie, Cullen, Portsoy, Tillynaught and Huntly. There were connecting trains from Banff and Keith and the Third Class Return fare from the Coast stations was 3/-. The train departed Elgin at 10.55am and the return left Aberdeen at 7.15pm. The special ticket was only valid for the day of issue and no luggage was allowed but, rather paradoxically, supporters were allowed to extend their trip and return on any train on Monday 12th February on payment of one half of the extra fare at the Aberdeen Booking Office. Presumably those supporters who stayed on for a couple of nights simply tucked a toothbrush into their pocket! Supporters of the Highland League Clubs also travelled to games by the Coast Line, especially those of Deveronvale, Buckie Thistle, Elgin City and Lossiemouth.

The Great North published a Tourist Guide to complement the excursions as well as a list of Furnished Lodgings which were issued free from all stations. The Company held sets of Lantern Slides.... *"showing the splendid scenery and places of interest on the Railway"* along with accompanying Lectures which could be obtained free of charge from the Company Head Office in Aberdeen. An example of the excursions on the Coast Line for the Summer Season of 1914 is shown in the table on the right.

Additionally, on Thursdays 18th June, 16th July, 20th August and 17th September, an excursion train ran from Elgin (8.20am), Garmouth (8.36am), Fochabers (8.41am), Portgordon (8.46am), Buckie (8.53am), Findochty (9.00am), Portknockie (9.05am), Cullen (9.11am) and Portsoy (9.25am) to Aberdeen (11.15am). The train returned from Aberdeen at 7.25pm and arrived back in Elgin at 10.15pm. The Third Class return fare was 3/9d from all stations.

There were cheap fares for golfers on Wednesdays and Saturdays from May to October from Elgin to Fochabers on condition that they purchased admission tickets to Spey Bay Golf Course at Elgin Booking Office. The return fare was 1/6d First Class and 9d Third Class valid for all trains on the day of issue. The Company highlighted the golf courses at Banff (via Golf Club House Halt), Banff (Duff House), Portsoy, Cullen, Buckie, Spey Bay, Elgin and Lossiemouth in their promotional literature with details of the number of holes and the charges.

Looking further afield, the Great North offered Cheap

Summer Season 1914 Excursions		
From	To	Days & Dates
Aberdeen	Banff, Portsoy, Cullen, Buckie, Fochabers, Garmouth, Elgin.	Wed & Sat, 30th May-30th Sep.
Banff	All Coast stations to Elgin excl. Spey Bay, Urquhart, Calcots.	Wed, Jun-Sep.
Buckie	Banff, Elgin, Lossiemouth.	Wed, Jun-Sep.
Buckpool	Elgin, Lossiemouth.	Wed, Jun-Sep.
Cullen	Banff, Elgin, Lossiemouth.	Wed, Jun-Sep.
Elgin	Garmouth, Fochabers, Portgordon, Buckpool, Buckie, Portessie, Findochty, Portknockie, Cullen, Lossiemouth.	Wed & Sat, Jun-Sep.
Findochty	Banff	Wed, Jun-Sep.
Glassaugh	Banff	Wed, Jun-Sep.
Huntly	Banff, Portsoy, Cullen, Buckie, Fochabers, Garmouth, Elgin.	Wed & Sat, 30th May-30th Sep.
Huntly	Banff, Portsoy, Cullen, Portknockie, Findochty, Buckie.	Thu 9th & 30th Jul, 27th Aug.
Insch	Banff, Portsoy, Cullen, Portknockie, Findochty, Buckie.	Thu 9th Jul, 27th Aug.
Keith & Keith Town	All Coast stations to Garmouth.	Wed & Sat, Jun-Sep.
Portessie	Banff, Elgin, Lossiemouth.	Wed, Jun-Sep.
Portknockie	Banff	Wed, Jun-Sep.
Portsoy	Banff, Elgin, Lossiemouth.	Wed, Jun-Sep.
Tochieneal	Banff	Wed, Jun-Sep.

Excursion Tickets on Thursdays in May, June, July, August and September to England and Wales (mainly London, Liverpool and Manchester but also to most principal towns) on specified trains. These were only issued at certain stations which included Banff, Buckie, Cullen, Elgin, and Portsoy. Travel had to be via Aberdeen.

In the opposite direction Tourist Tickets targeted holiday-makers from England between 1st May and 31st October, valid for six months from a large range of English stations to certain Great North stations. Elgin and Keith were amongst these from where the visitors could link with the Coast Line. However, Tourist Tickets issued in London (a range of stations) could be purchased for return travel to Banff, Buckie, Cullen, Fochabers, Lossiemouth and Portessie. The First Class return fare to all Coast Line stations was £7.6.11d (Lossie £7.7.11d); and Third Class £3.3.0d (including Lossie). And these tickets were also issued at Birmingham, Manchester, Liverpool and some other towns in the North of England to Banff. The tickets were issued in reverse at the same prices. Again, travel had to be via Aberdeen in all cases.

Closer to home, the Great North enticed Glaswegians to the north-east through excursion tickets valid for 8 and 16 days from Glasgow to all stations on the Great North network via Aberdeen. The special fares were only valid on Wednesdays in June, July and August and reflected a return for the price of a single except in high season when the fare increased to the single rate plus a quarter. No doubt many a wean arrived on the Coast Line complete with bucket and spade!

Appendix 5: LNER Instructions for the Working of Blairshinnoch Crossing

Blairshinnoch Crossing was about ½ mile west of Ladysbridge. The Down home signal carried the distant for Ladysbridge. The same instructions were issued to Ladysbridge.

1. Particular attention must be paid to Rules 99, 100, 101, 102, 104, 106 and 107.
2. Position of Gates: The Level Crossing Gates are always to be kept shut and locked across the Railway except when required to be opened for the passage of trains.
3. Operation of Gates: The Gates must always be opened from the Railway and closed to Road traffic in sufficient time to prevent risk and delay to trains.
4. Telephone Communication: Telephone Communication is provided between the Crossing and Banff Signal Box.

Before a Down Train or Engine is accepted from Tillynaught the Signalman at Banff must first telephone to Blairshinnoch Crossing and advise the Crossing Keeper of its running. If attention cannot be obtained on telephone the Signalman at Banff must advise Signalman at Tillynaught to warn Driver to approach Blairshinnoch Crossing cautiously and be prepared to stop clear of any obstruction.

Prior to the departure of an Up Train or Engine from Banff the Signalman at Banff must telephone to Blairshinnoch Crossing and advise the Crossing Keeper of its running. If attention on telephone cannot be got the Signalman must stop the train and advise the Driver as shewn above.

The Signalman, Banff, will also give two rings on telephone for Up trains leaving Banff, and one ring for Down trains leaving Tillynaught to the Crossing Keeper at Boyndie, and these rings must be acknowledged by repetition by Crossing Keeper Boyndie.

The Crossing Keeper must not rely entirely upon the telephone, however, but must be on the alert for trains approaching without having been previously advised.

All telephone messages passing between the Crossing Keeper and Signalman respecting the running of special trains, etc., must be acknowledged by the Crossing Keeper repeating them and no message must be taken as having been received until it has been correctly repeated to the place from which it was forwarded.

Edinburgh, February 1940   R. Gardiner, Superintendent

Note: Immediately after the Second World War, Blairshinnoch Crossing was known locally as Gurlay's Crossing after the surname of the 'keeper. There was a tiny outbuilding in the garden of the keeper's cottage which served as a tea-room for the public. Local children from Ladysbridge would walk along at weekends for a bottle of lemonade.

At night, a standard railway handlamp was mounted on a special stand to give a green light, indicating to drivers that the gates were open for trains to pass.

BIBLIOGRAPHY

Barclay-Harvey, Sir Malcolm, *History of the Great North of Scotland Railway,* Locomotive Publishing Company, 1949
Rosemary Burgess and Robert Kinghorn, *Moray Coast Railways*, 1990.
Mike Cooper and Graham Maxtone, *Then and Now on the Great North* Vol. 2, GNSRA, 2020.
Louise Davidson, Susan McGruer, Morag Shearer and David Flett, *Memories of The Railway in Cullen*, Cullen Primary School, June 1986.
A.G. Dunbar, The Centenary of the Great North of Scotland, *Railway Magazine*, Oct 1954.
J.A.N. Emslie, The Circus comes to the Great North of Scotland, *Railway Magazine*, Oct 1954.
Keith Fenwick and Graham Maxtone, *Great North of Scotland Railway Signal Boxes*, GNSRA website
Keith Fenwick and Neil T. Sinclair, *The Inverness & Aberdeen Junction Railway*, Highland Railway Society, 2008.
Peter Fletcher, *Directors, Dilemmas And Debt*, GNSRA and HRS, 2010.
F. A. Gosling, *Register of Closed Signal Boxes 1st Jan 1887 – 31st Dec 1967*, July 1968.
GNSRA, Abstracts: 2,4,5,6,9,12,13,15,16,21,22,26,31,32.
GNSRA, *Great North Memories* Nos. 1 and 2, July 1978 and September 1981.
Dick Jackson & John Emslie, *Great North Memories: The LNER Era 1923-1947*, GNSRA, January 1993.
Great North of Scotland Railway, Buckie Extension Contract, 1883.
Great North of Scotland Railway, *The Moray Firth Coast: The Scottish Riviera*, 1913.
Great North *Review*, The Journal of the Great North of Scotland Railway Association, Various 1964 – 2023.
Roger Griffiths and John Hooper, *Great North of Scotland Railway Engine Sheds,* Steam Days, July 2022.
Keith & Dufftown Railway Association, *Tales with Trains*, June 2018.
Keith Jones, The Moray Firth Coast Railway, *Steam Days*, November 1999.
Keith Jones, Steam Days at Elgin, *Steam Days*, October 2009.
Keith Jones, Fish Traffic From North-East Scotland, *Steam Days,* October 2010.
Keith Jones, Elgin to Lossiemouth, *Steam Days,* February 2018.
David M. E. Lindsay, Great North of Scotland Railway Statistics, undated.
LNER Camping Holidays Guide, April 1936.
G. R. Maxtone, *The Railways of the Banff & Moray Coast*, KDRA, 2005.
Duncan McLeish, *Rails to Banff, Macduff and Oldmeldrum*, GNSRA, 2014.
Mike Mitchell, *Great North of Scotland Railway Road Services*, GNSRA 2016
Railway and Sporting Guide to the Highlands, Munro & Co (Publishers), 1937.
David Ross, *The Great North of Scotland Railway*, Stenlake Publishing, 2015.
John Ross, *The Spey Viaduct*, GNSRA, 2006.
John Ross, *The Travellers Joy*, author, 2001
W. J. Scott, Little And Good/Bigger And Better, *Railway Magazine*, 1897.
Signalling Record Society, *Signal Box Register*, Volume 6, 2012.
Andrew Simpson and Eleanor Gillespie, *The Spirit of Banffshire*, 2022.
David Spaven, *Steam Memories North East Scotland: Images from the Neville Stead collection*, The Transport Treasury, 2021.
David Spaven, *Scotland's Lost Branch Lines: Where Beeching Got It Wrong*, Birlinn Ltd, 2022.
Stephenson Locomotive Society Journal, Great North of Scotland Railway 1854-1954 Vol. XXX, No. 352,12th September 1954.
H. A. Vallance, *The Great North of Scotland Railway*, (House of Lochar revised edition), 1989.
West Highland News Plus, Summer 2022 (Friends of the West Highland Lines).
Brian Wilkinson, *The Heilan Line*,1988.

INDEX

A

Aberdeen, Banff & Elgin Railway 9
Area Managers 88

B

Banff **17**, **18**, **20**, **21**, **23**, 24, 58, 62, 63, **78**, 85, **95**, **100**, **118**
Banff, Macduff & Turriff Extension Railway 14
Banff & Moray Junction Railway 18
Banff, Portsoy & Strathisla Railway 13
Banffshire Railway 19
Barry 19
Beeching Report 85
Blaikie Brothers 38
Boyndie Crossing, **110**
Bridgefoot 65
Buckie 18, **26**, 27, 28, **35**, **49**, **50**, 80, 82, **89**, **90**, **118**
Buckpool **51**, 83, **108**
Buffalo Bill circus 101

C

Cairnie Junction 34, 43, 61, **62**, 64, 70, **82**, **83**, 93
Calcots **54**, 82, 86
Callander, contractors 28
Camping coaches **73**, 74, 80
Cathcart, Lady Gordon 31
Class L **107**
Cornhill 14, 16, 23, **43**, 55, 58, 78
Cullen **29**, **30**, 36, **46**, **57**, **85**, **94**

D

Dandaleith **12**
Donald, John 97
Duncan, John 25

E

Elgin **11**, 32, 33, **56**, 63, **70**, 72, **76**, **81**, 85, 95
Elphinstone, Sir James 25

F

Ferguson, William, of Kinmundy 25, **27**
Findochty **7**, 47, **48**, 61, 93
Fish traffic 57
Fishworkers 57
Fochabers & Garmouth Railway 18
Fyfe, contractor 38

G

Garmouth 32, **53**, **58**, 86
Geddes, John 97
Glassaugh 31, **45**, 81, 86
Glenbarry 14, 19, 22, 59, **60**, **86**, **103**
Golf Club House 65, **66**
Grange **13**, 14, 83
Grange North Junction 34, **83**, **92**, **117**
Granger, contractor 29
Great North of Scotland (Eastern Extension) Railway 9
Great North of Scotland (Western Extension) Railway 9

H

Highland Buckie branch 70
Highland Railway 28, 33, 59, 63
Hind, contractor 38

I

Inverboyndie Distillery **68**, 96
Inverness & Elgin Junction Railway 9

K

Karam Dad **109**
Kintore, Earl of 27
Knock **2**, 14, 21, 22, **59**

L

Ladysbridge 14, 16, 19, **22**, **24**, 87, 95, **110**, **115**
Lossie Junction **54**, 86, **118**
Lossiemouth **10**, 11, 85

M

Macduff 14, 17, 21
Marindin, Major 31, 32, 33, 40
Merrilees, William 98
Millegan 16, 19, 20, 22
Moffatt, William 25, **28**
Morayshire Railway 11

O

Ordens 16, **19**

P

Portessie 28, **32**, 33, **48**, **49**, 80, **84**, 86, **96**
Portgordon 20, 25, 51, **52**, 66, 86, 97, **98**
Portknockie **47**, 61, **76**, **87**
Portsoy **14**, **15**, **17**, 20, **44**, **45**, 63, **69**, 82, 86, **93**, 96, **116**
Post Office Sorting Van 55, 101

R

Richmond and Gordon, Duke of 27, 37, 42
Road services 71–72
Runabout Tickets **79**, 80
Rutland, Duke of 18

S

Seafield, Earl of 18, 30
Snow plough **105**
Spey Bay **52**, 64, **77**, 86, **88**, **94**, **116**
Spey Viaduct **37–42**, 93, **95**
Spies 97
Strathlene **74**, **96**

T

Tillynaught 23, 31, **44**, 61, **75**, 78, 81, 86, **91**, 93, 117
Tochieneal **31**, 81, 86, 87
Train services 77
Train Tablet 35
Tyer's No. 6 tablet instrument **112**

U

Urquhart **53**, 86

V

von Donop, Colonel 62

W

West Buchan Light Railway **95**

Bold page numbers indicate an illustrations; those pages may also contain text.

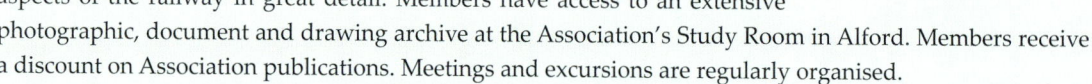

The last Down train calls at Buckie on Saturday 4th May 1968. Some people had gone for a last trip on the train while others had turned out to watch the railway pass into history.

(Mike Stephen)

Great North of Scotland Railway Association

Founded 1964

The Association caters for all those interested in the history of the Great North of Scotland Railway and its constituent companies, as well as the lines during the LNER and British Railways periods and continuing to the present time. The Association promotes the study and collection of information, documents and illustrations relating to all aspects of the north-east's railways. It also facilitates and co-ordinates members' research and provides information for modellers.

Members receive a quarterly *Review* containing articles, photographs, drawings and news of the railway, both historical and current. The Association has produced a comprehensive range of books and technical papers covering aspects of the railway in great detail. Members have access to an extensive photographic, document and drawing archive at the Association's Study Room in Alford. Members receive a discount on Association publications. Meetings and excursions are regularly organised.

For further information, please look at the Association's website

www.gnsra.org.uk